access to history

The British Empire c1857–1967 for AQA

ALAN FARMER

The Publishers would like to thank the following for permission to reproduce copyright material:

Photo credits: p13 Everett Collection Historical/Alamy Stock Photo; **p16** Hulton Archive/Getty Images; **pp51, 52** Wikimedia Commons/Public domain; **p66** Pictorial Press Ltd/Alamy Stock Photo; **p81** Wikimedia Commons/Public domain; **p84** Chronicle/ Alamy Stock Photo; **p99** Wikimedia Commons/Public domain; **p142** Library of Congress/LC-DIG-npcc-17934; **p156** Wikimedia Commons/Open Government Licence.

Acknowledgements: Hodder Education, *The British Empire 1815–1914* by Frank McDonough, 1994. Hodder & Stoughton, *Britain: Foreign and Imperial Affairs 1939–64* by Alan Farmer, 1994. Macmillan Press, *The British Empire and Commonwealth: A Short History* by Martin Kitchen, 1996. Orbis/TimeLife/BBC, 'A Most Superior Person' by David Dilks, *British Empire Magazine*, 1973. Oxford University Press, 'Critics of Empire in Britain' by Nicholas Owen, in *The Oxford History of the British Empire, The Twentieth Century*, edited by Judith M. Brown and W.M. Roger Louis, 1999; 'The dissolution of the British Empire' by W.M. Roger Louis, in *The Oxford History of the British Empire: The Twentieth Century*, edited by Judith M. Brown and W.M. Roger Louis, 1999. Palgrave Macmillan, *Histories and Controversies, British Imperialism* by Robert Johnson, 2003. Pearson, *The Lion's Share: A Short History of British Imperialism 1850–2004* by Bernard Porter, 2004. Routledge, *British Foreign and Imperial Policy 1865–1919* by Graham Goodlad, 2000. Vintage Books, *The Decline and Fall of the British Empire 1781–1997* by Piers Brendon, 2008.

Orders: please contact Bookpoint Ltd, 130 Milton Park, Abingdon, Oxon OX14 4SE. Telephone: +44 (0)1235 827827. Fax: +44 (0)1235 400401. Email: education@bookpoint.co.uk. Lines are open from 9 a.m. to 5 p.m., Monday to Saturday, with a 24-hour message answering service. You can also order through our website: www.hoddereducation.co.uk

First published in 2018 by
Hodder Education
An Hachette UK Company
Carmelite House, 50 Victoria Embankment
London EC4Y 0DZ

www.hoddereducation.co.uk

Impression number	10	9	8	7	6	5	4	3	2	1
Year	2022		2021		2020		2019		2018	

Cover photo: © Classic Image/Alamy Stock Photo
Produced and typeset in Palatino by Gray Publishing, Tunbridge Wells
Printed in the UK by CPI Group Ltd

A catalogue record for this title is available from the British Library.

ISBN 978 1510423480

Contents

Dedication

Keith Randell (1943–2002)

The *Access to History* series was conceived and developed by Keith, who created a series to 'cater for students as they are, not as we might wish them to be'. He leaves a living legacy of a series that for over twenty years has provided a trusted, stimulating and well-loved accompaniment to post-16 study. Our aim with these new editions is to continue to offer students the best possible support for their studies.

Colonial-era names are used in this book and this table shows the colonial names alongside the present-day names

Colonial-era name	Present-day name
Basutoland	Lesotho
Bechuanaland	Botswana
Bombay	Mumbai
British Guiana	Guyana
Burma	Myanmar
Calcutta	Kolkata
Ceylon	Sri Lanka
Gold Coast	Ghana
(British) Malaya	Malaysia
Mesopotamia	Iraq
Northern Rhodesia	Zambia
Persia	Iran
Portuguese East Africa	Mozambique
South-West Africa	Namibia
Southern Rhodesia	Zimbabwe
Tanganyika	Tanzania
Transjordan	Jordan

The development of imperialism, c1857–c1874

In 1857, Britain was the world's greatest colonial power. By 1874, its Empire had grown even larger. Yet – somewhat ironically – British governments and people seemed to show relatively little interest in imperial expansion. This chapter will examine the development of imperialism in Britain in the period c1857–c1874 by examining the following themes:

- ★ The British Empire in 1857
- ★ India, 1857–74
- ★ The colonies of settlement
- ★ Expansion of the Empire in Africa
- ★ Relations with indigenous peoples

Key dates

1857–8	Indian Mutiny
1858	Government of India Act
1860	Britain acquired Kowloon
1861	Annexation of Lagos
1867	British North America Act federated the Dominion of Canada
1868	Basutoland became a Protectorate
1869	Opening of the Suez Canal
1871	Annexation of Griqualand West

1 The British Empire in 1857

▸ *To what extent did Britain exert control over its colonies?*

The development of British imperialism before 1857

It is possible to argue that the English Empire began with the conquest of Ireland, a long process from the Norman period to the reign of Elizabeth I. However, it is a moot point whether Ireland was an English (and later British) colony. The word colony tends to imply a degree of geographic separation between the colony and the imperial power. Thus, the expansion of the Russian Empire eastwards and the USA's expansion westwards in the nineteenth century are not usually seen as colonisation processes. Given Ireland's proximity to England, it is possible to claim that it was not a colony in the usual sense of the word.

England began building its world empire in the early seventeenth century, establishing colonies in North America and the West Indies. The East India Company, founded in Queen Elizabeth I's reign, also established trading posts and took over territory in India. In the eighteenth century, Britain (following the unification of England and Scotland in 1707) fought a series of successful wars with France and Spain, ensuring the British Empire grew. By the end of the Seven Years' War in 1763, Britain was able to lay claim to most of North America and large parts of India. Britain thus became the world's greatest imperial power.

The loss of Britain's thirteen North American colonies, resulting from British defeat in the American War of Independence (1775–83), was a serious blow to Britain's prestige and imperial ambitions. However, in the late eighteenth and early nineteenth centuries, the British Empire again expanded, due largely to Britain's naval and commercial power. The defeat of Napoleonic France in 1814–15 and expansionist policies thereafter ensured that Britain had become the world's greatest imperial power by the mid-nineteenth century.

Imperialism

Imperialism is an action that involves a country, usually an empire or a kingdom, extending its power by the acquisition of territories – often called colonies. The word imperialism (which originated from the Latin word *imperium*, meaning supreme power) was rarely used before the 1870s. It tended then (and still tends) to have negative connotations, being seen as a process by which colonies were exploited by the **mother country**. The word now is mainly applied to Western (and Japanese) political and economic dominance, especially in Asia and Africa, in the nineteenth and early twentieth centuries. It is almost interchangeable with the word colonialism.

KEY TERMS

Mother country The home country of colonists.

Afrikaans Language spoken by Boers, meaning 'African-Dutch'.

Boers People of Dutch origin who settled in southern Africa.

The nature of the British Empire in 1857

In 1857, the British Empire was a complex mix of territories, which had little in common with each other except that Britain had some kind of control over them.

Colonies of settlement

These colonies had been founded and settled by people of British or European origin. In many respects they were very different from each other:

- (What was to become) Canada contained many French-speaking colonists.
- Newfoundland did not regard itself as part of Canada.
- Cape Colony and Natal in southern Africa contained many **Afrikaans**-speaking **Boers**.
- Although originally settled by European colonists, Britain's West Indian islands were mainly populated by people whose ancestors had been enslaved Africans. (Slavery ended in the British Empire in 1834.)
- Australia was a collection of separate colonies.

- Maori chiefs had ceded **sovereignty** of New Zealand to Britain in 1840. Fewer than 100,000 Maoris had lived in New Zealand before British settlers arrived. By the 1850s, people of British stock outnumbered the Maoris.

KEY TERMS

Sovereignty Ultimate power.

East India Company A commercial company that established considerable political power in India in the eighteenth and early nineteenth centuries.

British settlers

- The Irish potato famine in the 1840s drove large numbers of Irish to emigrate. Many went to Britain and the USA, but others went to Australia, Canada and New Zealand. Irish emigration remained high throughout the 1860s.
- Economic hardship resulted in many Scots emigrating, particularly to Canada.
- After 1870, most emigrants were English.
- Transportation, an alternative punishment to imprisonment, had been used by Britain since the seventeenth century. Australia was used as a dumping ground for British convicts until 1868. Some 160,000 were transported there between 1783 and 1868.
- The Colonial Land and Emigration Commission funded assisted passages from the proceeds of land sales in Australia. Between 1840 and 1872, it paid for 340,000 Britons to emigrate to Australia.
- The arrival of steam-powered ships by the 1850s made the sea passage to the colonies much speedier.

British rule

By 1857, most of the colonies with substantial numbers of British settlers had been granted self-government. However, Britain retained control of their foreign relations and defence. The general British view was that these colonies would quickly become independent nations, but there was also a strong hope that the colonies might become part of a 'Greater Britain' – an extension of Britain. Many Australians, New Zealanders, Canadians and people of British descent in southern Africa took a similar view.

Dependent/Crown colonies

Dependent colonies contained few British/European settlers. These colonies, albeit often called Crown colonies, were essentially controlled by the British Parliament or by British trading companies by the mid-nineteenth century:

- India was the largest and most important dependent colony. In 1857, it was ruled by a Governor-General who worked in association with the privately owned **East India Company**.
- Some areas, like Ceylon and Malaya, were highly profitable.
- Some dependent colonies seemed to offer relatively little economic opportunity. Britain's colonies in west Africa, for example, had lost much of their economic importance with the abolition of the trans-Atlantic slave trade (1807).
- Islands like Malta and Mauritius provided the Royal Navy with bases.

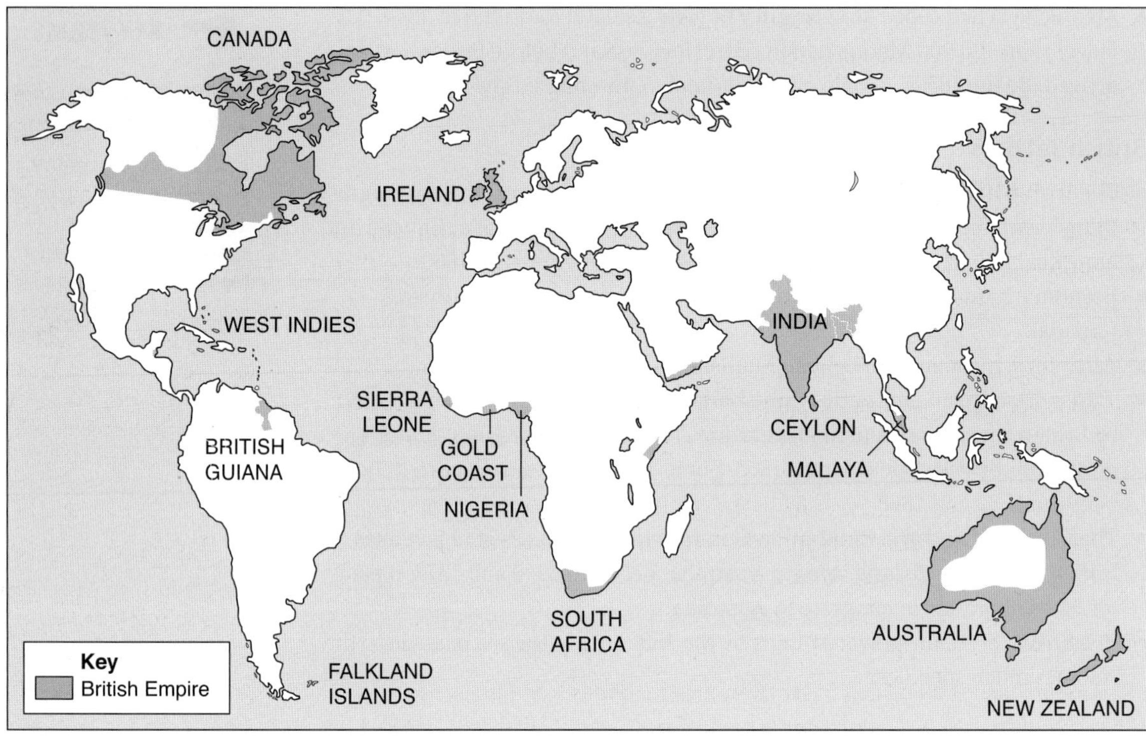

Figure 1.1 The British Empire in the 1850s.

KEY TERMS

Executive power The right to administer and manage.

Autocratically Non-democratic rule which is often conducted by one person.

Colonial rule

In the Crown colonies, British-appointed governors had full **executive power**. However, British rule almost everywhere depended on the support of local elites: hereditary rulers, great landowners or rich merchants. This avoided the need for expensive British officialdom and large military forces.

British governments ultimately decided colonial policy. Governments delegated day-to-day matters to colonial secretaries who presided over the Colonial Office. The Colonial Office, in turn, delegated responsibility to colonial administrators or (in the case of the colonies of settlement) to the colonists themselves.

The Empire had no legal coherence. Britons carried their own law with them to settler colonies but Roman–Dutch law was retained in the Cape, Ceylon and British Guiana. Varieties of French law prevailed in Lower Canada, St Lucia, Mauritius and the Seychelles. Trinidad had Spanish law, Cyprus had old Turkish law. Nor was there judicial impartiality: in theory, all people were equal before the law. In reality, white men were considered superior to all other races while women did not have the same legal rights as men.

While Britain ruled its colonies **autocratically**, most British administrators thought British rule was enlightened and civilising. They believed that it would rescue the colonies from backwardness, chaos and violence. It was expected that

Britain would have to maintain order in these areas for a considerable time – for the good of the **indigenous** peoples. Local opposition was dealt with harshly. A successful rebellion in any part of the Empire might encourage trouble elsewhere.

Racial assumptions

The Empire was profoundly racist (in today's terms and by today's standards). Most Britons assumed that they were God's chosen race and that this gave them the right to rule over other 'lower' races. (Such assumptions were also held by white settlers in Canada, Australia, New Zealand and southern Africa). To dilute white authority by making it subject to indigenous assemblies, or by recruiting indigenous officials, was opposed at every level of white society. The white 'elite' maintained a deliberate social distance from indigenous peoples and there was a strict codification of almost all social contact. Mixed-race marriages were particularly taboo. Nevertheless, in all the colonial areas there were a minority of white people who believed in studying local languages and traditions with a view to gaining a better understanding of indigenous peoples.

A free-trade Empire

The Empire had initially been based on **mercantilism**. However, by the 1850s, British politicians were committed to **free trade**. Unlike conventional imperialism, which profited the imperialists at the expense of their subjects, free trade, in theory, profited both Britain and its trading partners. The notion of an empire of free trade went further. Britain believed that free commercial relations would allow free passage of ideas as well as goods. Britain would eventually export its institutions and values as well as its manufactured products – all of which were considered to be more advanced than those of the rest of the world. Britain saw itself as a liberator, opening up 'closed' societies. In the meantime, if free trade was rejected or resisted by indigenous peoples, Britain was prepared to impose it. The British government believed that it was in its own interests to do so. However, it also believed that it would ultimately be in the best interests of indigenous peoples themselves.

The imperialism of free trade

Historians Ronald Robinson and John Gallagher claimed (in the 1950s) that British imperialism was shaped as much by 'informal' imperialism as by 'formal' **annexation**. They stressed the importance of free trade, regarding British imperialism as essentially an 'imperialism of free trade'. Britain, they claimed, undertook formal – expensive – colonisation only as a last resort. Robinson and Gallagher's implication that Britain was reluctantly imperialist may be at odds with the enormous territorial gains. Nevertheless, their work is vital in stressing that the Empire was a complex entity with tentacles reaching beyond formal political borders. Britain was determined to safeguard its commercial interests. If this could be done without annexation, so much the better.

KEY TERMS

Indigenous People who are native to the area they inhabit.

Mercantilism The belief, widely held in Europe in the seventeenth and eighteenth centuries, that economic self-sufficiency is the key to national wealth and prosperity. European states envisaged that colonies would provide them with valuable raw materials and also provide markets for their goods.

Free trade International trade that takes place without tariffs being imposed.

Annexation Taking permanent possession of a country.

Informal Empire

As well as its formal Empire, Britain possessed what is usually called an 'informal' Empire. While not directly controlling countries, Britain could rely on the influence of its bankers and merchants, its consuls and the Royal Navy to ensure that it exerted a great deal of control. However, the 'informal' Empire was essentially a sphere of influence, not an 'empire'. British influence varied according to circumstances, not least the cooperation of local politicians and the policies of rival powers.

China

Britain's main problem with regard to its informal Empire was to persuade China to open its doors to trade. The First Opium War (1839–42) was fought for this end. By the time of the Treaty of Nanking (1842), China was compelled to cede the islands of Hong Kong to Britain, to open five ports to British merchants (including Shanghai and Canton) and to reduce the import duty on British goods. Some thought the acquisition of Hong Kong showed Britain's intent to take over the whole of China at some future date. China, itself, seemed in a state of terminal decline, with a decadent leadership, an inefficient bureaucracy and a stagnant culture. However, most British politicians wanted to exploit China, not to bring about its collapse. So long as Chinese emperors provided security for existing trade, Britain left them alone. When they did not, Britain was prepared to fight. Britain used the Second Opium War (1857–60) to extend its trading rights. Five more Chinese ports, as well as the interior of the country, were opened to foreign trade. The opium trade was legalised and Britain also acquired Kowloon, extending its power in the Hong Kong region. By the 1870s, Britain was responsible for 75 per cent of China's overseas trade.

The Ottoman Empire

Britain's main aim in the eastern Mediterranean and the **Middle East** was strategic rather than economic – to keep Russia from gaining power over the area. Thus, Britain supported the tottering **Ottoman Empire**. Lord Stratford de Redcliffe, Britain's ambassador at Constantinople in the mid-nineteenth century, exercised enormous authority in the Sultan's Court.

KEY TERMS

Middle East The mainly Turkish and Arabic-speaking area around the eastern end of the Mediterranean Sea and in the Arabian Peninsula.

Ottoman Empire The huge empire controlled by the Ottoman Turks in the Middle East.

Latin America

British financiers played an important role in much of Latin America, especially Argentina and Uruguay. Consequently, Britain had considerable influence in much of South America.

Reluctant imperialism?

Historian Sir John Seeley, writing in the 1880s, claimed that Britain's Empire was acquired in a 'fit of absence of mind'. Other scholars, not pushing the point quite so far, see the British political establishment after 1850 as 'reluctant' imperialists, unwillingly annexing territory. Certainly, some politicians were more reluctant than others. But given the vast areas brought under British control between 1857 and 1874, the notion of 'accidental' or even 'reluctant' imperialism is not particularly persuasive. Nevertheless, the Empire expanded in a haphazard fashion – by conquest, by settlement, by **cession** and in a variety of other ways. At times, it was not so much pushed out from London as pulled out from the extremities. There were many cases of the British dog being wagged by its colonial tail.

KEY TERMS

Cession The process of giving up power or ceding territory.

Industrial Revolution The economic and social changes arising out of the change from industries carried out in the home with simple machines to industries in factories with power-driven machinery. This led to a great change in the scale of production.

Gold Coast Present-day Ghana.

Imperialist attitudes

There seems to have been no great enthusiasm for Empire in Britain in the 1850s:

- As a result of the **Industrial Revolution**, Britain dominated world trade. It seemed that the country no longer needed extensive and expensive colonies.
- In the mid-nineteenth century, Britain and its overseas possessions (except India) seemed relatively free from external danger – given the power of the Royal Navy (see page 8). There was therefore no need to expand for such defensive purposes as acquiring a safer frontier line.
- The loss of Britain's American colonies (in 1783) suggested that colonies, like ripe apples, were bound to fall from the tree. Given this expectation, there seemed little point acquiring them.

However, between 1844 and 1870, in a period when there was supposed indifference to Empire, Britain acquired or annexed New Zealand, the **Gold Coast**, Hong Kong, Natal, Lagos, Sierra Leone, Lower Burma, Kowloon, Basutoland and large areas of India. From 1837 to 1872, the Empire grew on average by 100,000 square miles a year – almost the same rate of expansion as that in the second half of Victoria's reign, which is usually regarded as the 'golden age' of territorial expansion. Why did this happen?

British interests

British imperial expansion was not the result of a co-ordinated policy of conquest. Nevertheless, British governments were determined to maintain Britain's economic, political and strategic interests. Thus, there was little prospect of Britain abandoning its Empire – and certainly not its possessions in India. Threats to perceived interests often led to further expansion. Lord Palmerston, champion of an aggressive British foreign policy, and prime minister 1855–8 and again 1859–65, was keener to foster commerce than to acquire territory. But sometimes one enterprise involved the other. Whatever the case, Palmerston had an infallible guide: 'the interest of England is paramount'.

But Britain also had high-minded justification for imperial expansion. Christianity and civilisation followed the Union Jack. Many Britons felt it was their country's duty to improve the world. Even the critics of Empire regarded

KEY TERMS

Manifest destiny A God-given right. The term is more widely used with regard to the USA's expansion westwards in the course of the nineteenth century.

Evangelists People who do their best to spread (what they believe to be) good ideas.

Gross national product (GNP) The total value of all goods and services produced within a country plus the income from all investments abroad.

British settlement and rule over large parts of the world as a 'good thing'. For critics of the Empire, as well as ardent imperialists, it seemed Britain's **manifest destiny** to be the liberator, protector, transformer and liberal **evangelist** of the world beyond Europe. Politicians might deplore the Empire's trouble and cost. Nevertheless, most believed that it was essential to Britain's greatness.

British strengths

The Empire was able to expand for a number of reasons, as detailed below. Military and economic strength were key, although other factors such as emigration contributed too.

Military strength

In the mid-nineteenth century, the Royal Navy ruled the waves. During the 1850s and 1860s, it was converted from a fleet of wooden sailing ships into a fleet of iron, coal-fuelled steamships. It protected Britain, its colonies and its trade routes.

The British army was also a major force. Far better trained and equipped than any of its colonial enemies, it proved to be a highly effective instrument for the defence and enlargement of the Empire. It fought 15 major wars between 1857 and 1899 and won them all.

Emigration

British expansion in part resulted from the propensity of Britons to migrate. Nineteen million people, twice as many as from any other part of Europe, emigrated from Britain between 1815 and 1930. Britain's rapid economic development encouraged population growth. Some parts of Britain, particularly Scotland and Ireland, were notable exporters of people because of economic misery at home.

Economic strength

Britain's economic strength was crucial to its imperial power. By 1870, Britain was at the height of its commercial and industrial power:

- it accounted for half the world's trade in textiles and metal manufactured goods
- its **gross national product (GNP)** was higher than that of China and Russia combined
- its merchant fleet carried half the world's sea-borne trade.

As well as being the workshop of the world, Britain was the world's financial centre. Income from commercial services, for example, shipping and insurance, continued to increase. Britain had capital to spare and some of that capital went into its colonies. Britain's economic and financial strength helped tie the colonies to Britain. Colonies, as well as purchasing British goods, produced goods either for Britain or for other British colonies. Indeed, Britain provided a market for almost every colonial product. Colonial economies thus became dependent on the commercial apparatus for long-distance trade that Britain provided. Once hooked up to this trade and reliant on it for local prosperity, it was difficult to withdraw. The British connection was important to maintain certain people's status and wealth.

Imperial weaknesses

Although seemingly strong, the Empire carried within it what historian Piers Brendon in 2007 called an 'ideological bacillus' (a potentially deadly idea) that was always likely to prove fatal. This was the **paternalistic** doctrine that colonial government was something that had essentially been entrusted to Britain. It was to be exercised for the benefit of subject people until such time as they would attain their birthright – freedom. Already, by 1857, Canada, Australia and New Zealand had almost achieved independence from Britain.

KEY TERM

Paternalistic A system or tendency in which well-meaning supervision is apt to be seen as unwelcome interference.

Another weakness was that Britain, remote from its overseas possessions, had a small human and geographic base. While Britain had huge industrial, commercial and naval advantages in 1857, it was likely that rivals would eventually challenge these advantages. By 1860, the population of the USA (31 million) had overtaken that of the UK (29 million) and it was on its way to becoming a serious rival.

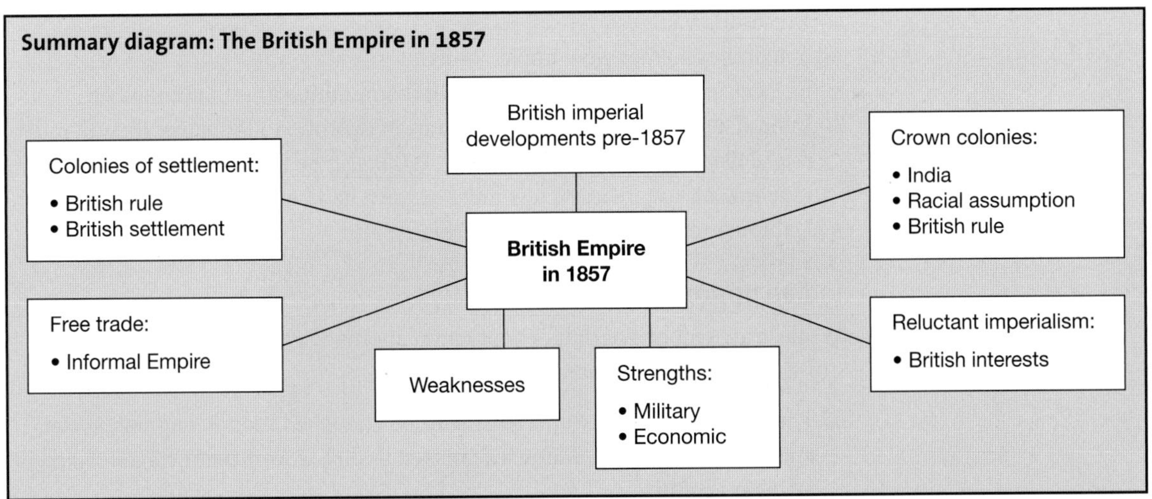

2 India, 1857–74

▶ *Why was Britain so determined to maintain its Indian Empire?*

KEY TERMS

Jewel in the crown The greatest asset.

Missionary A person sent on a mission to convert people, usually to a particular form of religion.

India was the '**jewel in the crown**' of the Empire, providing Britain with considerable wealth and trading opportunities. All British governments believed that it had to be protected, whatever the cost.

East India Company rule

In 1857, British rule in India was theoretically in the hands of the East India Company. Company rule was helped by the fact that:

- Indians were hugely divided – politically, religiously and socially
- many Indians were prepared to collaborate with the company and Britain
- it commanded a large Indian army.

In the mid-nineteenth century, East India Company policy in India was generally to develop India along British lines, extending the benefits of European civilisation. Two governor-generals in particular, Lord William Bentinck (1828–35) and Lord Dalhousie (1848–56), promoted reform in these ways:

- English was made the official language of law, administration and education.
- Several traditional Indian customs such as *sati* or *suttee* (the practice of widows being burned to death on the funeral pyres of their dead husbands) were outlawed.
- Irrigation schemes were implemented.
- Dalhousie set out to create a system of communications that united all India. The building of the great road from Calcutta to Peshawar (begun in the 1840s) was a major undertaking. Work also began on building a railway network, although only a few miles of track had been completed by 1857.
- Dalhousie reformed the tax-gathering system.

Indian opposition

While large sections of India's population approved of the reforms, there was a growing resentment towards British rule:

- The policy of Westernisation disregarded cherished Indian religious, social and regional customs. Many Indians felt that they were being forced to accept an 'alien' culture.
- Some of the reforms alienated specific groups. Reforms of the revenue system, for example, disaffected the traditional tax-gatherers.
- The Christian **missionary** fervour displayed by some British officials and soldiers alarmed both Hindus and Muslims.
- Britons often treated Indians with contempt and arrogance.
- There were economic grievances. For example, India was swamped by cheap British goods, and British property developers purchased land, introduced a landlord system and imposed high rents.

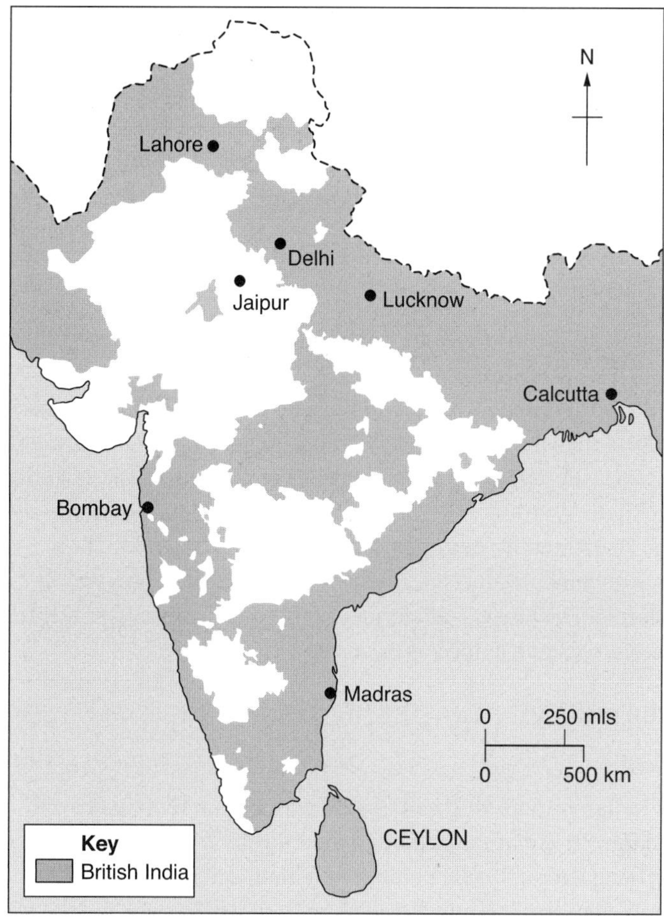

Figure 1.2 India in 1857.

- In the 1840s and 1850s there were political grievances as Britain annexed a spate of territories – Punjab and Sind (1843), Berar (1853) and Oudh (1856). Dalhousie also annexed princely states when the ruler left no direct heir, flouting the Hindu tradition of adoption.

Sepoy resentment

The British rulers failed to realise the resentment caused by their actions. They also failed to recognise the weakness of their own situation. British security depended on the East India Company army. In 1857, this army numbered 270,000 men, but only 40,000 were of European origin. The bulk of the men were **sepoys** – soldiers recruited from the local Indian community. The army had served the company amazingly well over the previous century. But by 1857 the native infantry were increasingly discontented – at the level of pay, loss of allowances, treatment by British officers, and a general enlistment order of 1856 making all troops liable for overseas service. (High-caste Hindu Indians had a ritual objection to crossing the sea.)

Dalhousie, disregarding warnings that the sepoys were close to mutiny, planned to equip the Indian army with the new Enfield rifle. The paper cartridges for the weapon were supposedly coated with grease made from pork and beef fat. Given that the ends of the cartridges had to be bitten off, most sepoys were offended: the pig is considered to be unclean by Muslims while the cow is sacred to Hindus. The cartridges were quickly withdrawn by the army command. But not all sepoys in 1857 were convinced.

The Indian Mutiny

In May 1857, 85 sepoys at Meerut were court-martialled for refusing to accept the new cartridges. They were sentenced to ten years' hard labour in prison. The next day, three sepoy regiments at Meerut mutinied, killing all the British officers. The mutineers then marched on Delhi, quickly capturing India's ancient capital, and killing every European they could find. The mutiny spread to Oudh, Cawnpore and Lucknow. Within weeks, Britain lost control of much of north-central India. Some 70,000 sepoys mutinied; a further 30,000 deserted. The sepoy mutiny was complemented by civil rebellions, resulting from grievances arising from British rule. The 80-year-old former Emperor Bahadur Shah, heir to the **Mughal** emperors, was proclaimed as ruler.

KEY TERM

Mughals A Muslim dynasty which claimed to rule much of India from 1526 until 1858.

The impact of the mutiny

Fortunately for Britain:

- The majority of Indian princes who had treaties with Britain remained loyal.
- Britain raised a large 'irregular' force though the Punjab's tribal chiefs.
- Sepoy troops in Bengal, the Punjab, Bombay and Madras remained loyal.
- The mutiny or rebellion was confined to northern India. Even here, many Indians opposed the rebels.
- No outstanding Indian leader emerged. There was thus no unified command, no coherent strategy and little co-ordination.
- The rebels lacked (for the most part) Enfield rifles, which were far more accurate than muskets.

Nevertheless, Britain faced massive problems. It took three months for British troops to restore order at Delhi. Not until large numbers of British reinforcements arrived – some 90,000 in total – did Britain begin to recapture lost cities. British officers generally showed skill and courage. The struggle for Lucknow, the capital of Oudh, lasted twelve months before British troops regained full control in March 1858. British and loyal sepoy troops effectively put down the revolt in mid-1858 when they retook Gwalior. Nevertheless, resistance in some areas continued into 1859. A state of peace was finally declared by the Viceroy in July 1859.

Terrible atrocities were committed by both sides. Mutineers slaughtered British men, women and children. (Some 200 British women and children were murdered at Cawnpore.) British reprisals were brutal. Huge numbers of

SOURCE A

A contemporary illustration of Indian rebels being blown away by guns.

What does Source A show about the nature of the Indian Mutiny?

mutineers and rebels were executed, often without any pretence of a trial. Most were hanged. Some were tied to cannon mouths and blown to pieces. Large numbers of rebel villages were burned to the ground. Britain lost some 2000 killed in military action. A further 9000 died from disease. Indian casualties probably exceeded 100,000.

Many Indians concluded that attempting to overthrow British rule by force could lead only to catastrophe. The defeat of the mutiny/rebellion thus helped to solidify British rule.

The mutiny and historians

The Indian Mutiny (to use its British name) has been the subject of heated debate. Indian historians once viewed the mutiny as a national revolution against British rule. Today, however, most Indian scholars think that 'rebellion' is a better description than 'revolt'. The mutiny is increasingly seen as backward-looking, with the rebels/mutineers focusing their dislike of British rule on the policy of Westernisation. Their main desire was not a new united India but a return to past ways, not least a regionalised 'old' India. For historian Jadunath Ghosh (writing in the 1930s), the mutiny was the last gasp of the Mughal Empire rather than the first flowering of Indian nationalism.

While British historians once viewed the mutiny as a localised army revolt, sparked by the introduction of the Enfield rifle and new cartridges, most now emphasise the importance of broader social, economic and political discontent, resulting from the policy of Westernisation. They tend to see the mutiny as historian Christopher Hibbert (1973) saw it: 'the last swan song of Old India' – an event that was more than an army mutiny but a good deal less than the 'first Indian war of independence'. Confined to northern India, it was a mixture of military uprising, political coup, religious war, peasant revolt and race riot: a reaction against both long-standing and immediate grievances.

Indian reforms

In 1858, the administration of India was taken from the East India Company and put directly under the British Crown and Parliament. A secretary of state and a council of fifteen ministers were appointed to run Indian affairs. A viceroy replaced the governor-general as the new ruler.

The Indian army was also reformed:

- Indian soldiers were never to outnumber British troops by more than two to one.
- All artillery in India was put under British control.
- The new Indian army was recruited almost entirely from loyal Punjabis and hardy hill farmers – the so-called 'martial races'.
- After 1858, British officers treated Indian troops with greater respect.

The military reforms ensured that British rule would continue. India's armed forces could be – and were – used for imperial purposes, holding down Britain's other territories around the Indian Ocean.

British rule after 1858

After 1858, rather than train a new Western-educated elite (which was the aim pre-1857), Britain sought to work with India's traditional rulers. Britain hoped that the latter would ensure that most Indians remained loyal. Princes and other traditional rulers thus became an important collaborating class. Social, religious and cultural matters were left in their hands. Accordingly, British administrators made no effort to overthrow the caste system (see box below). Nor, after 1857, did they challenge Hinduism or Islam. Christian evangelism was discouraged. The new emphasis was on holding India rather than preparing it for self-rule.

The caste system

This system, which existed in large parts of India, ensured that people's position in society was fixed and mobility from one caste to another (for example, by marriage) was prevented. In the Hindu caste system there were four main caste divisions: brahmins (priests), ksatriyas (warriors), vaisyas (merchants) and sudras (serfs). Outside these groups were the 'outcastes' or untouchables. Each system was elaborately subdivided. The 1901 census identified 2378 main castes, some of which had several hundred subcastes.

Economic improvement

British administrators focused on economic policies designed to improve Indians' material welfare:

- The chief priority was building railways. In 1857, there were just 288 miles of track. In the 1860s some 5000 miles of track were laid. The Indian government financially backed the railway system. Given its involvement, the track was laid out to serve military purposes, strengthening Britain's hold on India. Nevertheless, the growing railway network also made it easier to relieve famines.
- There was progress in other areas including irrigation programmes, road and canal building, and the extension of telegraphic and postal services.
- A number of public health measures reduced deaths from diseases such as cholera. This resulted in an increase in the population. The first Indian census, held in 1872, showed that the population had reached 206 million.

Nevertheless, Indian taxes were mainly spent on maintaining the Indian army, rather than on Indian improvements. Hundreds of thousands of Indians continued to die, as they had done in the past, as a result of famines.

British administration

Indians, who paid for the **Raj**'s administration and for the Indian army, had no say in how India should be run. By 1870, some 1000 British administrators ruled the whole of India. Most administrators:

- had been educated in public schools which tried to instil certain qualities – courage, self-assurance and self-sacrifice
- lived totally apart from Indians
- believed India was a long way from being peaceful enough to rule itself.

KEY TERM

Raj Used to describe British rule in India, 1858–1947. It encompasses attitudes and styles of living as well as Britain's actual governing of India.

In British eyes, firm, honest and efficient British officials governed an inferior race, keeping anarchy at bay and promoting Western technology and education. While some British civil servants looked on India as simply an opportunity to make their fortunes, most worked diligently. 'Collectors', who headed a district, played a vital role by presiding over courts, collecting taxes and watching out for any sign of political unrest. In theory, Indians could take new, supposedly competitive examinations and apply to join the Indian Civil Service, but in practice, very few Indians were admitted. They had to sit the examinations in England. Even if they passed, they were unlikely to be appointed. However, thousands of Indians had lower administrative jobs in the Indian government.

The princely states

The Raj covered just over 61 per cent of Indian territory. The remainder consisted of some 565 despotic (dictatorial) princely states. Although technically not part of British India, nearly all these states had made treaties with Britain by which they accepted allegiance to the British Crown. Britain controlled their foreign

SOURCE B

What does Source B suggest about British rule in India?

A photograph of a British administrator with Indian servants in c1870.

and defence policies. Most states also had British 'residents', drawn partly from the Indian Civil Service and partly from the British officer corps. Despite their presence, corruption and intrigue within governments remained rife in the semi-independent Indian states.

Summary diagram: India, 1857–74

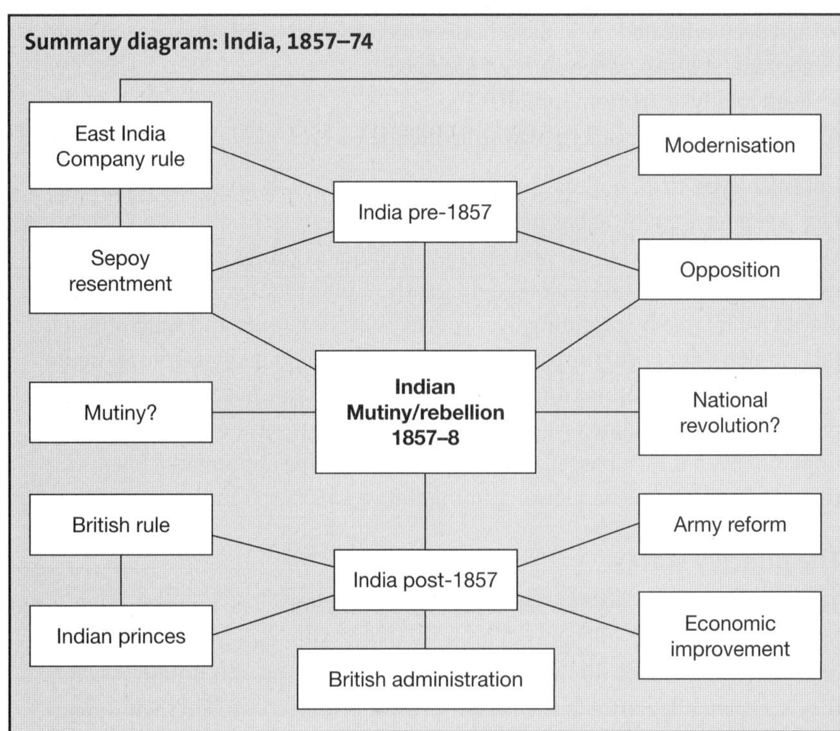

The colonies of settlement

▸ *To what extent were the colonies of settlement effectively independent by 1874?*

The West Indies

Britain had acquired several West Indian islands during the course of the seventeenth, eighteenth and early nineteenth centuries. The production of sugar made them valuable assets. The sugar plantations were the property of wealthy British landowners who imported large numbers of Africans to work as slaves on the plantations. The emancipation of slaves in the early 1830s had been carried out without undue difficulty in most of the British West Indies. The sugar-growing economy ran well enough until foreign – and much cheaper – slave-grown sugar captured the British market after the removal of the tariff preference policy in 1849. This damaged Britain's West Indian islands quite severely. Economic problems led to increased political tension. In 1865, there were extensive riots by downtrodden black people in Jamaica. Governor Edward Eyre suppressed the rioting by imposing **martial law** and hanging or flogging many hundreds of black people. William Gordon, a Baptist preacher and politician of mixed race descent, was executed on the grounds that his speeches had incited rebellion. Eyre's harsh measures divided British opinion: some thought he had taken appropriate action to check rebellion, others thought Gordon's execution an act of judicious murder.

KEY TERM

Martial law The imposition of military power by a government in time of emergency, resulting in the temporary suspension of ordinary administration and policing.

It was clear that people of mixed race, whom Gordon represented, were soon going to dominate the self-governing assemblies in most West Indies colonies, given that there was a relatively low property qualification for voting. The British government could see problems arising from black-dominated assemblies making laws in colonies with a rich white minority. The white minority also realised the problem. Thus, in 1865, the assembly of Jamaica, still dominated by white people, asked Britain to annul the island's constitution. The assemblies of other islands soon followed Jamaica's lead. In a few islands, like Barbados, Bermuda and the Bahamas, where the white population was not so obviously exposed, the assemblies survived. In these islands there was a governor with executive authority and an assembly which could pursue an independent line on taxation and legislation. In Jamaica, and other dependent colonies, governors exercised a great deal of personal power.

Australia

In the mid-nineteenth century, there was no Australia as such, instead just a number of separate colonies: New South Wales, Victoria, South Australia and Queensland. The population of the colonies increased massively after 1850, especially in Victoria and New South Wales. The Australian colonies were quickly given representative institutions.

New Zealand

Between 1841 and 1861, some 100,000 British emigrants settled in New Zealand – outnumbering the indigenous Maori population. By 1860, the settlers had acquired provincial self-government. They had also acquired about half of New Zealand's total area. In the 1860s, disputes over land led to wars between Maoris and settlers. The Maoris fought well but were eventually defeated by the arrival of 18,000 British soldiers, sent in response to Sir George Grey's exaggerated accounts of Maori aggression. British taxpayers met the cost of the Maori wars. In 1869, British troops were withdrawn from New Zealand despite pleas that they should remain. The Colonial Office told New Zealanders that self-government involved taking care of local problems, using local resources. In the event, Britain did give New Zealanders loans for defence against the perceived Maori threat.

Fortunately, the wars did not cause any deep or lasting animosity. The Maoris managed to retain control of a great deal of land and also gained a constitutional voice in the settlers' assembly. They were treated less harshly by white settlers than indigenous peoples in other colonised regions.

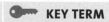

KEY TERM

Confederation
An association of states which unite permanently by treaty. Those states retain specific local powers.

Canada

British North America was huge geographically. But the population in 1860 of the provinces that would soon form the Canadian **confederation** was 3.3 million, less than that of London at that time. Federation seemed the best solution to colonies which were geographically tied together. Federation created a central government while the original colonies kept considerable local powers. Despite serious divisions, in 1865 proposals for a federal union of Canada were agreed by Canadians. In 1867, the Dominion of Canada came into existence, comprising Ontario, Quebec, New Brunswick and Nova Scotia. In 1869, the Canadian government bought the vast central tract known as Rupert's Land from the Hudson's Bay Company for a mere £300,000. British Columbia joined the Canadian Confederation in 1871. By 1871, Canada had thus taken a giant stride towards independence. As yet, few Canadians wanted complete separation from Britain. But that was now their free choice.

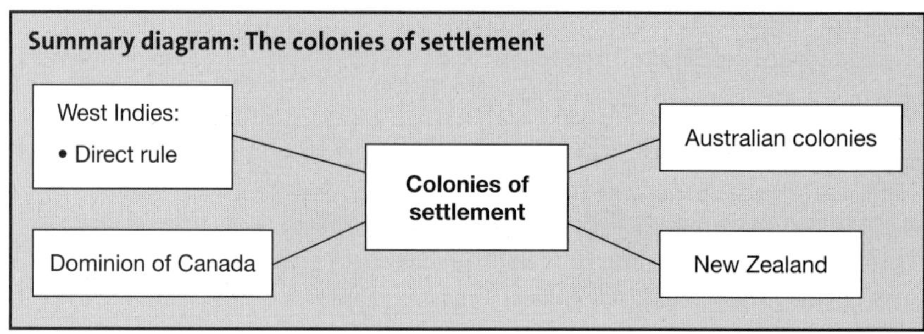

4 Expansion of the Empire in Africa

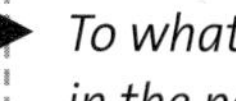

To what extent did Britain deliberately expand its Empire in Africa in the period 1857–74?

Before 1857, Britain's involvement in Africa was on a relatively small scale. For most of the period 1857–74 successive British governments believed that most of Africa was of little economic value. Nevertheless, they were averse to sacrificing Britain's position of power to potential European rivals.

Southern Africa

In 1857, British territory comprised Cape Colony (with 100,000 white and 150,000 black people – mainly **Bantu** – Africans) and Natal (with 10,000 white and 100,000 black people). Cape Colony was a vital staging post for ships sailing to eastern markets. Both colonies had assemblies. While British-appointed governors decided day-to-day policy, they could not make the assemblies pass laws or vote taxes.

KEY TERM

Bantu An African people who speak a common group of languages. In the apartheid era, the white minority used 'Bantu' or 'native' to refer to Africans in South Africa, often in a derogatory way.

The boundaries of British control were not fixed. Settlers continued to expand their territory. In the 1830s, Boer settlers (see page 2) had 'trekked' into the interior of Africa to escape British control. They set up their own republics: Transvaal and the Orange Free State.

European expansion led to wars with indigenous African people: the Xhosa (at the Cape) and the Zulus (further north). The Xhosa and the Zulu peoples proved to be formidable enemies. The fighting on the frontier posed a threat to peace and stability. British authorities endeavoured to control the situation – with mixed success:

- Costly efforts were made to annex frontier areas.
- Efforts to entrust defence to white colonists foundered: the colonists were not numerous enough or sufficiently wealthy.
- Efforts to unite British-controlled areas with the Boer republics in a great federation failed, mainly because Boers opposed the idea.

In 1868, Gladstone's government annexed Basutoland to protect it from the Boers. The discovery of diamonds in Griqualand in the late 1860s meant that southern Africa became potentially a huge economic asset. In 1871, Britain annexed Griqualand, hoping that by so doing it might reduce the cost of British involvement in southern Africa. In 1872, the Cape Parliament agreed to undertake responsible government. In the past, the financial and military burdens of self-government had held Cape politicians back, but the wealth from diamonds made expenses easier to bear.

West Africa

In West Africa, Britain controlled several small coastal areas: Gambia, Sierra Leone and a number of forts on the Gold Coast. It safeguarded its interests by cooperating with local rulers. When that cooperation broke down, Britain occasionally intervened:

- In 1861, Lagos was annexed.
- In 1873, the local Ashanti attacked Africans who lived on the Gold Coast. Sir Garnet Wolseley waged a successful campaign against them. In 1874, the Gold Coast became a Crown colony.

But the British government did not encourage its small colonies to expand inland or to acquire coastal territory so that they linked together.

East Africa

British politicians' lack of interest in acquiring territory in east Africa was shown by the Abyssinian expedition in 1868. General Napier led 13,000 troops (mostly Indian), 50,000 camp followers, 18,000 mules, 17,000 camels and 44 elephants to rescue 60 European hostages imprisoned by the Emperor Theodore. After crossing 400 miles of hazardous terrain, Napier's force destroyed Ethiopian forces at Magdala. Theodore killed himself and the prisoners were released. Napier then returned home. Although the expedition had cost £8 million, there were no suggestions that Britain should keep Abyssinia.

Egypt

In 1859, the Egyptian government gave Ferdinand de Lessop's French company permission to build a canal from the Mediterranean to Suez. British Prime Minister Palmerston opposed the venture because he feared it would inevitably lead to increased British involvement in the region – given the Suez Canal's potential importance to Britain's communications with the east. British bankers, aware of the Canal's likely importance, invested considerably in the project. The Canal was finally opened in 1869, reducing the length of a voyage to India by two months. Its completion meant that Britain was forced to take an interest in Egypt (see pages 39–40).

Explorers and missionaries

Britain's commercial and strategic interests were not alone in fuelling imperial expansion in Africa.

The opening up of Africa

Few Europeans penetrated Africa's interior pre-1850. The continent seemed to provide little opportunity for quick profit and the risk of disease and death was great. However, in the decades after 1850, advances inland became more practicable because of advances in medicine and technology:

- By the 1850s, explorers found that quinine was an effective drug against several tropical diseases, enabling them to explore more and for longer.
- Steamships, which could make their way up rivers, made water transport much easier.
- The spread of **breech-loading** rifles in the 1850s and 1860s meant that Europeans had far superior weapons to those of the Africans.

In the 1860s and 1870s, the European map of Africa was filled in by a few lone explorers:

- **John Hanning Speke** discovered Lake Victoria, the main source of the Nile, in 1858.
- **Richard Burton** discovered Lake Tanganyika with Speke in 1858.
- **Samuel White Baker** discovered Lake Albert (now Lake Mobutu) in 1864.
- **Joseph Thomson's** exploits paved the way for Britain's later claims to Kenya and Uganda.

David Livingstone

While most of the British pioneers had adventure, plain curiosity or hope of gain in mind, others thought more in terms of civilising their fellow men and women. One of the most famous explorers was missionary **David Livingstone** (1813–73), who explored south-central Africa in the 1850s and 1860s. Brought up in a crowded tenement near Glasgow and sent to work in a cotton mill at the age of ten, Livingstone hoped to end slavery and convert Africans to Christianity. His exploits, well publicised by an efficient missionary press, were eagerly read by the British public. When he was lost, an American newspaper sent journalist Henry Stanley to find him. Stanley duly obliged, locating him on the shore of Lake Tanganyika in 1871.

Missionary work

Many Victorians were inspired by Livingstone. The publicity resulting from his work helped to make Africa the focus of popular romanticism. It gave impetus to the idea that Christianity and commerce would together civilise Africa. Thus, in the second half of the nineteenth century, the work of missionary societies grew. Hundreds and later thousands of salaried missionaries travelled to Africa, hoping to convert its people to Christianity. Missionaries, mainly male initially but increasingly female over time, more than any other class of colonisers, lived and worked among local peoples. They were usually the only conduit for Western health care and education in remote areas. Missionaries were not agents of the British state: indeed, they were frequently at odds with colonial bureaucrats, although they were not necessarily critical of imperialism. They were more critical of imperial politics which, in their view, did not usually do enough to extend Christianity.

Initially, missionaries themselves were not very successful in spreading the Christian faith. Missionaries invariably faced opposition from those who

KEY TERM

Breech-loading Firearms that loaded at the side rather than down the barrel (like a musket).

KEY FIGURES

John Hanning Speke (1827–64)

Speke accompanied Richard Burton on an expedition to discover the source of the Nile in 1857–8. They discovered Lake Tanganyika and then Speke went on alone to discover Lake Victoria, which, on a second visit in 1860, he established to be the main source of the River Nile.

Richard Burton (1821–90)

After military service in India, Burton travelled in Arabia and Somaliland. He made two attempts (1855 and 1857–8) to discover the source of the Nile, discovering Lake Tanganyika (with Speke) in 1858. Burton later served as a British diplomat and also published splendid translations of oriental books, including the *Arabian Nights*.

Samuel White Baker (1821–93)

In 1861, accompanied by his wife, Baker set off from Cairo to discover the (still disputed) source of the Nile. In 1864, he found Lake Albert (now Lake Mobutu). He later led an expedition to annex the South Nile basin where, as Egypt's governor-general (1869–74), he abolished slavery.

defended traditional religious practices. Rather than making overt efforts to convert, missionaries often preferred to set up schools. This proved a better way to establish credibility. In Africa, as elsewhere, the great expansion in the number of professed Christian believers did not occur until after 1900.

Social reform

Missionaries, who tried to promote Western values, were a part of imperial conquest. They demanded reform in a wide range of 'native' activities. Along with feminists, humanitarians, doctors and teachers, missionaries called on colonial governments to end what they saw as barbaric practices. This led to the common and sincerely held view that 'uncivilised' peoples benefited from colonial administrations that educated them, helped them to curb disease and poverty, and improved their chances of a place in the afterlife.

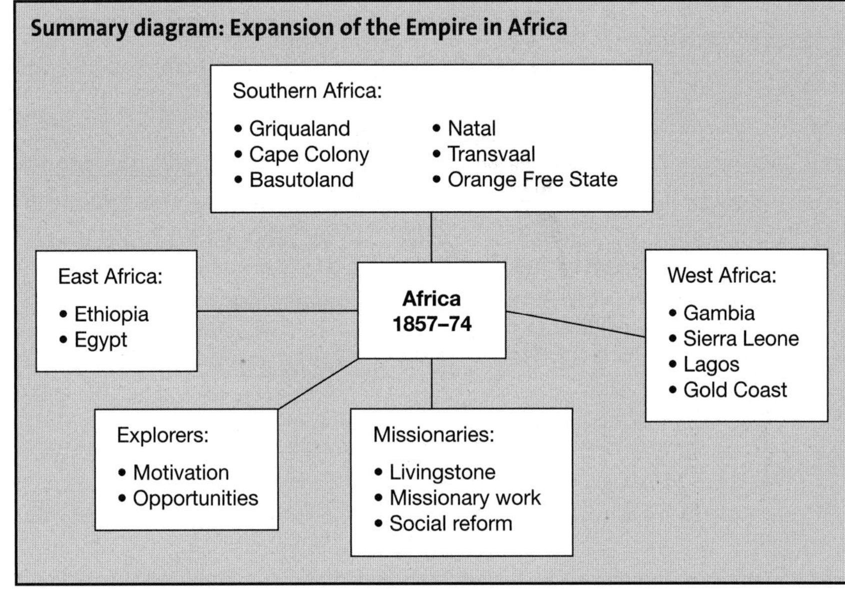

KEY FIGURES

Joseph Thomson (1858–95)

A Scottish geologist, Thomson led an important expedition to East Africa in the late 1870s. He was later employed by Cecil Rhodes to explore north of the Zambesi River.

David Livingstone (1813–73)

Livingstone was a Scottish missionary and explorer of Africa. He traced long stretches of the Zambesi, Shire and Rovuma Rivers and discovered the Victoria Falls and Lane Ngami. He was less successful as a missionary, converting very few Africans to Christianity. Nevertheless, stories of his 'good work' inspired many Britons to go to Africa as missionaries. Livingstone, having been 'found' by American Henry Stanley, died in Africa in 1873.

5 Relations with indigenous peoples

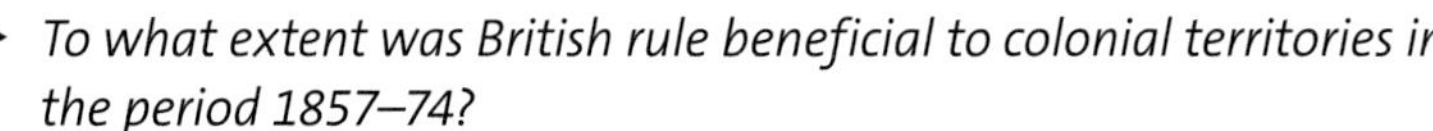

To what extent was British rule beneficial to colonial territories in the period 1857–74?

Relations with, and within, the colonies of settlement

By 1860, Britain had granted responsible government only to those colonies with a substantial number of white settlers. Britain generally had good relations with the governments in (what became) Australia, New Zealand and Canada. These governments, however, had little sympathy with indigenous people:

- Aborigines in Australia found themselves outcasts.
- Native tribes in Canada were 'encouraged' to settle on reservations.
- New Zealand Maoris managed to retain some of their land. They were also given political rights: four seats in the New Zealand Parliament were reserved for Maoris.
- In southern Africa, white settlers were too few and indigenous people too many and too useful to be driven out. While black people were often dispossessed of their land, they worked for their new white masters.

The impact of British rule

Journalists, politicians, missionaries and explorers claimed that Britain intended to bring civilisation to other countries and was preparing colonial subjects for home rule. Central to that argument was that freedom was some distance away. In the meantime, colonial peoples were far from free.

Government

There was little democracy outside the settlement colonies. Nevertheless, British officials, few in number, were often forced to cooperate with local political, religious and cultural leaders. Thus, far from attacking local cultural traditions, Britain usually worked with – not against – the traditions of the people they ruled.

Economic impact

The economic impact of colonisation created winners and losers. Some people benefited from commercial connections. Urbanisation and the building of railways in Asia and (later) in Africa produced work opportunities for indigenous men, as did the growth of large-scale agriculture, ports and shipping, and mining. But those who lost out might be trapped in dreadful conditions. Indigenous workers' wages were far lower than those of white people and they

KEY TERM

Indenture A written agreement, often between workers and employers, agreeing terms of employment – usually for a long period.

had few rights. Leaving a job 'without lawful cause', careless work or insulting a master could lead to withdrawal of wages, flogging or imprisonment. Large numbers of Indians were used as an **indentured** workforce, not just in India but in the Caribbean, Africa and the Pacific. Usually agreeing to work for five years (for very low pay), they were transported to where they were needed. Relatively little British investment went into new colonies.

Famine and disease

More than 6 million people died in famines in India in the 1870s. Cholera, plague, influenza and a host of other diseases had devastating effects in India and Africa. This was not the result of colonisation. Famines and disease had long been a terrible problem in the Indian subcontinent and large parts of Africa. But colonial governments were initially not very effective at dealing with the problems.

Education

It was mainly missionaries who provided education in the colonies, albeit at a very basic level. The sons of the elite, British and local, in India, Ceylon and Hong Kong usually received a better education, either in Britain or in British-style schools in their native country.

British administrators did their best to spread Western thought and technology and to instil British values, beliefs, institutions and habits. Those who opposed British rule were seen as backward, foolish and ignorant – their civilisation was seen to be at a standstill or in regression.

Was British rule beneficial?

British rule eventually impacted on every aspect of indigenous people's lives – job opportunities, property ownership, marriage, laws, religious practice, education, leisure and entertainment – for better and for worse. Many administrators certainly had a strong sense of duty to the people they governed. British rule did bring some economic investment, the establishment of law and order, and the end of some abhorrent practices, such as cannibalism and human sacrifice.

However, the Empire was a place of deep inequality between coloniser and colonised. A few elite groups, useful to the British, prospered. But many indigenous peoples lost their lands and their movement was restricted. Oppression, constraint and the uneven distribution of wealth and privilege were the norm. Many indigenous labourers in Africa and Asia were treated with routine brutality.

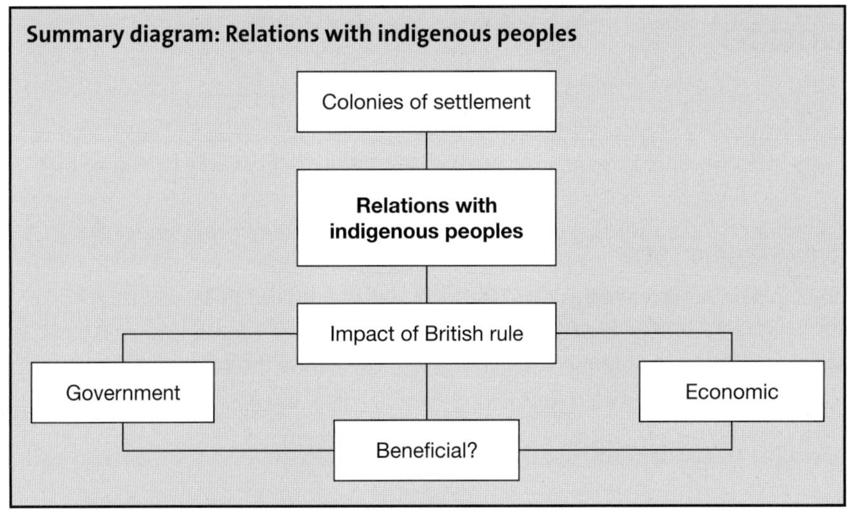

Chapter summary

The British Empire was far from a unified concern – or concept – in the period 1857–74. Colonies of settlement had little in common with Crown colonies. The acquisition of the Empire was not the result of a co-ordinated policy of conquest. Many British politicians were reluctant imperialists, preferring informal to formal empire. Nevertheless, British governments were generally determined to maintain British economic and strategic interests. Threats to these interests often led to Britain adding more territory to its Empire. Britain fought to put down the Indian Mutiny and keep control of India – the most valuable part of the Empire. Important reforms in India resulted from the mutiny. While Britain was granting increased independence to its colonies of settlement, it was extending its control in Africa. British rule had a major impact on the lives of indigenous peoples.

 Refresher questions

Use these questions to remind yourself of the key material covered in this chapter.

1 How were colonies of settlement different from Crown colonies?
2 To what extent was the Empire an empire of free trade?
3 To what extent was Britain a reluctant imperialist power?
4 What were Britain's main imperial strengths in the period 1857–74?
5 What caused the Indian Mutiny in 1857?
6 What were the main results of the Indian Mutiny?
7 How strong were Britain's relations with the colonies of settlement?
8 Why did Britain expand its territory in Africa in the years 1857–74?
9 What was the main impact of British rule on indigenous peoples?

Question practice

ESSAY QUESTIONS

1 'Britain acquired its empire in a "fit of absence of mind in the years 1857–1874".' Explain why you agree or disagree with this view.

2 'British rule in India was dependent on Indian support in the years 1857–74.' Explain why you agree or disagree with this view.

3 'The expansion of the British Empire in Africa between 1857 and 1874 was essentially the result of economic factors.' Assess the validity of this statement.

4 'There was no great enthusiasm for Empire in Britain in the period 1857–74.' Assess the validity of this statement.

CHAPTER 2

The development of imperialism, 1874–90

Between 1874 and 1890, most Britons were seemingly far more enthusiastic towards imperialism than they had been in earlier decades. This was to have a major effect on the development of the British Empire. This chapter will explore both the growth of imperialism and the Empire by examining the following themes:

★ British governments and imperialism
★ Growing threats to the Empire
★ British policy in Asia and the Pacific
★ The scramble for Africa
★ Trade and commerce

Key dates

1874	Fiji became a Crown colony
1875	Disraeli purchased the Khedive's Suez Canal shares
1876	Queen Victoria proclaimed Empress of India
1878	Cyprus placed under British administration
1879	Anglo-Zulu War: Zululand became a protectorate
1880	First Anglo-Boer War
1881	End of First Boer War Britain recognised self-government for Transvaal
1882	Occupation of Egypt
1885	General Gordon killed at Khartoum Formation of Indian National Congress
1886	Annexation of Burma
1888	Charter granted to British East Africa Company
1889	Charter granted to British South Africa Company

British governments and imperialism

▶ *To what extent did the British public support imperialism in the years 1874–90?*

Party political conflicts

In the early 1870s, Conservative leader **Benjamin Disraeli** believed he could win political capital by attacking the imperial policies of **William Gladstone's** Liberal government.

KEY FIGURES

Benjamin Disraeli (1804–81)

Seemingly committed to Empire, Disraeli became Conservative prime minister in 1874. He bought Britain a major stake in the Suez Canal in 1875 and in 1876 secured passage of a bill that conferred the title 'Empress of India' on Queen Victoria. In 1879, he took Britain into the Zulu War and the Afghan War.

William Gladstone (1809–98)

Gladstone dominated British politics in the second half of the nineteenth century. He was Liberal prime minister on four occasions: 1868–74, 1880–5, 1886 and 1892–5. He supported Irish Home Rule and was generally seen to be anti-imperialist.

Benjamin Disraeli

In his famous Crystal Palace speech in 1872, Disraeli criticised Liberal policy regarding India, and the Liberal government's decision to offer self-government to the colonies of settlement without accompanying arrangements for a **customs union**. Disraeli's attack seemed to resonate with voters. Helped by his beating of the imperialist drum, Disraeli defeated Gladstone in the 1874 general election. Disraeli, assisted by his colonial secretary the Earl of Carnarvon, then appeared to take the initiative in imperial matters:

- In 1874, Britain took control of Fiji (see page 36).
- In 1875, Disraeli purchased the Suez Canal shares (see page 39).
- In 1876, Disraeli supported a bill which gave Queen Victoria the title Empress of India. This seemed to emphasise the prime minister's firm commitment towards British imperial rule, both in India and elsewhere. Initially, the new title was unpopular in some quarters, especially among Liberals. Gladstone denounced it as 'theatrical folly and bombast'.
- In 1879, Britain went to war in Afghanistan (explained in more detail on page 34) and against the Zulus in southern Africa (see page 38).

KEY TERM

Customs union A group of states having free trade among themselves, and a common tariff policy towards non-member states.

Queen Victoria 1837–1901

Victoria, the Empress of India after 1876, came to espouse and embody imperial rule. The name Victoria was bestowed on mountains, lakes, rivers, waterfalls, harbours, provinces, districts and towns. Statues of the queen took pride of place in every large imperial city.

Disraeli, who put the consolidation of British power in India at the heart of his imperial crusade, created the image of a patriotic party for the Conservatives – a party rising above class loyalties to represent the British people as a whole. Not all contemporaries were impressed. Many viewed Disraeli as an unprincipled opportunist who supported imperialism in order to gain popularity, rather than as a matter of principle. After all, he had called the colonies 'millstones round our necks' in the 1860s. It is certainly possible to argue that Disraeli's conversion to imperialism was mainly for 'show' – not principle. Disraeli himself largely ignored imperial matters, leaving most decisions to his colonial secretary, the Earl of Carnarvon, who was a lukewarm expansionist. Once in power, Disraeli's government spent little on Empire and added little to it. In fairness to Disraeli, however, for much of his premiership he was concerned with problems in the eastern Mediterranean, particularly relations with Russia. In a sense, this was imperial action. Russia posed a threat to India which Disraeli was determined to counter. There is no doubt that by 1880 most Britons considered the Conservatives the imperialist party – as Disraeli intended. Ironically, this did Disraeli no favours electorally, as he was defeated by Gladstone in the 1880 general election.

Gladstone's Midlothian campaign

Gladstone was the dominant British politician of the second half of the nineteenth century. He won four general elections and was associated with high-minded Liberalism, the main principles of which were peace, retrenchment (cutting down government spending) and reform. After Disraeli's success in 1874, he resigned his parliamentary seat and retired from politics. But during the 1870s he was appalled by Disraeli's imperial drum-beating, describing the Afghan War of 1879 as 'a crime against God'. Indeed, he was so alarmed at Disraeli's '**jingoism**' that he emerged from retirement and stood as a candidate in the Scottish constituency of Midlothian. In the campaign, he attacked Disraeli's 'imperialist ambitions'. He argued that the only way to counteract this 'slide towards imperialism' was to champion the cause of peace, and to avoid needless imperial engagements. The Midlothian campaign was a triumph for Gladstone and helped the Liberals to win a convincing victory in the 1880 general election. Gladstone returned to office committed to the view that imperial adventures were both wrong and extravagant.

KEY TERM

Jingoism Extreme patriotism. (The word came from a popular song of the 1870s when Disraeli threatened war with Russia. According to the lyrics, 'We don't want to fight but by jingo if we do; we've got the ships, we've got the men; we've got the money too'.)

Gladstone in office, 1880–5

Gladstone and his type of high-minded Liberalism soon came under attack:

- He was naturally criticised by Conservatives, most of whom regarded Disraeli as a national hero.
- Queen Victoria viewed Gladstone as a 'dangerous revolutionary'.
- He even faced critics from within his own – divided – party. Some Liberals were supporters of Empire. Others, such as the radicals, supported welfare reforms to help the poor.

Despite Gladstone's opposition to imperial expansion, his government soon found itself involved in entanglements all over the world. Gladstone opposed what he called 'annexationism' – annexing countries merely because they could be annexed. Somewhat ironically, his government acquired more territory than

Disraeli's had done. His decision to occupy Egypt in 1882 (see page 39) dealt a severe blow to his policy of non-intervention and seemed to contradict the moral principles which he had declared would be the basis of Liberal policy. (He was concerned about Britain's economic interests in Egypt and perhaps mindful of the fact that much of his own personal wealth consisted of Egyptian stocks and shares.) However, of all the new acquisitions in the early 1880s, only Bechuanaland (now Botswana) could strictly be called a colony (see page 39). The rest were **protectorates** or spheres of influence, allowing Gladstone to claim that he had kept out of the scramble for Africa (see pages 38–42).

KEY TERMS

Protectorates States or territories which have effectively been taken over and run by another (more powerful) state without being officially annexed.

Irish Home Rule The idea that Ireland should have its own Parliament and be essentially independent from the rest of Britain.

Growing imperialist sentiment and concern

If imperial sentiment helped Disraeli to win the 1874 election, it did not save him from defeat in 1880. Most voters in the 1880 general election were concerned with domestic matters, not imperial issues. Nevertheless, all governments in the 1870s and 1880s were affected by growing imperialist sentiment:

- Politicians, whether or not they let it affect their decisions, assumed that public opinion was on the side of the imperialists.
- Governments that appeared to ignore British interests did so at their peril. The public reaction to Major-General Gordon's death at Khartoum in 1885 (see page 40) showed the strength of imperialist passion. Gladstone was not in sympathy with it, and suffered accordingly. Newspapers such as *The Times* and the *Daily Telegraph* and periodicals such as the *Spectator* and *Punch* turned sharply away from Gladstonian Liberalism. By 1885–6, a growing number of imperialists in the Liberal Party were also on the verge of revolt.

By the 1880s, newspapers expressed concern about the state of the Empire. Britain had struck a bad patch, both at home (with economic depression) and abroad (with growing tensions). It could be that 'popular' imperialism, usually associated with national self-confidence, had more to do with national self-doubt, as Britain's position in the world was challenged (see pages 48–9).

The 1886 election

The question of **Irish Home Rule** was the issue which finally split the Liberal Party. Gladstone, sympathising with the Irish Nationalists, decided to introduce a Home Rule Bill in 1881. This decision left him open to the charge that what he granted in Ireland today would be granted to India and the other colonies tomorrow. Over 50 Liberal MPs formed a separate Liberal Unionist group. Allying with the Conservatives, the Conservative/Unionists gained an overwhelming victory in 1886. Thereafter, they worked closely in Parliament, particularly as Gladstone remained as Liberal leader and continued to champion Home Rule for Ireland.

Lord Salisbury

Lord Salisbury, Conservative leader 1886–92 and 1895–1902, was cynical about high-minded justifications of Empire. 'If our ancestors had cared for the rights of other people', he said, 'the British Empire would not have been made.' Its purpose was not to spread sweetness and light but to increase Britain's wealth and power. He was very much a pragmatist. Aware of the expense of Empire, he was reluctant to get sucked into Africa except to counter the moves of other great powers. Even then, he was content for British commercial companies to take on enormous administrative responsibilities. Essentially, he was determined to maintain Britain's national interest but to do so at the cheapest cost. The responses he made to increasing challenges were not the maximum responses he thought he could get away with, but the minimum responses compatible with Britain's interest. Retrenchment thus remained a fundamental part of colonial policy in the late 1880s as it had been in the 1850s.

Lord Salisbury (1830–1903)

Salisbury was Conservative prime minister 1886–92 and 1895–1902. For much of that time, he also served as foreign secretary. He is usually associated with Britain's policy of 'splendid isolation' – no entanglements or alliances with other major powers. In 1899, he led Britain into the Boer War.

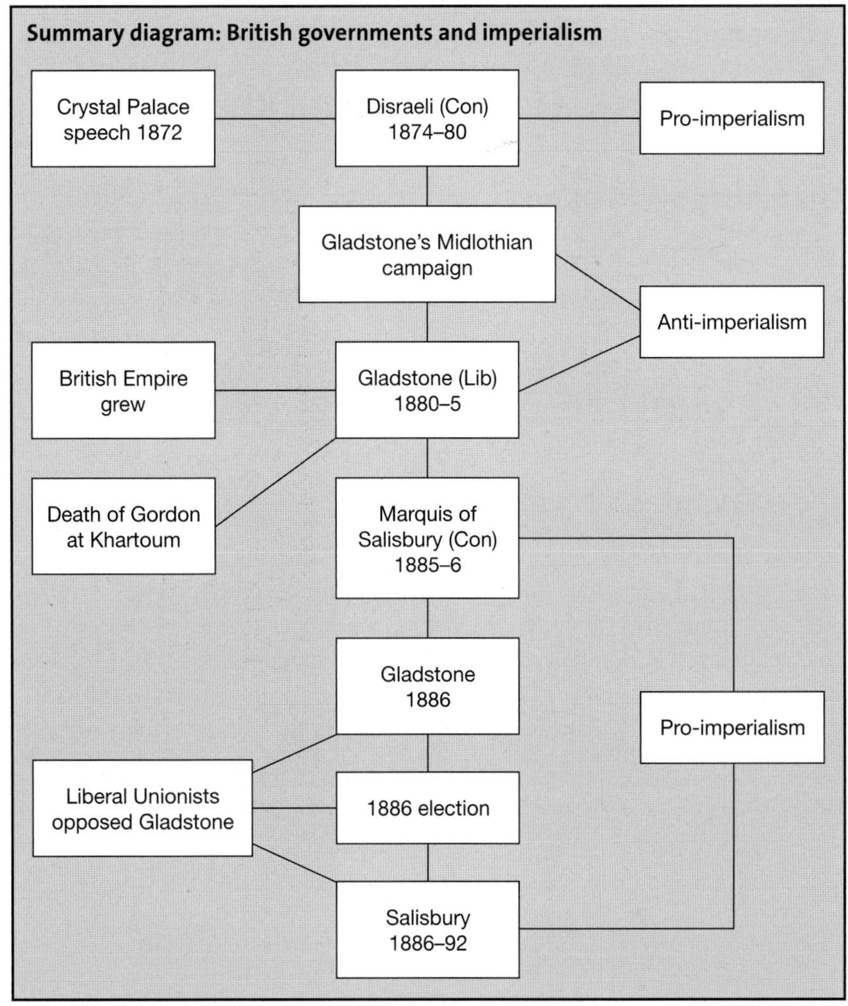

2 Growing threats to the Empire

▶ *How serious were the threats facing the British Empire in the years 1874–90?*

In the 1870s and 1880s, Britain faced a number of challenges to its imperial dominance. Nevertheless, Britain remained a strong and hugely important imperial power.

The Russian threat

In the 1870s, Russia posed the greatest threat to British interests:

- Military activity from the 1860s ensured that Russia accumulated a swathe of territory in central Asia. This brought Russia close to Afghanistan and thus made it a potential threat to India.
- Russia also had designs on the Ottoman Empire. As Russian expansion at the Ottoman Empire's expense might pose a threat to the Suez Canal, Britain felt it necessary to prop up the tottering Empire. In 1878, Disraeli acquired Cyprus from the Ottomans as a reward for supporting their Empire against Russian threats.

The European situation

By 1880, the European situation had changed:

- Germany, now a united nation, dominated central Europe.
- France, defeated by Germany in 1870–1, was determined to recover its prestige by increasing its empire in Africa and South-East Asia.
- Many Germans and Italians wished to emulate Britain's pathway to great power status by acquiring empires.

The economic challenge

By 1880, it was clear that other countries (notably Germany and the USA) were growing in industrial strength, challenging British pre-eminence. Since the 1840s, Britain had supported the idea of free trade. However, by the late nineteenth century, its industrial rivals imposed high duties, designed to protect their own economic interests. If Britain's competitors acquired colonies, Britain might be unable to trade with large areas of the world. To make matters worse, in the 1870s and 1880s economic depression led to falling profits and growing unemployment. This added to the fears of scarcity of markets. Many Britons believed that the country must expand its Empire to secure export outlets.

British strengths

Despite the challenging international situation, new technological developments favoured Britain's imperial position:

- Steamships and railways made most parts of the world more accessible.
- The electric telegraph and the submarine cable (which reached India in 1870) tightened the bonds and widened the bounds of Empire.
- Medical improvements gave Europeans a better chance of survival in the tropics.
- Britain enhanced its military supremacy over indigenous forces. Early prototypes of the machine gun – the Gatling gun and the Maxim gun – cut down local troops with ease. Similarly, new breech-loading rifles, developed in the 1860s, were far more deadly than the old musket. Accordingly, imperial troops had an overwhelming advantage in the colonial wars of the period.

However, Britain had no monopoly of the new technology. Other advanced nations had access to it. Other races could share it. Indian terrorists, for example, could make better bombs while Zulus could acquire modern rifles. Developments in communication made it easier for opponents of Britain to meet, share views and discuss possible courses of action.

British imperial and colonial policy

To many politicians, Britain's best hope of retaining its great power status was imperial expansion. Not all were convinced.

- Many Liberals remained **Little Englanders**.
- The men who made colonial policy, whether Liberal or Conservative, were generally cautious, concerned as always about the cost of Empire.

Nevertheless, established British interests appeared vulnerable. If Britain stood still, it might lose ground. Accordingly, politicians took stronger measures to secure imperial interests than previously.

Little Englanders Opponents of British imperialism.

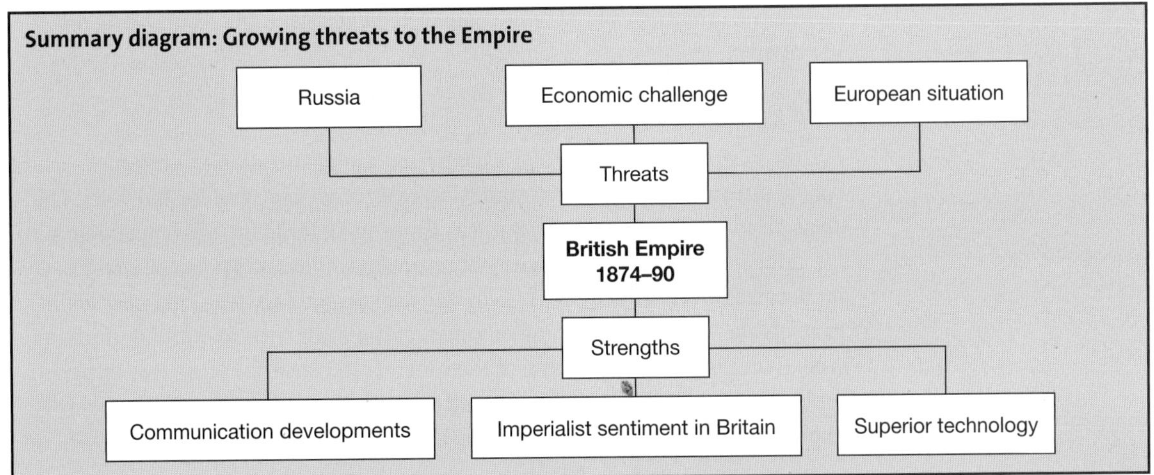

British policy in Asia and the Pacific

▶ *How effectively did Britain respond to the threats to its position in Asia and the Pacific in the years 1874–90?*

Afghanistan

In the 1860s, the British government had stuck to a policy of leaving Afghanistan alone, trusting to the effects of great distances and difficult terrain to keep India safe from potential Russian action. Disraeli, however, tried to encourage Thomas Baring, First Earl of Northbrook, the Indian viceroy at the time, to adopt a more active policy to stop Russian meddling in Afghanistan. When Northbrook resigned rather than do so, Lord Lytton replaced him:

- In 1876, Baluchistan, an unsettled area south of Afghanistan, became a British protectorate.
- In 1878, the Emir of Afghanistan accepted a Russian **envoy** at his court. Lytton, more aggressive than his instructions from London allowed, responded by insisting that the Emir should also accept a British envoy. When he refused, Lytton sent troops to Afghanistan and imposed a British envoy.
- In 1879, the people of Kabul rebelled against the British and the envoy was killed. Disraeli now declared war on Afghanistan. General Sir Frederick Roberts invaded the country, defeated Afghan forces, and reinstalled a British envoy. A new Emir agreed to accept British control of his foreign policy.

In effect, Afghanistan thus became a British protectorate.

KEY TERMS

Envoy A diplomat sent to transact business with a foreign government.

Raison d'être The main purpose.

The Raj

Enlightened Victorians insisted that good government was the ***raison d'être*** of British rule in India. Unfortunately, the British did not rule India particularly well. If the intentions of the white elite were benevolent, the results were not impressive.

Lord Lytton

Lytton, viceroy from 1876 to 1880, continued the post-Indian Mutiny approach of conciliating the princely class, mainly to avoid provoking any fresh revolts. The decision to proclaim Queen Victoria as Empress of India in 1876 helped reassure the princes that the British would not return to Dalhousie's policy of drastic modernisation (see page 10). A great imperial assemblage was held near Delhi to celebrate Victoria's becoming empress, at the same time as 5 million Indians were dying in the worst famine of the nineteenth century. Lytton was criticised for holding a public display of magnificence at such a time. His policies also alienated the emerging Indian middle class:

- He tried to create a two-tier civil service whereby Indians would be excluded from top levels, claiming that race distinction (essentially keeping races separate and with white people in a dominant position) was fundamental to Britain's position as the conquering power.
- He removed duties on imported cotton goods, thus further sacrificing Indian products to those of Britain.
- He imposed a Vernacular Press Act (1878) to gag criticism in non-English newspapers.

Table 2.1 Viceroys of India: 1864–1916

Sir John Lawrence	1864–9
Earl of Mayo	1869–72
Sir John Strachey	Feb 1872
Lord Napier	Feb–May 1872
Lord Northbrook	1872–6
Lord Lytton	1876–80
Marquess of Ripon	1880–4
Earl of Dufferin	1884–8
Marquis of Lansdowne	1888–94
Earl of Elgin	1894–9
Lord Curzon	1899–1905
Earl of Minto	1905–10
Lord Hardinge	1910–16

Lord Ripon

Lytton's successor, Lord Ripon, was a Gladstonian Liberal who governed India more sympathetically. He believed it was vital to make 'educated natives the friends, instead of the enemies, of our rule'. Thus, he repealed the Vernacular Press Act and introduced a measure of local self-government – albeit very limited in scope. His endeavour to permit Indian judges to try Europeans in court outraged the British community and he was forced to back down. Ripon left India in 1884, respected by Indians but not by Anglo-Indians.

Improvement

British civil servants, continuing to claim that they were the selfless guardians of India's downtrodden masses, pushed ahead with modernising India. More money was spent on irrigation, promotion of agricultural improvement, public health and railway building. The Indian railway system was the largest and costliest project of the colonial era.

The formation of the National Congress

Technological development – railway building, the telegraph, improved steamships, the building of the Suez Canal – all drew India closer to Europe. The circulation of information and ideas between Europe and India, and across India, began to accelerate. By the 1880s, more Indians could speak English and their knowledge of the situation in Britain increased. Indian intellectuals were aware that Gladstone stressed the need for a close political bond between people and government. Some claimed that British rule in India was thus 'unBritish'. Well-educated Indians, who had once been committed to Britain and modernisation, were less confident about the situation by 1880. Those who had hoped to join the ruling elite by passing the civil service exams realised that they stood little chance of doing so (see pages 15–16).

In the 1880s, educated Indians founded societies to discuss their problems. In December 1885, the first meeting of the **Indian National Congress** was held in Bombay. The new viceroy, Lord Dufferin, approved the organisation. When members of the Congress met in Calcutta in 1886, he held a reception for them. Dufferin hoped that he could use the organisation to discover what educated Indians thought and adjust the Raj accordingly. But those British civil servants who predicted that the movement was likely to develop a spirit of nationalism

KEY TERM

Indian National Congress Initially a society set up by educated Indians, it eventually became a major political force, campaigning first for home rule and then for independence for India.

were proved right. By 1890, members of the Congress were asking for home rule. While British officials accepted the need to work with Indians and allowed them to participate in local government, the Indian Civil Service was determined to preserve the racial solidarity of the white ruling caste.

Malaya

Britain expanded its grip on Malaya. The British governor in Penang was authorised to send residents to the courts of the sultans who still ruled much of the Malayan peninsula. This began the process of undermining the sultans' power.

Fiji

In the 1860s, British traders and settlers had begun to show interest in Fiji. By 1872, the King of Fiji, fearing that he might lose his authority, decided to hand the island over to the British government in the hope that it would be a conservative force. In 1874, a government commission's report urged the government to take over Fiji. Disraeli's government accepted the report. Fiji, in historian T.E. Lloyd's view (1997), is a good small-scale example of the way British possessions often grew: the British government did not encourage the activities of its expansion-minded subjects but eventually was forced to take action as a result of their activities.

Borneo

KEY TERM

Rajahs Indian and other Asian princes or kings.

The southern parts of Borneo had long been a Dutch colony. But on the north-west coast an English family – the Brookes – had established themselves as **rajahs**. The Brookes continued to be British subjects but their territory had no definable connection with the British Empire. When British businesses wanted to develop the timber found in north-east Borneo, they did not feel that an extension of Brooke rule would meet their needs. Instead, they asked for a charter to run their chosen territory with the sort of power that the East India Company had possessed in the eighteenth century. Gladstone's government granted the charter in 1881. The British Borneo Company limped along for many decades without doing very well economically. The precedent of granting a company a charter was to have important results in Africa.

New Guinea

In 1883, Germany began to show interest in New Guinea. Fearful of German annexation, the Queensland government proposed to annex the half of the island that the Dutch had not colonised. Other Australian colonial governments joined Queensland in demanding that Britain should do something – preferably, annexing all islands in the Pacific south of the equator that had not previously been occupied by a European power. The British government was unenthusiastic. It saw no reason to suppose that these islands could pay for themselves, no reason why British taxpayers should pay for the occupation, and no reason why Britain should quarrel with Germany or other countries over such a policy of universal annexation. Instead, in 1884, Britain set up a protectorate on the south-east coast of New Guinea but made it clear that the Germans were welcome to the north-east quarter of the island.

Burma

In 1885, Britain, concerned about French advances in Indo-China, invaded and annexed Upper Burma. (Lower Burma had been seized by Britain in the mid-1850s.) The Burmese king ruled his subjects brutally enough for British opinion to feel that suppressing him would be a humane policy. Indian Viceroy Lord Dufferin incorporated Burma into the Raj, destroying the old framework of government. His actions provoked a long and fierce **guerrilla war**. British forces responded savagely, burning villages and executing suspected terrorists. Burma, while part of the administrative structure, was never absorbed into India. Burmese national feeling remained strong and resentful of British rule.

KEY TERM

Guerrilla war Conflicts in which irregular forces harass an enemy rather than fight pitched battles.

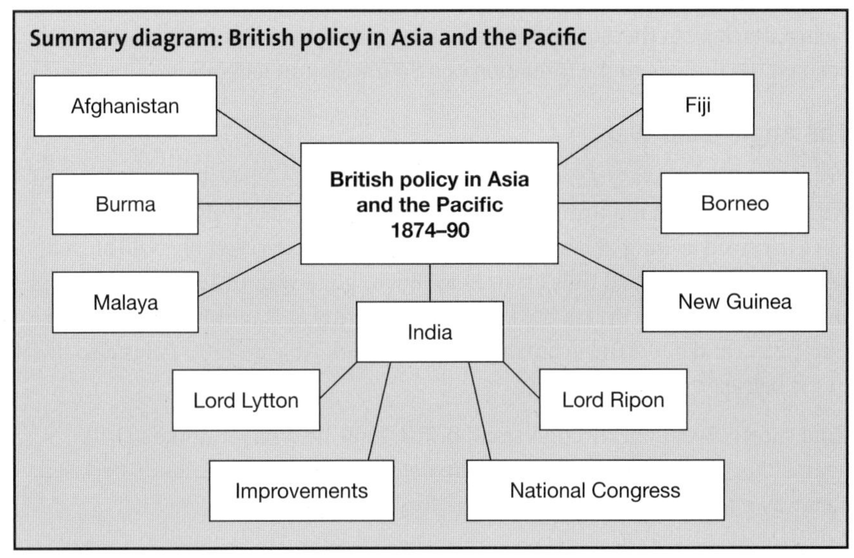

4 The scramble for Africa

▶ *To what extent were British actions in Africa successful in the period 1874–90?*

In the 1870s, but particularly in the 1880s, Britain was involved in a scramble for territory in Africa. Between 1884 and 1886, Otto von Bismarck, the German chancellor, who had previously shown no interest in colonies, suddenly seemed to become a convert to imperialism. Germany acquired South-West Africa, the Cameroons, Togoland and Tanganyika (see map on page 42). Bismarck was also instrumental in establishing Belgium's King Leopold as proprietor of the Congo. Gladstone professed not to be concerned and even welcomed Bismarck's colonial zeal, seeing him as a partner in 'civilising' Africa. But there was the danger that Britain might be squeezed out of African markets by German tariffs. At the same time there were threats from France in west Africa and from the Boers in southern Africa.

Zulus and Boers

Given that confederation had proved successful in Canada (see page 18), British officials hoped that a similar policy might be adopted in southern Africa. Their aim was to unite Cape Colony and Natal with the Boer republics, Transvaal and the Orange Free State (see page 19). In 1877, Transvaal, almost bankrupt and facing attack from the Zulu King Cetewayo, agreed to accept British rule. This seemed the prelude to the formation of a South African federation.

The Anglo-Zulu War

Britain's next step was to end the Zulu threat. In 1878, Cetewayo was presented with an ultimatum requiring him to disband his army. No Zulu king would have survived as king of his people if he had attempted to comply with such a demand. Cetewayo had thus little choice but to go to war. In 1879, 20,000 Zulus invaded territory the British held, defeating its army at Isandhlwana. Some 700 Europeans and 500 African auxiliaries were killed. At least 1500 Zulus also died in the battle.

Zulu success was short lived. A small British force held out at Rorke's Drift against huge odds. In June 1879, Britain defeated the Zulus at Ulundi, deposed Cetewayo, and annexed more Zulu territory.

The First Boer War

Britain's victory over the Zulus did not win Boer gratitude. Given that there was no longer a Zulu threat, the Transvaal Boers wished to be independent again. In 1880–1 they rose in rebellion, defeating a small British force at Majuba. Gladstone, sympathetic to the Boers, was not prepared to fight. Therefore, in 1882, Britain recognised Transvaal and the Orange Free State as self-governing nations. Two years later, the Boer states were given almost complete home rule except that Britain still claimed **suzerainty**, although it was far from clear at the time exactly what this meant.

KEY TERM

Suzerainty Having supreme power over someone.

Britain's hope of unifying southern Africa appeared to have collapsed.

Bechuanaland

In 1884, Germany established a protectorate over South-West Africa. This gave the Transvaal a possible outlet to the sea through Bechuanaland. Accordingly, in 1885, Britain annexed Bechuanaland, in an attempt to strengthen its position in southern Africa.

The Transvaal threat

In 1886, vast quantities of gold were discovered in Transvaal, potentially making it the richest nation in southern Africa. Transvaal's gold threatened to tilt the balance of power between Britons and Boers in favour of the Boers. Given that thousands of Boers lived in Cape Colony and Natal, it was possible that Transvaal might try to take over the whole of southern Africa.

Britain's response

Britain's response to these developments was further territorial expansion:

- Between 1885 and 1887, Britain took over Zululand and the remaining parts of the coastline between Natal and Mozambique to stop Transvaal reaching the sea.
- In the late 1880s, diamond millionaire Cecil Rhodes formed a commercial company to occupy Matabeleland and Mashonaland (see page 61), hoping to discover even more gold. He was granted a charter in 1889 which entitled his company, the British South Africa Company, to administer the territory north of the Limpopo River.

British involvement in Egypt and the Sudan

Egypt, nominally under the control of the Ottoman Empire (see page 6), was essentially independent. From 1863 it was ruled by Ismail Pasha. In the 1860s, Pasha supported the building of the Suez Canal.

The purchase of the Khedive's shares

Completed in 1869, the Canal halved the maritime distance between London and India: British steamers could now do the journey in four weeks. Three-quarters of the shipping using the Canal was British. Although the Canal was a potential money-maker, Ismail's government (the Khedive) borrowed money unwisely and by the mid-1870s was in debt to French and British creditors. In 1875, Disraeli purchased the Egyptian government's shares (nearly half the total) in the Suez Canal Company to check the spread of French influence in Egypt.

The occupation of Egypt

Despite the shares' sale, Egypt went bankrupt in 1876. Egypt's British and French creditors took over the running of the country. Harsh financial measures, including the reduction of the Egyptian army, provoked a nationalist uprising in 1881, which threatened the Suez Canal's security. Initially, the French took the lead in claiming that the authority of the debt commissioners must be recognised, and Egypt brought under control, while Gladstone had some sympathy for the rebels' demand of 'Egypt for the Egyptians'. However, in June 1882, riots in Alexandria led to the death of 50 Europeans. It seemed that Egypt was sliding into anarchy. Britain now intervened: the Royal Navy bombarded Alexandria, and British troops led by Sir Garnet Wolseley defeated the Egyptians at Tel-el-Kebir and occupied Cairo after a brilliant campaign.

Gladstone's government announced that the British occupation was to be a temporary measure. The British confined themselves to giving the Egyptian government advice through a consul-general (who, legally, was the equal of the diplomatic representative of any other nation). As none of the other diplomats had an army on the spot, British advice came to be seen as a command. In 1883, Sir Evelyn Baring was appointed consul-general, with the task of restoring stable and honest government. By 1885, Britain, through Baring's influence, had assumed control over Egypt – to the anger of France. For the next two decades Anglo-French relations were blighted by Britain's occupation of Egypt.

The Sudan

By occupying Egypt, Britain became involved in the Sudan. Egypt had claimed the Sudan (see map on page 42) as Egyptian territory for half a century, without much success. In 1881, an extremist religious leader, Mohammed Ahmed, known as the Mahdi, led a rising against Egyptian occupation. In 1883, the Mahdi's forces annihilated an Egyptian army, but Egyptian garrisons continued to hold out in Khartoum and a number of other Sudanese towns. Rather than becoming embroiled in a war to defeat the Mahdi, Gladstone decided to evacuate the Egyptian forces. The man chosen for the task was Major-General **Gordon**, a fervent imperialist.

Gordon reached Khartoum in February 1884 and soon convinced himself that it was neither humane nor necessary to abandon the Sudan to the Mahdi. Instead, he set about organising the defence of Khartoum. After much dithering, Gladstone (who believed that Gordon was trying to force Britain to annex the Sudan) decided to send a relief force to save Gordon. Two days before it arrived, Gordon was killed in January 1885 when Khartoum was overrun by the Mahdi's forces. Gordon became a hero figure among the imperialists. Many Britons blamed his death on Gladstone's indecision, but Gladstone stuck to his policy of staying out of Sudan – to the disgust of Queen Victoria and many ordinary Britons.

KEY FIGURE

Charles Gordon (1833–85)

Gordon served in the Crimean War and in China, where he suppressed a major rebellion in 1864. In 1874, he was employed by the Khedive of Egypt and from 1877 to 1880 was British governor of the Sudan. In 1884, he was sent back to the Sudan to evacuate Europeans and Egyptians, following the Mahdi's revolt. He was besieged for ten months in Khartoum, which fell two days before a relief force arrived. Gordon, who was killed, became a British hero.

West Africa

Although for many years the leading trading force in the region, Britain took little action as France and Germany seized territory in west Africa in the 1880s. The one exception was on the River Niger, where British commercial interests (buying palm oil in exchange for guns and liquor) were greatest, and where there was an agency at hand to carry the burden of administration – Sir George Goldie's Royal Niger Company. In 1886, Goldie's company was allowed to levy taxes, enabling him to eliminate competition. The company was also given powers of government in the River Niger basin, north of the coastal region. Goldie and his administrators were able to compete successfully with France in inducing African chiefs to sign treaties which were necessary to give legal validity to expansion. With Conservative leader Salisbury's backing, Goldie ensured that the Niger Company's claims to large areas of what became Nigeria were accepted. This prevented France annexing the region.

East Africa

In 1884–5, Germany claimed much of east Africa. Rather than quarrelling, Britain reached an agreement with Bismarck at the Berlin Conference whereby much of east Africa was divided into spheres of influence. In 1888, Salisbury, fearing that Germany was about to seize more territory, supported William Mackinnon's British East Africa Company. The company's charter allowed it to hold and rule the section of east Africa that lay between German East Africa and Italian claims in Somaliland. Mackinnon sent an expedition to Uganda, establishing the company's authority over the area. Bismarck, who had no wish to quarrel with Britain, was keen to reach a settlement. In 1890, Salisbury gave up the North Sea island of Heligoland in exchange for:

- German acceptance of the British annexation of Zanzibar
- recognition of Britain's occupation of Egypt
- recognition of Britain's interests in east Africa.

The chartered companies

Most African colonies, initially unprofitable, were dependent on subsidies from their respective governments. The British government was rather less willing to give subsidies than most of its European competitors. Instead, it relied on chartered trading companies absorbing administrative, police and transport costs from their trading profits. This ensured that British taxpayers did not have to bear these costs. However, there were disadvantages in giving commercial companies licence to rule colonial territories:

- They discouraged free competition.
- Their exploitative functions were rarely compatible with their subjects' welfare.

- None of the charters granted in the 1880s gave the companies the monopoly of the British market. Accordingly, profits were in most cases not large enough for the companies to maintain an administration and an army.

The 'men on the spot'

The British government was by no means in control over 'men on the spot' who often drove imperial expansion:

- It did not exert much control over missionaries who went to Africa to convert people to Christ rather than to act as cultural assistants of British power.
- It did not necessarily control the actions of men such as Goldie and Rhodes, who did their best to encourage British government involvement in Africa. Such men worked with local power brokers to realise their grandiose schemes (see, for example, page 61). Once the schemes were launched, they sought the support of the British government to complete the process.
- The government did not necessarily have much control over its own officials. Technology meant that many parts of the world were scarcely in contact with London. Thus, governors of particular colonies wielded considerable power.

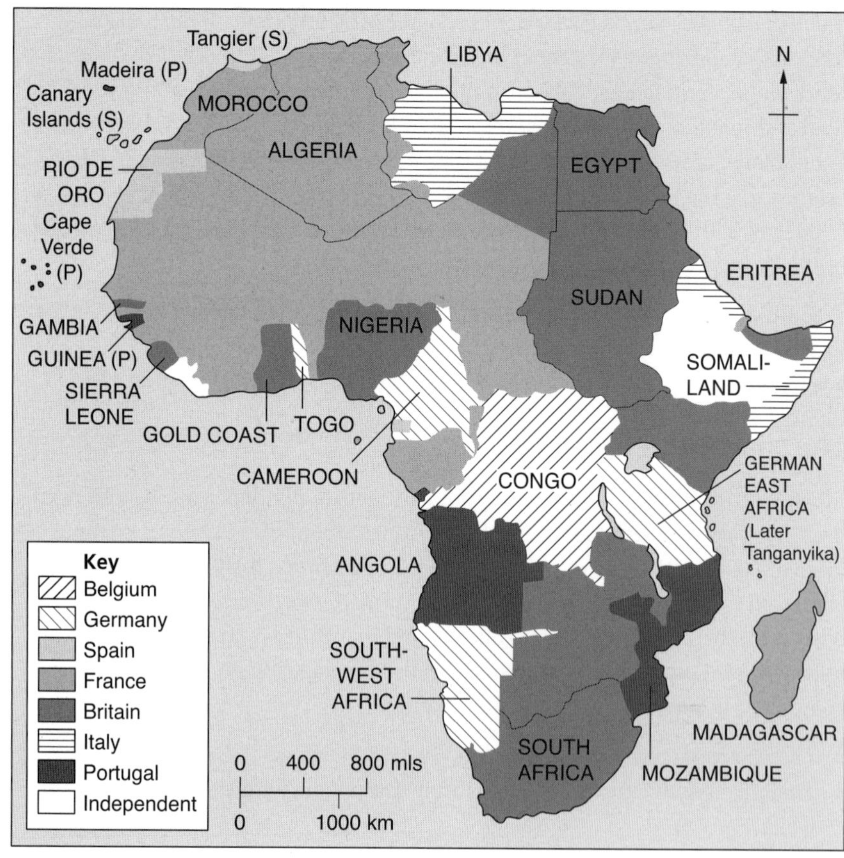

Figure 2.1 Africa in 1890.

Conclusion

Britain acquired large parts of Africa in the 1880s. Political annexation was not undertaken lightly – usually only to safeguard established British interests. It was regarded as a last resort. The difference between the 1860s–1870s and the 1880s was that in the latter period, the last resort had to be resorted to more often. By 1890, treaty-making had run ahead of map-making as Britain, France and Germany worked out partition frontiers without having much idea of the nature of the land they were acquiring. But at least diplomacy had ensured there was no risk of immediate conflict between the European powers arising from the situation in Africa.

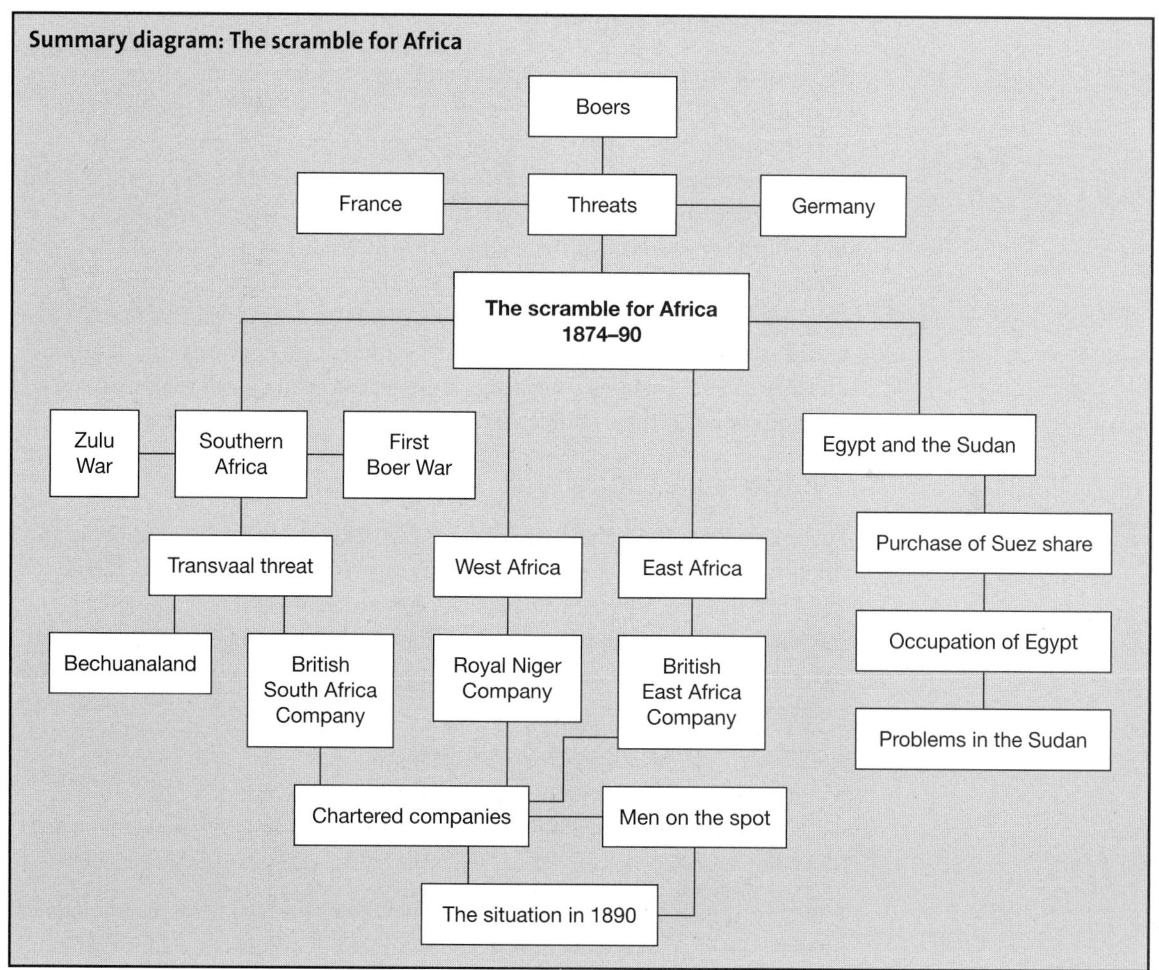

 5 Trade and commerce

▶ *To what extent was British imperial expansion the result of trade and commerce in the period 1874–90?*

By the 1880s, Britain's commercial dominance was contracting. As Britain's 'informal' Empire was challenged, Britain's formal Empire expanded. This was no accident. Imperial expansion in the 1880s, rather than a sign of British power, was more a reflection of its decline. Instead of enjoying a vague ascendancy over the world as a whole, Britain now had more definite ownership over just part of it.

The colonial economies

Prohibitive tariffs imposed by Britain's competitors (for example, Germany from 1879 and France from 1881) undermined the principle of free trade. Consequently, British commercial interest shifted towards the colonies. In theory, the colonies operated in a free-trade environment, but in practice Britain dominated as supplier and as buyer. In most colonies, the encouragement to produce goods for the British market helped Britain more than it did the producers. Colonial production tended to be focused on a narrow range of commodities. This lack of diversity made colonial economies vulnerable to market shifts. However, there was a wide economic gulf between 'settlement' and 'dependent' colonies. The former experienced economic development on a scale unknown in the dependent colonies.

'Gentlemanly capitalism'

Historians Peter Cain and Tony Hopkins (2001) claimed that City of London financiers had a major impact on imperial expansion. According to Cain and Hopkins, these 'gentlemanly capitalists', concerned about their commercial interests and overseas investments, were able to 'persuade' governments to act in their best interests. However, many scholars question this interpretation. They point out that:

- northern manufacturers also had 'influence'
- City financiers often competed with each other
- there is little evidence of financiers actually 'persuading' governments to act as they wished.

In reality, British governments acted in what they perceived to be the 'national interest'. Their actions were affected by a number of influences: public opinion, strategic interests, prestige, as well as financial, economic and commercial considerations.

Fair trade

By the 1880s, British economic supremacy was under threat. Whereas Britain produced nearly a third of the world's manufactured goods in 1873, by 1883 the figure had shrunk to less than a quarter. Given the economic challenge, some Britons thought it was time to see a major change in policy. In the 1880s a number of politicians and businessmen talked about 'fair trade'. By this, they meant Britain and its Empire establishing protective tariffs, ending the previous commitment to free trade. Although a few Conservative MPs took it seriously, the 'fair trade' movement did not win the unequivocal support of any leading British politician in the 1880s.

The Imperial Federation League

In Britain there was increasing concern about the rise of larger and potentially stronger nations, especially Germany, Russia and the USA. All had a greater number of workers and more natural resources than Britain. If large nations and empires were to dominate the future, then the British Empire could be the largest of all. In 1884, the Imperial Federation League was created with this in mind. The League was not committed to federation in the technical sense of wanting a structure of government with a central legislature. It simply asked for the 'closer union' of the Empire. At times, however, it did discuss possible constitutions for an Empire with a central parliament. The organisation was dominated by Conservatives although Lord Rosebery, a future Liberal prime minister, was an enthusiastic recruit.

In 1887, the League persuaded Salisbury that the celebration of Queen Victoria's Golden Jubilee (the fiftieth anniversary of her reign) would be an excellent opportunity for the British government and colonial leaders, who would be coming to London to join in the ceremonies, to discuss the imperial future. In the event, nothing was agreed. Although supportive of a system of imperial preference, the self-governing colonies valued their autonomy. They had no wish to surrender it to a united parliament dominated by Britain. Few British politicians, by contrast, were prepared to abandon the doctrine of free trade.

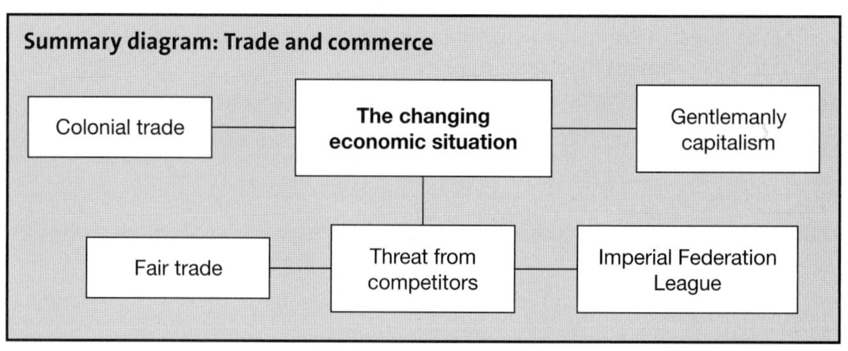

Chapter summary

In the 1870s, the Conservative Party (under Disraeli) espoused the imperialist cause. Although more Britons were enthusiastic towards imperialism, this did not guarantee the Conservatives electoral success. Liberal leader Gladstone, who was opposed to imperial expansion, was re-elected in 1880 and again in 1892. Ironically, the Empire grew more under Gladstone than under Disraeli. The Empire faced economic and territorial challenges from Russia, France, the USA and Germany. Britain responded to the challenge by expanding its Empire in Asia, the Pacific and Africa, where it made use of chartered companies which bore many of the costs of Empire. Concerned at the economic challenge posed by its tariff-imposing competitors, some Britons supported the creation of an imperial customs union. Despite colonial support, such hopes came to nothing.

Refresher questions

Use these questions to remind yourself of the key material covered in this chapter.

1 To what extent did the Conservative and Liberal parties disagree about imperial matters?
2 To what extent was the British electorate imperialist?
3 Which country posed the main threat to Britain?
4 How successful were British policies in India?
5 How successful were British policies in Africa?
6 What role did chartered companies play in Africa?
7 How important were 'men on the spot'?
8 How important were economic and financial factors in Britain's imperial expansion?

Question practice

ESSAY QUESTIONS

1 'The British electorate was far more enthusiastic towards Empire in the period 1874–90.' Explain why you agree or disagree with this view.
2 'The economic challenge was the main reason for the growing imperial sentiment in Britain in the years 1874–90.' Explain why you agree or disagree with this view.
3 'Britain won the scramble for Africa in the years 1874–90.' Assess the validity of this statement.
4 'British imperial expansion was the result of trade and financial concerns in the years 1874–90.' Assess the validity of this statement.

CHAPTER 3

Imperial consolidation, c1890–1902

Throughout the 1890s, Britain continued to feel threatened by European rivals and was forced to expend more of its resources in resisting the perceived challenge. It also faced challenges from the Boers in southern Africa. This chapter will examine Britain's problems by focusing on the following themes:

★ The strengths and weaknesses of the Empire in the 1890s

★ British imperialism, 1890–1902

★ Britain in Asia, 1890–1902

★ Consolidation and expansion of the Empire in Africa

★ Problems in southern Africa, 1890–7

★ The causes and course of the Second Boer War

Key dates

1895	Jameson raid	**1899**	Start of the Second Boer War
1898	Battle of Omdurman	**1901**	Australia acquired a national constitution
	Fashoda incident	**1902**	End of the Second Boer War
	Wei-hai-wei leased to Britain		

1 The strengths and weaknesses of the Empire in the 1890s

▶ *To what extent was the period from 1890 to 1902 the high point of British imperialism?*

In the 1890s, Britain ruled the largest empire the world had ever seen. The representations of Empire and the way it featured in popular culture, such as Queen Victoria's Diamond Jubilee (her sixtieth year as monarch) procession in 1897 (see page 49), seemed proof that Britain had never been greater. But beneath the display there was an awareness that Britain was weaker – economically, militarily and diplomatically – in the world than two decades earlier.

The threats to Britain

After 1890, the British Empire faced challenges from several quarters.

Economic decline

In the 1890s, Britain's economic dominance was under threat:

- There was a decline in Britain's old export staples of cotton and woollen textiles.
- Britain was overtaken in steel production by the USA and Germany.
- By 1900, Britain's imports were greater in value than its exports. The deficit was bridged partly by the interest on investments abroad and partly through service industries.

Some people saw the economic threat as an argument for overseas expansion. Even if a colony did not directly favour British goods, it would still be helpful to keep territory out of the hands of countries that would set up tariffs to exclude British goods.

Military weakness

Britain's armed forces seemed insufficient to defend its scattered possessions. The army, excepting the Indian army, was relatively small. The Royal Navy was also a growing source of concern. In 1889, the government had adopted the 'two-power standard': British naval strength should always exceed that of the next two strongest navies combined. A large naval building programme was inaugurated. But other countries – France, the USA, Germany, Japan and Russia – were also building new fleets. After 1900, Germany increasingly posed a threat to British naval supremacy.

Diplomatic weakness

Britain had no allies. Its diplomatic isolation was called 'splendid' as if it were an aloofness deliberately chosen. But many statesmen regarded it with unease, fearing that other countries (most likely France and Russia) might combine against Britain. Some Liberals refused to regard all foreigners automatically as rivals or enemies and believed in peaceful cooperation. But they were a minority. The governments of the 1890s, mostly Conservative, made a virtue of realism: they acknowledged the amorality of the world – and thus the dangers.

The Empire's fragility

The Empire looked strong on maps simply because it appeared to be so large. The reality was different:

- A bigger Empire resulted in Britain having more frontiers to defend and longer supply lines to maintain in the event of war.
- New colonies were occupied by peoples who had no loyalty to Britain. Indeed, in the event of a major war, they might side with the enemy.

- The Empire was full of weak spots in the 1890s. Northern India was threatened by Russia, and Egypt and the Sudan by France. Southern Africa was not secure while the Boer republics were so rich and so hostile.

British strengths

Despite fears about decline, Britain remained a great imperial power. By the mid-1890s its Empire covered 11 million square miles and contained 400 million people. In many respects, its imperial strengths outweighed its weaknesses.

Imperial enthusiasm

According to historian Piers Brendon, writing in 2007, the years between 1897 and 1900 'probably witnessed the most fervent devotion to the Empire ever manifested in Britain'. Imperial enthusiasm took two distinct forms in the Empire post-1890:

- enthusiasm for closer relations between Britain and the self-governing colonies, most of whose inhabitants were of British descent
- enthusiasm for expansion by the acquisition of new territory.

Closer union and territorial expansion were expressions of nationalism. Many people in the self-governing colonies, proud of their Britishness, shared this feeling.

Military strength

The Royal Navy continued to rule the waves and the Indian army continued to rule India. Britain was strong enough to deal with internal threats in Africa and Asia.

Economic and financial strength

Britain continued to be a great manufacturing nation and the world's greatest trading nation. As a result of its service industries – shipping, banking and insurance – it continued to have a healthy balance of payments surplus.

Representing Empire: Queen Victoria's Diamond Jubilee

Queen Victoria's Diamond Jubilee in 1897 was a celebration of Britain's imperial greatness. London was festooned with garlands, banners and bunting. Eleven colonial premiers took part in a great procession. So did dozens of Indian maharajahs. Some 46,000 troops marched past the queen. At the Spithead naval review more than 160 warships were arrayed in three lines, almost 30 miles in length.

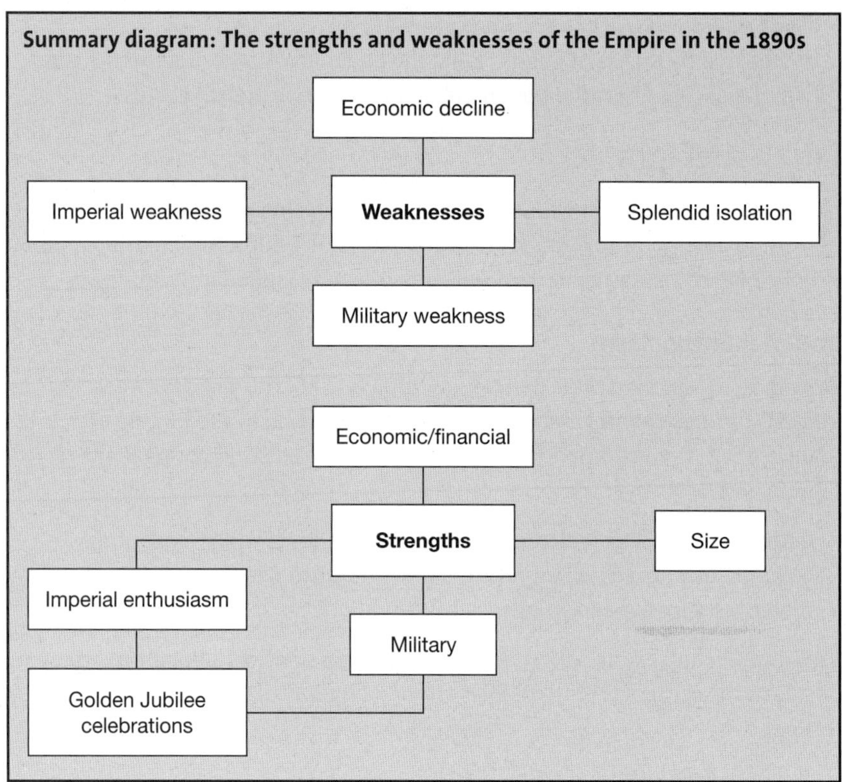

2 British imperialism, 1890–1902

▶ *To what extent did the roles and influence of Cecil Rhodes and Joseph Chamberlain epitomise British imperialist opinion in the years 1890–1902?*

In the 1890s, a more strident form of imperialism emerged. Imperialists had various visions of how Britain might strengthen the Empire and how the Empire might strengthen Britain.

Key supporters of imperialism

Cecil Rhodes and Joseph Chamberlain were leading supporters of British imperialism.

Cecil Rhodes

Cecil Rhodes played a crucial role in southern Africa. Arriving at the Cape in 1870, he made a fortune from diamond- and gold-mining. He was Cape prime minister (from 1890) and developed a 'big idea' for the expansion of the Empire. Convinced that the British were 'the first race in the world, and that the more of

Cecil Rhodes

1853	Born, the son of a vicar of Bishop's Stortford
1870	Travelled to southern Africa, hoping to improve his health
1870s	Made his fortune from Kimberley diamonds
1881	Entered the Cape Colony Parliament
1888	Paid for mining concessions from King Lobengula, who ruled an area north of the Limpopo River
1889	Secured a Royal Charter for his British South Africa Company to exploit mineral resources north of the Transvaal
1890	Sent a Pioneer Column from Kimberley to Mashonaland – an invasion masquerading as a mining expedition
1890	Became prime minister of the Cape; he aimed to form a British Union of South Africa stretching from the Cape to the Belgium Congo
1895	The area controlled by Rhodes' South Africa Company was named Rhodesia in his honour
1895	Responsible for the Jameson raid (see page 61)
1896	Forced to resign as Cape prime minister for his involvement in the Jameson raid
1902	Died

Rhodes believed that the ends justified the means. He was often ruthless and sometimes reckless. President Stephanus Johannes Paulus 'Paul' Kruger of the Transvaal described him as 'one of the most unscrupulous characters that have ever existed'. He believed that every man had his price. Historian Bernard Porter (*The Lion's Share: A Short History of British Imperialism 1850–2004*, published in 2004) had this to say about Rhodes:

> *Rhodes' influence in South African affairs was partly the outcome of his wealth and the use he made of it, partly the result of the favour shown to him by British government ministers for reasons of their own. The two things were connected, of course. Rhodes used his wealth to cultivate ministers' favour and ministers favoured him partly because of the power he wielded through his wealth. The threads of politics and finance were finely entangled; but they were distinct. Rhodes's power had been built up out of the Kimberley diamond fields, which he came to monopolise in 1888 and the gold reefs of the Witwatersrand, which he never could control absolutely, but which he shared with two or three other great magnates in the 1890s. With the wealth from these two gigantic concerns at his back, and with winning ways with all kinds of men which none of his rivals could begin to compete with, he established for himself a predominant position in South African politics.*

the world we inhabit the better it is for the human race', he dreamed of bringing Africa, Latin America, the Middle East and China under British rule, recovering the USA in the process. In the meantime, he hoped to see the construction of a railway from Cape Town to Cairo which would go through British-controlled territory.

Joseph Chamberlain

Joseph Chamberlain, leader of the Liberal Unionists (formed in 1886, see page 60), had long advocated the notion of forging a more cohesive Empire – a federation of nations – bound together by economic interest and with an imperial Parliament in London. He took a positive view of imperial endeavour. He believed its aim was to spread civilisation and commerce abroad in order to promote prosperity and social reform at home. By providing markets, raw materials and outlets for Britain's surplus population, colonies could alleviate

? What point is the cartoonist in Source A trying to make?

SOURCE A

The Rhodes Colossus, a cartoon published in *Punch* magazine in 1892.

hardship in Britain. Chamberlain hoped that this would weaken the growing support for socialism, which he perceived as a major threat. Given the challenge from Germany and the USA, he believed that imperial unity was vital if Britain was to remain a great power.

In 1895, Chamberlain became colonial secretary. The post had not been considered particularly important in the past. The Foreign Office dealt with major international negotiations. But Chamberlain put a new spirit into the system, perhaps best expressed by his remark that the colonies were a 'neglected estate' which he determined would not be neglected in the future. But, short of (Treasury) money, Chamberlain's plans never developed as he wished.

In 1897, Chamberlain pressed for a federal council which would lay down a united foreign policy for the Empire. The prime ministers of the self-governing colonies drew back from this. While they talked of closer union, they did not want an institution based in London and dominated by Britain which might limit their freedom of action. Their idea of closer union was to persuade Britain to set up a protective tariff with preferential rates for colonial products.

Popular support for Empire

Most Britons seemed to have felt a sense of pride in the Empire and derived satisfaction from the thought that they constituted a successful imperial 'race'. Most Britons at the time regarded the superiority of white people over black people as self-evident. They also saw themselves as the best of all the white races. While the term 'Anglo-Saxon race' was often used, it was not usually thought of in purely biological terms: it was envisaged more as a carrier of a distinct set of values and institutions. In fact, the most common justification of Empire rested less on race than on the concept of 'mission'. There was a strong belief that Britain brought education, peace and better conditions of life to 'lower races'.

Historians generally agree that the greatest enthusiasm for Empire came from the upper and middle classes. However, there is evidence that working-class Britons were more imperialist than was once thought. Victorian music-hall songs and acts, popular with the working classes, had a strong imperial emphasis, supporting a jingoistic view of Empire.

By the early twentieth century, the most popular newspapers – the *Daily Mail* and the *Daily Express* – strongly supported British imperialism. Imperial enthusiasts created associations to work for imperial unity, for example, the British Empire League (1894).

Opposition to Empire

Not all Britons supported imperialism. Radical Liberals, members of the fledgling Socialist groups and Irish Nationalists were all critical of it, with some:

- arguing that the Empire exposed Britain to wars
- insisting that imperial ambitions distracted attention from social problems at home
- attacking the Empire for its exploitation of indigenous people.

The political impact of imperialism

It seemed that imperialism might provide the cement the Conservatives had been looking for to forge all classes into 'one nation'. Conservative/Unionist governments were in power for most of the period from 1886 to 1905. The Liberal Party was divided. Some Liberals, like Lord Rosebery, were committed imperialists. Others, like David Lloyd George, were anti-imperialist.

Greater Britain

Most of the self-governing colonies felt close to Britain. This owed much to the fact that most Canadians, Australians and New Zealanders had British roots. There was also pride in association with Britain which was in so many ways the leader of the English-speaking countries. Moreover, the self-governing colonies appreciated the tangible economic and financial benefits of links with Britain.

Australian unity

The various Australian colonies (see page 17) had begun to draw closer together during the 1880s:

- In 1882, an Australian cricket team defeated an English team. Cricket success helped the Australians to see themselves as a nation well before political union.
- Germany's brief period of advance in the Pacific from 1883 to 1885 (see pages 36–7) made Australians more concerned about their position in the world and more willing to look at ways of uniting the colonies. A Federal Council was created, comprising representatives of the six colonies.

Two meetings in 1890 and 1891 laid the foundations of an Australian constitution. It was taken for granted that the British monarch would be head of state. The colonies then set out to build a federal and democratic system, similar to that of the USA. In 1898, the proposed constitution was presented to the electorates to vote on in referendums. After some revisions, the constitution was accepted by all the colonies. Britain accepted the new constitution and Australia emerged as a self-governing colony in January 1901. Most Australians saw federation as a way of playing a more important part within the British Empire, not as a step away from it.

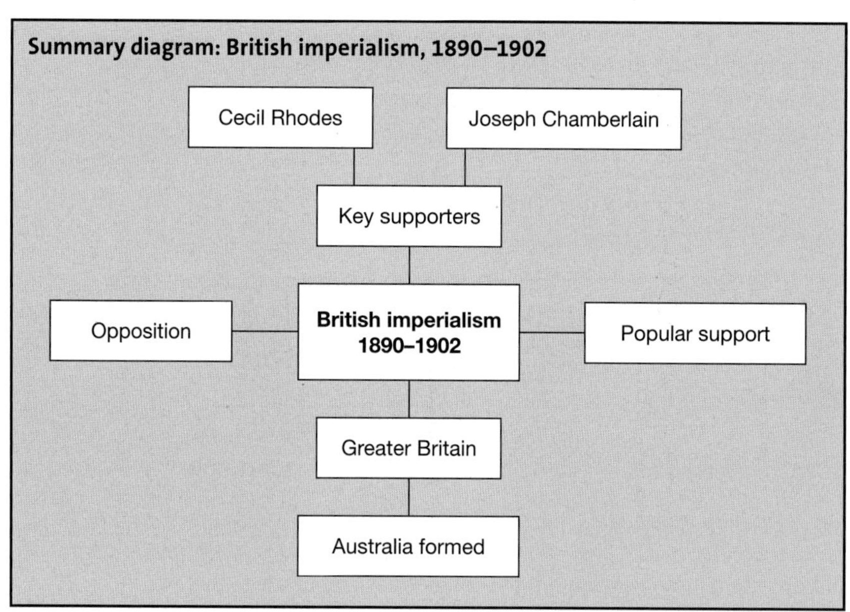

Britain in Asia, 1890–1902

▶ *What problems did Britain face in Asia in the years 1890–1902?*

Britain's main rival in Asia was Russia, which was still regarded as a major threat to India. Britain also saw Russia as a threat in China – a country which seemed to be stumbling towards extinction (see pages 6–7).

The problem of China

In the early 1890s, British manufacturers and financiers enjoyed free access to China, to Britain's advantage (see page 6). More than half of China's foreign trade was in British hands. Britain was aware that this situation could not last. Its commercial rivals were beginning to exploit the Manchu dynasty's crumbling authority by demanding exclusive concessions. Britain feared that China would eventually be partitioned among the stronger nations – a partition from which Britain was unlikely to benefit.

Although one-third of the world's population were Chinese, Anglo-Chinese trade never made up more than one per cent of total British overseas trade at any time pre-1914. However, it was the prospects for future growth rather than the current reality that concerned British merchants and the British government.

In 1895, China was defeated in war by Japan. As part of the peace agreement, China agreed to pay Japan a £30 million indemnity. China could raise this sum only by borrowing, mortgaging its resources as security. In 1897–8, there was a frantic scramble to lend China the money it needed – in return for ports, railways, banks, mining rights and control of customs revenues. Britain joined in the scramble, taking the port of Wei-hai-wei, more of Kowloon and 2800 miles of railway concessions. Effectively, China was divided into spheres of influence: Russia in the north, France in the south, Germany in Shantung, while Britain controlled the Yangtse valley – China's commercial heartland.

The Boxer rising

A Chinese reaction in 1900 (the Boxer rising) threatened to provoke a wholesale colonial grab by the powers. Fortunately for Britain, Russia and Germany did not want to expand or see others expand. They agreed to put down the rebellion in concert with other powers and to maintain the Manchus. Accordingly, the rebellion was supressed and order restored. In the end, China was saved from partition only because the various powers feared the ambitions of each other more than they wanted to rule China. The survival of an independent China was satisfactory for Britain: this had been its aim all along.

The north-west frontier

To the north and east of India, British policy towards Russia was cautious and conciliatory. The buffer states of Persia and Afghanistan helped to limit Russian advances. In India, Britain subdued rebellious tribes in areas bordering Afghanistan. A major rebellion was crushed in 1897. British policy thereafter was to persuade the tribes to police themselves and to use the Indian army in the last resort. This policy worked. The north-west frontier quietened down.

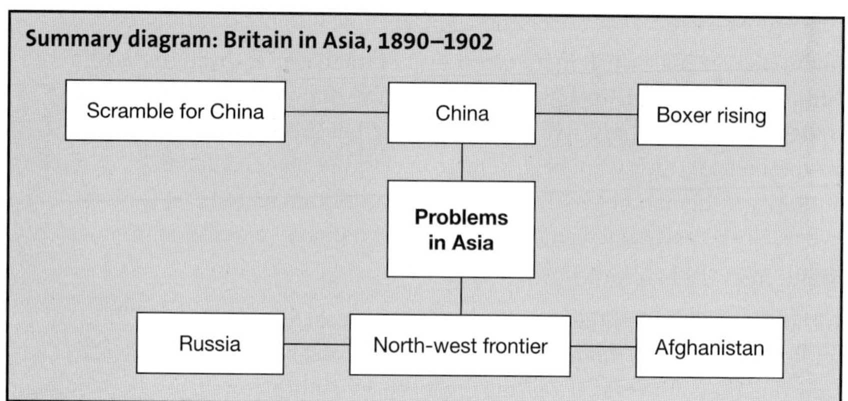

Summary diagram: Britain in Asia, 1890–1902

Consolidation and expansion of the Empire in Africa

▶ *To what extent was British expansion in Africa the result of challenges from other European powers in the period 1890–1902?*

The scramble for Africa in the 1890s had little to do with trade. As the British foreign secretary told the French ambassador in 1895, the vast areas of central Africa were nothing more than 'barren deserts or places where white men cannot live, dotted with thinly scattered tribes who cannot be made to work'. Lord Salisbury held a similar view. However, he was aware that winning territory in Africa helped to sustain Britain's international standing: France was Britain's main rival, and there was a danger that Anglo-French rivalry in Africa could lead to a major war.

East Africa

In 1890, Germany had recognised Britain's title to Uganda and the Upper Nile (see page 41). The British East Africa Company established a British presence in what became Uganda and Kenya without involving the British government. Sir William Mackinnon, founder of the company, was a wealthy shipping owner: devout, philanthropic and keen to spread civilisation to Africa.

In 1890, the company's representative Captain Frederick Lugard marched into an area known as Buganda (modern-day Uganda) and persuaded its ruler to accept the company as his overlord. This was politically satisfactory for the British government. However, it made little financial sense for the East Africa Company. There was not enough trade to justify going so far inland.

In 1894, Uganda was declared a British protectorate as the company drew back. By 1895, the company was bankrupt. Salisbury's government compensated it for the money it had spent on administration. Britain then built a railway line from Mombasa to Uganda. Commercially, the line was not much sounder than the company. East Africa was too poor and too short of people to fulfil British expectations. By 1900, the two colonies of Kenya and Uganda, into which the East Africa Company's territory had been divided, still depended on British grants.

West Africa

Britain controlled Sierra Leone, the Gold Coast, Lagos and the Niger in west Africa. The main question was how far their **hinterlands** should go. France was far more committed than Britain to west Africa. Moreover, it had armies there, ready to fight. Britain was not prepared to offer a serious challenge to French ambitions. The agreed boundaries of Sierra Leone, Gambia and the Gold Coast favoured France.

KEY TERM

Hinterland Inland territory.

On the River Niger, it was different. Sir George Goldie's Royal Niger Company had a firm claim to a large part of the hinterland and forces to support its claim. Goldie continued to persuade local rulers to sign treaties in which they gave up jurisdiction in return for protection. The French did much the same. Goldie's most effective agent was Frederick Lugard, who had proved his worth in East Africa. Lugard was successful because of the determination with which he approached the task but also because Africans usually preferred the Niger Company, which offered trade and gifts, to French military rule.

In 1897, the French moved into an area the Niger Company had been administering since the mid-1880s. The company asked the government for help. Salisbury's government accepted that it would do so. But it did not want to perpetuate a situation in which the company's board of directors could plunge Britain into a European war. The government began negotiations to buy out the political and administrative side of the company's activities. Meanwhile, the company's officials acted as the government's agents in defining the western frontier of Nigeria. British and French forces marched up and down disputed areas, hoisting their own flags as close to those of the other side as was practicable without bringing on a war. Salisbury and the Foreign Office were willing to give way to France, but Chamberlain stood firmly behind the claims of the Niger Company. Eventually, in 1898, the French agreed to Nigeria becoming larger in area than they would have liked.

In 1899, the process of buying out the company's right to govern was completed (for £850,000) and the British government prepared to rule its new, densely populated colony – Nigeria. Goldie likened the government's action to a highwayman, who not only robbed his victim but stole his clothes. Lugard became high commissioner for northern Nigeria in 1900. He refined Goldie's methods, recruiting local chiefs as collaborators and using force against those who did not collaborate.

Egypt and the Sudan

By 1890, the British government accepted that Egypt was a permanent responsibility and, given the Suez Canal's importance, its safeguarding became a top priority. Thus, the territories to the south of Egypt which straddled the Upper Nile were also a major concern. Salisbury was convinced that Britain must secure the whole of the Nile or some other power might dam it, cutting off Egypt's water supply. His government announced that it would regard the advance by a European power into the area whose rivers and watercourses flowed into the Nile as an 'unfriendly act'.

By the late 1890s, Baring (now Lord Cromer) had successfully reduced Egyptian government spending, ensuring that it had sufficient funds to consider using its re-equipped and retrained army to march south into the Sudan. The Mahdi (see page 40) had died shortly after the capture of Khartoum but the Khalifa (the successor) had established a reasonably stable state. The British controllers of Egypt supported an advance down the Nile to reconquer Sudan and avenge Major-General Gordon (see page 40).

Fashoda

Britain still feared French designs on the Nile valley, with good reason. France, which ruled much of north Africa, hoped to occupy the Sudan and prise Britain out of Egypt. In 1896 a French military expedition, led by Captain Marchand, set out to travel via the French Congo (see map on page 42) to claim the Sudan.

 **KEY TERM**

Dervishes Members of an Islamic sect who opposed Egyptian/British rule in the Sudan in the late nineteenth century.

In 1896, Britain, aware of the French challenge, sent a large Anglo-Egyptian force under General Kitchener into the Sudan. Kitchener subdued the **Dervishes** as he marched south. His advance was slow because as he headed to Khartoum, his forces laid a railway line – proof that Britain intended to hold on to the Sudan once it was conquered. The greatest battle came at Omdurman, near Khartoum, on 2 September 1898. Eleven thousand Dervishes were killed. Fewer than 50 British and Egyptians died. Britain and Egypt could now claim the Sudan by right of conquest.

Captain Marchand's small French force reached the Nile at Fashoda two months before the battle of Omdurman. Later, in September 1898, Marchand and Kitchener met at Fashoda. The two officers held friendly talks, agreed to differ and then waited for their governments to resolve the problem of who controlled the Sudan. It was no contest:

- Kitchener's army far outnumbered Marchand's force.
- Kitchener had a string of military conquests to confirm Egypt/Britain's claim.
- Britain had effective control over the region.
- Britain was prepared to fight a war with France in order to keep control over the Sudan.
- France was not prepared to fight a war it could not win.

Marchand returned to French territory and France withdrew its claims in the Nile valley. Britain now controlled the Upper Nile region.

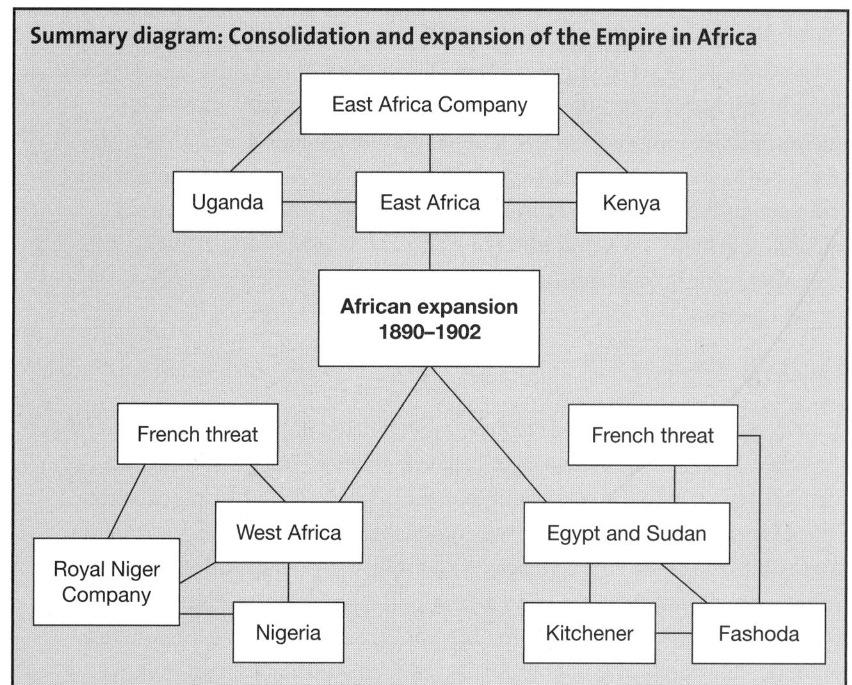

5 Problems in southern Africa, 1890–7

▶ *To what extent was Britain responsible for the tension in southern Africa in the period 1890–7?*

Although still claiming suzerainty over Transvaal and the Orange Free State (see pages 38–9), Britain had restored virtual independence to the two republics in the early 1880s. Then, in 1886, gold was discovered in Transvaal, making it the richest nation in southern Africa (see page 39). This situation threatened to tilt the balance of power between Britons and Boers in the region in favour of the Boers.

KEY TERMS

Uitlanders White foreigners living in the Transvaal and the Orange Free State.

Portuguese East Africa Modern Mozambique.

The problem of the *uitlanders*

Transvaal lacked the workers and the expertise to develop the gold mines on its own. Consequently, waves of immigrants – ***uitlanders*** – mainly from Britain, poured into Transvaal hoping to make their fortune. Some did so. Indeed, much of Transvaal's new wealth was soon in the hands of a few British and German mine-owners. By the mid-1890s, *uitlanders* exceeded the Boer inhabitants and paid nine-tenths of the Transvaal's taxes. Determined to maintain Boer supremacy, Transvaal's government, led by President Kruger, insisted that *uitlanders* had to reside for fourteen years in Transvaal before they could apply for full Transvaal citizenship.

Kruger's denial of voting rights to the *uitlanders*, coupled with irksome (some thought oppressive) taxation, gave the British government a pretext for interference in Transvaal, whose independent behaviour it was anxious to stop. Britain was particularly angry in 1894–5, when Transvaal's government proposed building a railway through **Portuguese East Africa**, thereby bypassing British-controlled ports in Natal and Cape Colony. As well as freeing Transvaal from British control, this would undermine the prosperity of the British colonies.

Salisbury's aims

In 1895, Salisbury returned as Conservative prime minister. He was also foreign secretary. His aims were to protect Britain's essential interests – security, India, the world sea lanes – by preserving peace. Salisbury's tenure of the Foreign Office is usually associated with 'splendid isolation': the idea that Britain did not need to make binding alliances with any other power. Parliament had little influence over Salisbury's foreign and imperial policy. Such disagreements as there were took place within the Liberal Party, where Little Englanders denounced Britain's imperial ambitions which necessitated high military expenditure. But Liberal leaders generally supported Salisbury's policies. Salisbury disliked the encroachment of democratic pressures into the diplomatic process, particularly fearing popular excitements, fanned by newspapers. However, he knew that public opinion could not be entirely ignored. Thus, he sometimes found himself being pushed in directions he did not wish to go. Joseph Chamberlain was one of those who 'pushed' him.

Joseph Chamberlain

Chamberlain, with other Liberal Unionists, had transferred his allegiance to the Conservatives because he opposed Irish Home Rule. In 1895, Chamberlain became colonial secretary (see page 81), aiming to forge a more coherent Empire. He quickly enhanced his own authority and raised the profile of the Colonial Office. His aggressive defence of British imperial interests, supported by a jingoist press, sometimes collided with Salisbury's quieter conduct of policy.

Cecil Rhodes and the British South Africa Company

Cecil Rhodes played a crucial role in southern Africa (see page 51). He dreamed of bringing the whole of Africa under British rule. Standing in the way of his ambitions were the Boer republics.

Through the British South Africa Company (see page 51), Rhodes sent men north of the Limpopo river into Mashonaland in 1890. He hoped that they would discover gold which would cancel out Transvaal's advantage. Rhodes' action led to the annexation of territories later known as **Southern Rhodesia** and **Northern Rhodesia**. However, no gold fields were discovered.

KEY TERMS

Northern Rhodesia
Modern Zambia.

Southern Rhodesia
Modern Zimbabwe.

By 1893, after a brief and decisive war against the Matabele people, the company's political authority was firmly established. Britain, which had taken over the Nyasa area, allowed the South Africa Company to administer the area. Rhodes' company thus controlled an area of some 750,000 square miles.

The Jameson raid

In the early 1890s, Rhodes encouraged *uitlanders* to agitate for voting rights. Transvaal's government correctly saw this as a deliberate plot to undermine its independence. In 1895, Rhodes hatched a scheme to seize control of Transvaal. An uprising of *uitlanders* would be supported by men from his company's mounted police. Rhodes left the planning to Dr Jameson, a company administrator. Rhodes expected Jameson to wait for a revolt to break out in Johannesburg before his force crossed the border to help. But, in December 1895, Jameson led 600 armed men into Transvaal. Unfortunately for Jameson, Boer authorities had warning of the raid and were prepared. Jameson's men were soon surrounded by Boer forces and, after a brief skirmish, forced to surrender. The uprising of *uitlanders* never materialised.

Consequences of the Jameson raid

There were several consequences of the raid:

- Instead of weakening President Kruger, the raid strengthened him and made him more uncompromising.
- The raid's failure was a deep humiliation for Salisbury and Chamberlain, both of whom denied any knowledge of the raid.
- Rhodes, severely censured at both a Cape inquiry and a London parliamentary inquiry, was forced to resign as Cape prime minister and as chairman of the South Africa Company.
- Transvaal's government handed its prisoners over to British authorities and they were put on trial in Britain. Jameson, regarded as a hero by the British public, was sentenced to fifteen months' imprisonment. For a time his wax model occupied a place of honour at Madame Tussaud's wax figures museum in London.

- The raid alienated many Cape Boers from the British.
- The British government realised that it could no longer pursue its southern Africa policies by relying on capitalists like Rhodes.
- The raid drew Transvaal and the Orange Free State (led by President Martinus Theunis Steyn) together in opposition to the British threat. In 1897, the two Boer republics signed a military pact.
- Kruger, convinced that war with Britain was likely, equipped Transvaal's army with the best European rifles and artillery.

Rhodesia

In 1896, both the Mashona and the Matabele tribes rebelled against the South Africa Company's rule in Rhodesia. They killed more than 370 Europeans, about ten per cent of the white population – but the white settlers, assisted by British soldiers, had the firepower to defeat the rebels, who retreated to strongholds in the Matopo Hills. Rhodes salvaged his reputation by riding forward alone to meet the Matabele leaders, and managed to bring the rebellion to a quicker and less bloody end than had seemed possible.

Summary diagram: Problems in southern Africa, 1890–7

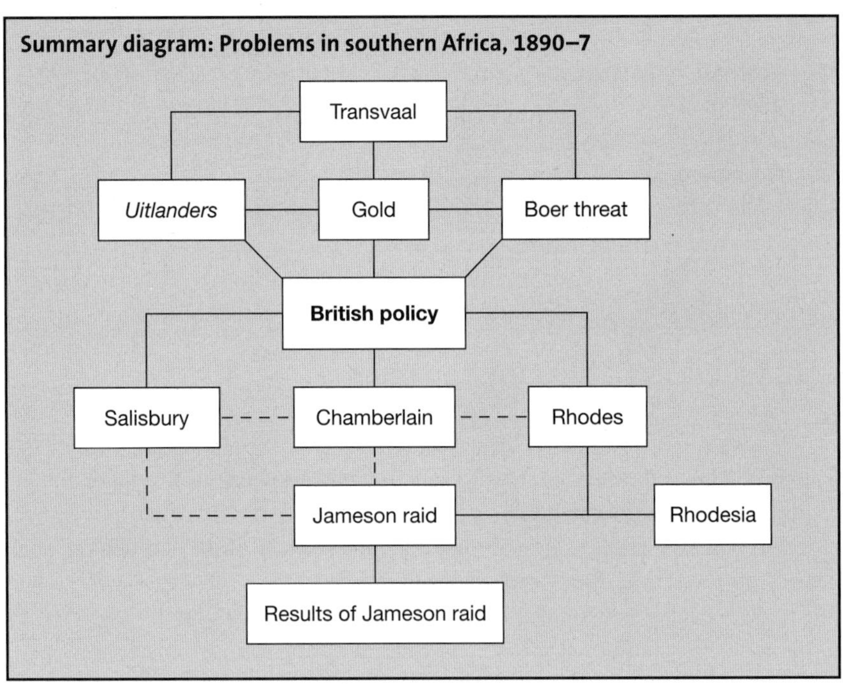

6 The causes and course of the Second Boer War

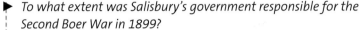

To what extent was Salisbury's government responsible for the Second Boer War in 1899?

The causes of the war, 1896–9

In 1897, the British government, very much influenced by Chamberlain, sent **Alfred Milner**, a passionate imperialist, as high commissioner to southern Africa. Milner told a friend that he was going to 'teach those bloody Boers a lesson'. He believed that gold-rich Transvaal, perhaps assisted by Germany or France, represented a threat to Britain. Once in Africa, he worked to mobilise pro-British elements and constantly exerted pressure on behalf of the *uitlanders*. In his dealings with **Kruger**, Milner took an uncompromising stance, demanding that *uitlanders* be granted full citizenship within five years. It is possible that he pressed for the *uitlanders'* right to vote because he thought an *uitlander*-dominated Transvaal would slip naturally into the British Empire. It is also possible that he thought that the issue would enable Britain to go to war on the popular slogan of Britons' right to vote in a territory under British suzerainty.

Many organised groups, as well as influential newspapers, supported Milner's efforts to uphold what were perceived to be Britain's interests in southern Africa. These included the Primrose League and the Imperial South African Association. However, not all Britons were jingoistic. Even Chamberlain felt some disquiet at Milner's 'forward' policy, believing that war with Transvaal would be unpopular in Britain.

The coming of war

In a last-ditch effort to resolve Anglo-Transvaal problems, Steyn, president of the Orange Free State, invited Milner and Kruger to attend a conference in Bloemfontein on 31 May 1899. At the meeting, Milner made several demands, including the enactment by Transvaal of a law that would immediately give *uitlanders* the right to vote. Kruger rejected these demands. Despite encouragement from Chamberlain to continue the talks, Milner walked out of the conference on 5 June.

Milner remained confident that Kruger would 'bluff up to the cannon's mouth' and then accept Britain's demands. As tension mounted, Salisbury's government did not send substantial reinforcements to southern Africa, fearing that such action would look too aggressive and might encourage a Boer attack rather than help bring about a negotiated settlement. This suggests that Salisbury did not want or expect war. Nevertheless, by the summer of 1899, the Cabinet, most

KEY FIGURES

Alfred Milner (1854–1925)

After serving in Egypt (1889–92) and as chairman of the Board of Inland Revenue (1892–97), Milner was high commissioner in southern Africa (1897–1906) and governor of Cape Colony (1897–1901). His inflexibility at the Bloemfontein conference (1899) helped bring about the Second Boer War. Milner proved himself a distinguished administrator as governor (1902–6) after the annexation of the Transvaal and the Orange Free State.

Paul Kruger (1825–1904)

A farmer of Dutch descent, Kruger settled with his parents in the Transvaal after taking part in the Great Trek. He led the struggle to regain independence for the Transvaal from Britain, achieved in 1881. He became president of the Transvaal in 1883 and remained so until 1902. As president, he resisted *uitlander* demands for political equality, a policy that led to the Second Boer War. He fled to Europe in 1900, seeking support for the Boer cause. Unsuccessful, he settle first in the Netherlands and then in Switzerland.

MPs and the British press were all of the view that the Boers needed 'teaching a lesson'. Salisbury believed that:

- Britain had an obligation to people of British descent in southern Africa.
- Transvaal aspired to a Dutch South Africa. This would be damaging to Britain's prestige and had to be stopped.

In September, Chamberlain sent an ultimatum demanding full equality for British citizens resident in Transvaal. Britain now began bringing in additional troops from India. Kruger, regarding war as inevitable, issued his own ultimatum on 9 October, giving Britain 48 hours to withdraw all of its troops from Transvaal's border, otherwise Transvaal and the Orange Free State would declare war. News of the ultimatum reached London on the day it expired. Most newspaper editorials shared the sentiment of the *Daily Telegraph*, which declared 'there can only be one answer to this grotesque challenge. Kruger has asked for war and war he must have'. The Boers declared war on 11 October.

Kruger's action, said Salisbury, has 'liberated us from the necessity of explaining to the people of England why we are at war'.

KEY TERM

Rand millionaires British and German mining magnates who made fortunes from Transvaal gold. The rand was the Boer currency.

Who was responsible?

The role played by the **rand millionaires** in the origins of the war remains controversial. Most gold-mine owners certainly viewed Kruger's obstinacy towards *uitlanders* as a handicap to attracting essential labour and investment. Radical Liberal J.A. Hobson claimed that the war was caused by a 'conspiracy of financiers' for whom the *uitlander* issue was a cloak to hide a desire for profit. Historian Thomas Pakenham, writing in 1991, agreed, claiming that mine owners were 'active partners' with Milner in the making of the war. However, historian Andrew Porter rejected the view that the British government was the puppet of the mining magnates. Indeed, most scholars now believe that Salisbury's government pursued its own broader strategic, political and economic aims in southern Africa. Moreover, many Transvaal mine owners preferred peace and profit with Kruger to war.

Salisbury did not want war and had misgivings about Milner's stubbornness at the Bloemfontein conference. Nevertheless, in the last analysis, he shared Milner's view that what was at stake was a struggle to make sure that 'we not the Dutch are Boss'.

Chamberlain had long expressed concerns about the dangers for British interests of an independent Transvaal. After 1895, he soured Anglo-Boer relations in several ways – not least by appointing Milner as high commissioner. Yet it is unlikely that Chamberlain did this as part of a deliberate plan to instigate war.

The leading candidate for 'warmonger' is Milner. He believed that there was 'a greater issue than the grievances of the *uitlanders* at stake … our supremacy in South Africa … and our existence as a great power in the world is involved'. Nevertheless, he did not expect war. He thought Kruger would ultimately accept Britain's terms.

Kruger must share responsibility for the war. Convinced that Britain wanted to end Transvaal's independence and unwilling to concede rights to the *uitlanders*, he believed war to be inevitable. He thus prepared for it. His resolve was stiffened by the fact that his leading generals were convinced that the Boers would win and that the outcome would be a United States of Southern Africa under Transvaal leadership.

The Boer War

British forces were reasonably well prepared for war. Many officers and men had been hardened in a succession of colonial wars in which they had invariably been successful. Once war was declared, mobilisation went like clockwork. The Admiralty transported men and supplies over a distance of 6000 miles without a hitch. Nevertheless, the war did not go to plan.

The Boer army

On paper, the Boer army looked no match for the British. The Boers could put fewer than 60,000 men in the field. (The total white population of the two Boer republics was only 300,000.) The Boer army was essentially a civilian militia. When danger loomed, all adult male citizens in a district were expected to form a commando unit, which elected officers. Each man brought his own weapon and horse.

But the Boers should not have been underestimated:

- The First Boer War (see pages 38–9) suggested that the Boers were likely to be tough opponents.
- The Boers were excellent horsemen and hunters.
- They were armed with Europe's best weapons.
- They had a greater familiarity with the terrain than British officers.
- Boer morale was strong and was sustained by the belief that they were engaged in a life-and-death struggle to preserve their distinctive culture.
- Many Boers in Cape Colony and Natal sympathised with Transvaal and the Orange Free State.

The war, 1899–1900

In the war's early months, Britain suffered a series of humiliating defeats, particularly in 'Black Week' (10–15 December 1899) as the Boers laid siege to Ladysmith (in Natal), Kimberley (in Cape Colony) and Mafeking (in Bechuanaland). British forces were forced to take the offensive sooner than was prudent in an attempt to relieve the besieged towns.

Comment on the soldiers' military appearance in Source B.

SOURCE B

Photograph of Boer soldiers in 1900.

More troops (450,000 in total) and better generals, notably Lord Roberts and Kitchener, were sent to southern Africa. By mid-1900, British forces, having relieved Ladysmith, Kimberley and Mafeking and captured the main Boer towns, seemed to have triumphed. Kruger fled to Europe and Roberts returned home, a hero.

The relief of Mafeking

News of the relief of Mafeking (on 17 May 1900) had a major impact on Britain. The celebration was not stirred up by jingoists of press, pulpit or soapbox. It was a spontaneous response to good news – an affirmation of imperial triumph.

Guerrilla war

Boer generals continued to fight a guerrilla war which dragged on for two years. Boer commandos returned to their home districts where they could rely on local support. Their tactics were to strike fast and hard against British forces, raiding outposts, ambushing columns and cutting railway lines. The commandos had hoped:

- to rouse the **Afrikaners** of Cape Colony to rise in rebellion
- that the British would get tired of war.

KEY TERM

Afrikaner A person born in South Africa of Dutch/Boer descent.

The vast size of the republics made it difficult for British troops to control territory effectively. As soon as British troops left a district, British authority faded away. Determined to defeat the Boers, Kitchener:

- divided Boer territory into zones, sectioning them off with barbed wire, making it difficult for Boers to raid
- built some 8000 fortified blockhouses, each housing six to eight soldiers
- continued Lord Robert's **scorched-earth policy**.

 **KEY TERM**

Scorched-earth policy
This involves burning farms, destroying crops, rounding up animals and poisoning the wells of the enemy.

Some 50 concentration camps were set up as refugee camps for Boer families who had been forced to quit their homes. Inadequate food, poor shelter, bad hygiene and sanitation, shortage of medical facilities and overcrowding led to the spread of disease. Over 20,000 Boer women and children died in the camps – about one in four of the inmates. Tens of thousands of black Africans were also forcibly removed from Boer areas and placed in separate camps. Conditions in these camps were worse than in the Boer camps. Fewer records were kept but over 12,000 black inmates probably died. The high death rate in the camps was the result of incompetence on the part of British military authorities. It was not a deliberate policy of extermination.

Criticism of the camps

In 1901, radical Liberals, led by David Lloyd George, denounced the concentration camps. Liberal leader Henry Campbell-Bannerman did not initially support the radicals. He saw it as his duty to support the government in time of war. Aware that the radicals were a minority group, he was also reluctant to press a matter which was certain to divide his party. However, Emily Hobhouse's description of camp conditions in June 1901 created a domestic and international outcry. Campbell-Bannerman now attacked 'the methods of barbarism' being used in southern Africa. Concerned by the public outcry, the government appointed a (uniquely) all-women commission, headed by Millicent Fawcett. Between August and December 1901, the commission conducted its own tour of the camps, confirming everything that Hobhouse had said. In November 1901, Chamberlain ordered Milner to ensure that 'all possible steps are being taken to reduce the rate of mortality'. Civil authorities now took over the running of the camps. By early 1902, the death rate for white inmates dropped to two per cent, a lower rate than that which occurred in many British cities.

Given the uproar over the camps, Kitchener in December 1901 instructed his commanders not to bring in women and children when they 'cleared' the country. This was a shrewd move. While seeming to appease his critics, it also handicapped the guerrillas, who now had to care for their desperate families.

A white man's war?

Boers and British alike feared the consequences of arming black Africans. The memories of the Anglo-Zulu War (see page 38) and other tribal conflicts were still fresh and there was a recognition that whoever won would have to deal with the consequences of a mass militarisation of the black population. At first there was an unwritten agreement that the war would be a 'white man's war'. But as the fighting continued, the British increasingly used armed black people as scouts and auxiliaries. By 1902, some 30,000 black people had served in the British army. Most black Africans were pro-British.

The end of the war

Kitchener's tactics of containment and harassment were ultimately successful. By early 1902, it was obvious, even to Boer 'bitter-enders', that further resistance was futile. The Boer War ended with the Treaty of Vereeniging (May 1902). The Boers recognised Britain's annexation of their two republics. Britain, in return, agreed to restore self-government in Transvaal and the Orange Free State at the earliest opportunity. The Boers were also given £3 million for reconstruction purposes.

The cost of the war

Over 22,000 British soldiers died. Nearly 8000 died in battle, the rest through disease. More than 7000 Boer soldiers died. The scale of the war exceeded all expectations. It required the services of 450,000 British and colonial troops and cost the British taxpayer £217 million. By 1901, it was costing the Treasury £140 to kill a single Boer combatant.

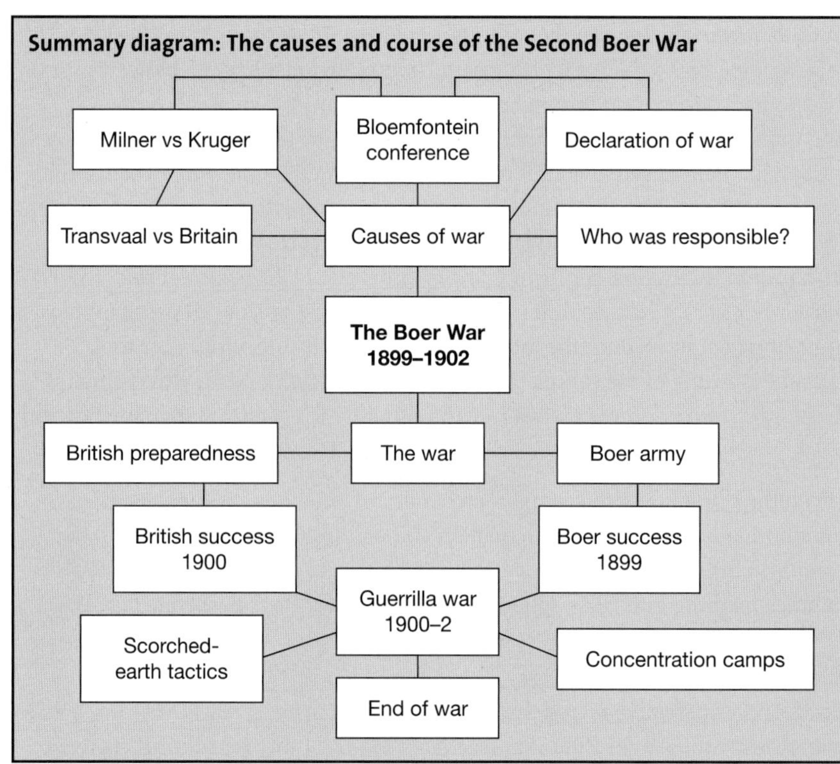

Chapter summary

Between 1890 and 1902, Britain faced increasing economic, military and diplomatic challenges. Nevertheless, it remained a great imperial power, confident enough to pursue a policy of 'splendid isolation'. Although there was some opposition to imperialist policies, most Britons enthusiastically supported the Empire, and the Conservatives, led by Salisbury, were in power for most of the period. In Asia, Britain achieved most of its aims in China. In Africa, it faced challenges from France. Goldie's Niger Company ensured that Britain acquired more territory than the French would have liked in (what became) Nigeria. Kitchener's occupation of Sudan and victory at Omdurman forced the French to back down. The most serious challenge to Britain came from the Boers in Transvaal. A number of incidents, notably the Jameson raid (1895), soured Anglo-Boer relations. In 1899, the Second Boer War began. Although the war did not go well initially and then turned into a difficult guerrilla conflict, Britain emerged victorious.

Refresher questions

Use these questions to remind yourself of the key material covered in this chapter.

1. To what extent did Britain's strengths outweigh its weaknesses in the 1890s?
2. How did the imperialist aims of Rhodes and Chamberlain differ?
3. How popular was imperialism in Britain in the 1890s?
4. Why was China a problem for Britain in the 1890s?
5. What problems did Britain face in east and west Africa?
6. Why was Britain successful in the Sudan in 1898?
7. Why were the British and Boers at odds in southern Africa in the 1890s?
8. Who was most responsible for the Boer War?
9. Why did the Boer War last so long?

Question practice

ESSAY QUESTIONS

1. 'British expansion in Africa was the result of challenges from other European powers in the period 1870–1900.' Explain why you agree or disagree with this view.
2. 'Britain's imperial strengths outweighed its weaknesses in the years 1870–1902.' Explain why you agree or disagree with this view.
3. 'Britain was very successful in protecting its interests in Asia in the period 1870–1900.' Assess the validity of this statement.
4. 'British policy was essentially to blame for increasing tension in southern Africa in the years 1870–99.' Assess the validity of this statement.

CHAPTER 4

Imperial liberalisation and representations of Empire, 1902–14

In the 1906 general election, the Liberal Party won a landslide victory. The Liberals, who remained in power until the First World War, were less imperial-minded than the Conservative/Unionists. However, imperial enthusiasm in Britain did not disappear. Nor did the Empire. This chapter will examine the imperial liberalisation of the period 1902–14 by examining the following themes:

★ The consequences of the Boer War

★ The administration of Egypt and India

★ The consolidation of British rule in Africa

★ Trade and commerce

The key debate on pages 83–6 of this chapter asks the question: To what extent did the Boer War lead to a decline of imperial sentiment in Britain?

Key dates

1904 Anglo-French entente

1905 Partition of Bengal

1906 Formation of Muslim League in India

1907 Responsible government granted to Orange Free State and Transvaal

1910 Creation of the Union of South Africa

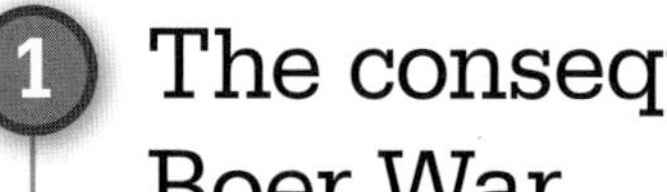

1 The consequences of the Boer War

▶ *How far-reaching were the consequences of the Boer War?*

The consequences of the war for southern Africa

Post-war reconstruction in southern Africa was presided over by Milner. Anxious to destroy Boer influence, he soon realised this was impossible. Britain, for all its sacrifices, had not secured total predominance in southern Africa. While the new leaders in Transvaal were prepared to work in harmony with Britain, the Orange Free State was more uncooperative. Milner and the Conservative government had hoped to consolidate Britain's position in southern Africa by encouraging large-scale immigration from Britain to increase the English-speaking population. The plan never stood much chance of success. The Afrikaners' birth-rate was too high.

In 1906–7, Britain restored self-government and free elections – for white people – in Transvaal and the Orange Free State. The Liberal government in Britain portrayed this as an act of reconciliation, designed to win the allegiance of former enemies by extending to them the hand of trust and friendship. In reality, ministers were not confident that their policy would succeed although it did, at least in the short term:

- In the 1907 elections, the Afrikaner *Het Volk* Party, committed to both a Union of South Africa and racial segregation, won a sweeping victory.
- The 1909 South African Act united Transvaal, the Orange Free State, Cape Colony and Natal in a Union of South Africa, which came into existence in 1910. The state was to be a unitary, not a federal system of the Canadian or Australian type (see page 54). South African politicians wanted a powerful central government that could deal effectively with rebellions like the one in Natal in 1906 (which was brutally crushed). Louis Botha, a famous Boer soldier, became the country's first prime minister.
- When Botha took South Africa into the First World War on Britain's side in 1914, it seemed as though the Liberal gamble had been vindicated. South Africa proved a valuable ally.
- The price for this achievement was the sacrifice of the black people of South Africa. Only white people could sit in the Union Parliament and vote in Transvaal and the Orange Free State.

The political consequences of the war for Britain

Initially, most Britons supported the Boer War. But by 1902 it was evident that not all Britons were committed to the war or to the Empire.

Khaki fever

In 1899–1900, '**khaki fever**' raged throughout Britain:

- There was a spate of popular jingoistic songs.
- Half a million people cheered off the First Army Corps as it embarked at Southampton for Africa in 1899.
- Men rushed to volunteer for the army.
- Joyous reaction greeted news of the lifting of the sieges of Ladysmith and Mafeking.

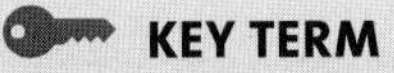

KEY TERM

Khaki fever British soldiers wore khaki (brown)-coloured uniforms.

The Khaki election

In September 1900, believing that the war had effectively ended, Salisbury called for a general election. In the campaign, Chamberlain declared that 'every vote given against the government is a vote given to the Boers'. The Conservative/

Unionist coalition was returned with a majority of 134 over all its opponents – eight seats fewer than it won in 1895.

Opposition to the war

A sizeable minority of the population – radical Liberals, socialists, Irish Nationalists – vehemently opposed the war from the start. They were backed by newspapers like the *Manchester Guardian* and the *Morning Star*. There were also a number of influential anti-war groups, including the Stop the War Committee. The setbacks in the early stages of the war, and the unexpectedly long-drawn-out closing stage, damaged imperial enthusiasm.

Financial problems

The Boer War cost over £200 million. Given that Britain seemed to be reaching the limits of tolerable taxation, there were issues about how to pay for the war and much-needed social reform. The Conservative/Unionist government, led by Arthur Balfour after 1902, was divided on what types of measures were necessary. Charles Ritchie, the new chancellor of the exchequer, favoured reducing government spending, rather than raising taxation. Joseph Chamberlain, by contrast, supported tariff reform. This was to have major political consequences (see page 82).

Changes in foreign policy

During the war, 'splendid isolation' had seemed far from splendid. Given that international opinion sympathised with the Boers, there were fears of invasion. Britain thus attempted to secure allies:

- In 1901–2, Chamberlain's efforts to secure an agreement with Germany failed. By 1902, the British public had become increasingly anti-German as a result of Kaiser Wilhelm II's pro-Boer stance, his imperial ambitions and his construction of a big navy.
- Britain, worried by the Russian threat in the Far East, allied with Japan in 1902.
- In 1904, Britain made an **entente** with France.

KEY TERM

Entente A friendly agreement not involving a binding commitment.

National efficiency

The fact that it took an imperial army of 450,000 men 32 months to defeat 60,000 Boers shattered national complacency and helped to create a sense of danger. Many believed that the British Empire might be brought down, like the Roman Empire, by decadence and incompetence. Analysis of society's problems preoccupied the political class under the guiding rule of national efficiency. The national efficiency 'movement', held together by an informal network of friends and acquaintances, generally wanted to:

- institute a career system open to talent
- ensure that all children received a good education

- modernise Britain's secondary schooling and higher education systems, particularly by taking science and technology seriously, so that the country retained its economic competitiveness
- harness all the Empire's resources – intelligence, capital, labour, even women's wombs.

National efficiency appealed to many different groups.

- Some socialists supported it, hoping it would lead to social reform.
- Many Liberals and Conservatives welcomed it on the grounds that it seemed both patriotic and progressive.

National efficiency supporters insisted that the old battles between Conservatism and Liberalism, even those between capitalism and socialism, meant little compared with the more serious battle taking place between the forces of competence and incompetence in many areas of British life, for example education, social reform and government administration. Germany was seen as a model for emulation but also as a rival whose very efficiency threatened Britain.

The war seemed to provide evidence of both physical and moral decline. There were doubts about the continuing superiority of the imperial race – often regarded as the key element in Britain's greatness. The spectre of 'racial deterioration' stalked the land. There were efforts to counter the fear by support for pauper emigration, birth control and the sterilisation of the unfit.

The impact of the war on the Empire

The Boer War indicated that many men within the Empire were loyal to it. Some 30,000 men from British South Africa volunteered to fight. By 1902, 16,000 Australians, 6000 Canadians and 6500 New Zealanders had also seen service in Africa.

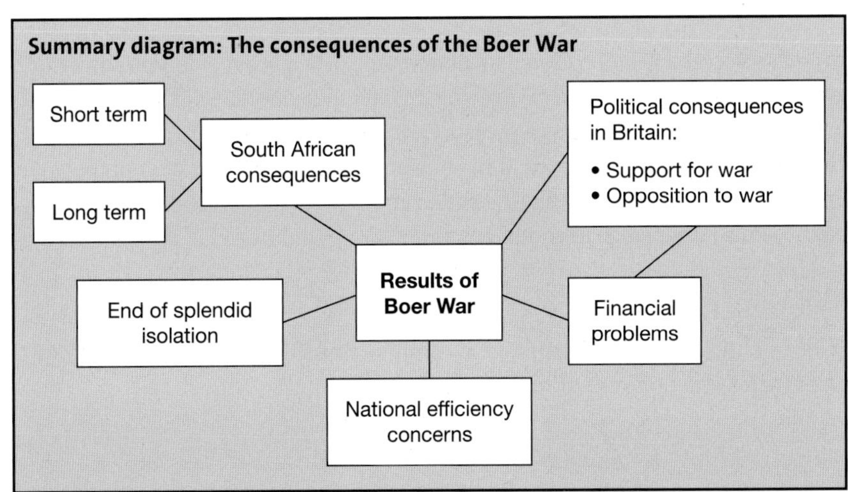

2 The administration of Egypt and India

▶ *To what extent did Britain try to rule Egypt and India by conciliatory means in the period 1902–14?*

Britain had long collaborated with the traditional ruling classes in India and Egypt. However, by the early twentieth century, Indian and Egyptian elites no longer commanded the loyalty of their peoples. The forces of nationalism were growing in strength. These forces needed conciliating or repressing.

Egypt

While British rule in Egypt helped to modernise the country, it was never popular.

Lord Cromer, consul-general of Egypt from 1883 to 1907, ruled with some success:

- He reduced government spending and also succeeded in lowering the rates of taxation.
- He reformed the civil service, reducing corruption.
- Engineers improved the system of irrigation.

However, Egyptian nationalists continued to challenge British rule. Cromer's efforts to win over moderate nationalists, for example, by appointing one to head his Education ministry, were generally unsuccessful. Cromer retired in 1907, believing that Britain could not govern Egypt indefinitely. In 1908, he wrote that Britain was striving for two imperial ideas that were mutually exclusive, 'the ideal of good government, which connotes the continuance of [its] own supremacy, and the ideal of self-government, which connotes the whole or partial abdication of [its] supreme position'.

Cromer's successor, Eldon Gorst, increased the participation of Egyptians in local government. However, failing to conciliate the nationalists, Gorst was forced to adopt more repressive measures. In 1911, Lord Kitchener replaced Gorst. Kitchener's enlargement of the powers and the representation of the Egyptian Legislative Assembly, instead of ending nationalists' complaints, only gave them a larger stage to complain on.

India

British politicians were determined to continue British rule in India. But the Raj faced increasing pressure from Indian nationalists.

Congress

By 1900, Congress members (see pages 35–6) were increasingly critical of the Raj. The best-known leaders of Congress before 1914 were Gokhale and Tilak:

- Gokhale, an admirer of British liberalism, pressed for the gradual introduction of self-government for India along the same lines as had occurred in Canada, Australia and New Zealand. Persuasion and non-violence were central to his strategy.
- Tilak, a devout Hindu, admired the national heritage of India and stressed how much of that heritage had been destroyed by British rule. Sympathetic to a more extreme form of nationalist protest which had developed in the 1890s, he favoured open confrontation with the British.

Before 1900, most Congress members, still essentially well-educated Indians, preferred Gokhale's moderate approach to Tilak's extremism.

Indian nationalist problems

Indian nationalists faced a number of difficulties in applying the European ideal of nationalism – the shared desire for self-government based on a common language, customs and culture – to Indian conditions:

- India was deeply divided in religious terms. The major religious division was between Hindus (70 per cent of Indians) and Muslims (21 per cent). The remaining religious groups included Sikhs, Christians and Jews.
- Each Indian province had its own history, local customs, laws, traditions and language or languages. Most Indians felt part of a distinct region: few had any concept of India as a modern nation-state.

India's divisions ensured that the growth of nationalism was a slow process. Even if nationalists managed to win mass support, they still faced the problem of overthrowing British rule.

Lord Curzon

Curzon, viceroy from 1898 to 1905, was 39 years old when he arrived in India. He had the self-confidence of someone who thought it was his divine right to lead. He believed that Britain was in India to stay. He ruled India with huge displays of pomp and ceremony which he thought would impress the Indian people. He declared that one of his objectives was to preside over the peaceful demise of Congress. He hoped to do this by giving India the best government it had ever enjoyed. Curzon undoubtedly worked hard to reform India, improving communications, developing irrigation, relieving famine, spreading education and promoting efficiency. Soon, however, Indians resented his imperial condescension. According to historian Piers Brendon, he even treated the princes as 'a pack of ignorant, unruly schoolboys who had to be disciplined' (2007).

The division of Bengal

Curzon's decision in 1905 to partition Bengal, India's largest province, into two regions – a mainly Hindu western half and a mainly Muslim eastern half – caused a nationalist outcry. While Curzon was concerned simply with administrative efficiency, most Indians regarded his action as an attack on India's ancient boundaries:

- Congress spread fears that other provinces might face the same fate as Bengal unless Indians took a stand against British rule. Accordingly, Congress organised street demonstrations and boycotts of British goods.
- The division of Bengal helped the creation of the Muslim League in 1906. Its members had no wish to be ruled by Hindus or the British. The League promoted civil disorder: some called it terrorism.

Lord Minto and John Morley

In 1905, Curzon was replaced by Lord Minto. The new viceroy viewed self-government for India as 'a fantastic, ludicrous dream'. Faced with Curzon's legacy of discontent, he took strong repressive measures, including deportations, and passed laws to control the press and curb public meetings. In 1908, Tilak was charged with sedition and received a six-year prison sentence. However, Minto had to work with Secretary of State for India John Morley, an admirer of Gladstone. Morley pressed Minto to release as many political prisoners as possible. He also introduced measures in 1909 which gave Indians more say in the running of India:

- An Indian was appointed to the viceroy's executive council in India.
- Two Indians were appointed to the secretary of state's Indian Council in London.
- More Indians were added to the Imperial Legislative Council. Twenty-seven of its 60 members were elected rather than appointed by the viceroy.
- Provincial legislative councils had more elected Indian members.
- The imperial and provincial legislatures were permitted to debate budgetary matters.

The reforms were mild enough to reassure the Indian Civil Service, which had little sympathy with Indian home rule, and generally welcomed by Indian moderates.

Lord Hardinge and Lord Crewe

In 1910, Lord Crewe took over the India Office from Morley while Lord Hardinge succeeded Minto. By reunifying Bengal in 1911, Hardinge appeased many Indians. But aware that India was essential to Britain's strength and prosperity, neither Crewe nor Hardinge supported Congress's demands for home rule. Publicly Hardinge appeared sympathetic towards Congress but privately he regarded Gokhale as 'the most dangerous enemy of British rule in this country'.

In 1911, Britain announced that the Indian capital was to be moved from Calcutta to Delhi. The new Delhi, planned by architects Sir Edwin Lutyens and Sir Herbert Baker, was designed to present an orderly contrast to the confusion of old Delhi. The new capital was probably the grandest monument ever erected to the Empire – a symbol of British strength. Yet, nationalist pressure continued. Hardinge was badly injured in a bomb attack as he made a state entry into Delhi in 1912.

Iran

In 1907, Britain reached agreement with Russia on Iran (see map on page 106), regarded as part of the outer defences of India. Iran, although nominally independent, was cut into three sections. The north became a Russian sphere of influence, Britain gained the south-east and the remaining third became a buffer zone between the two powers.

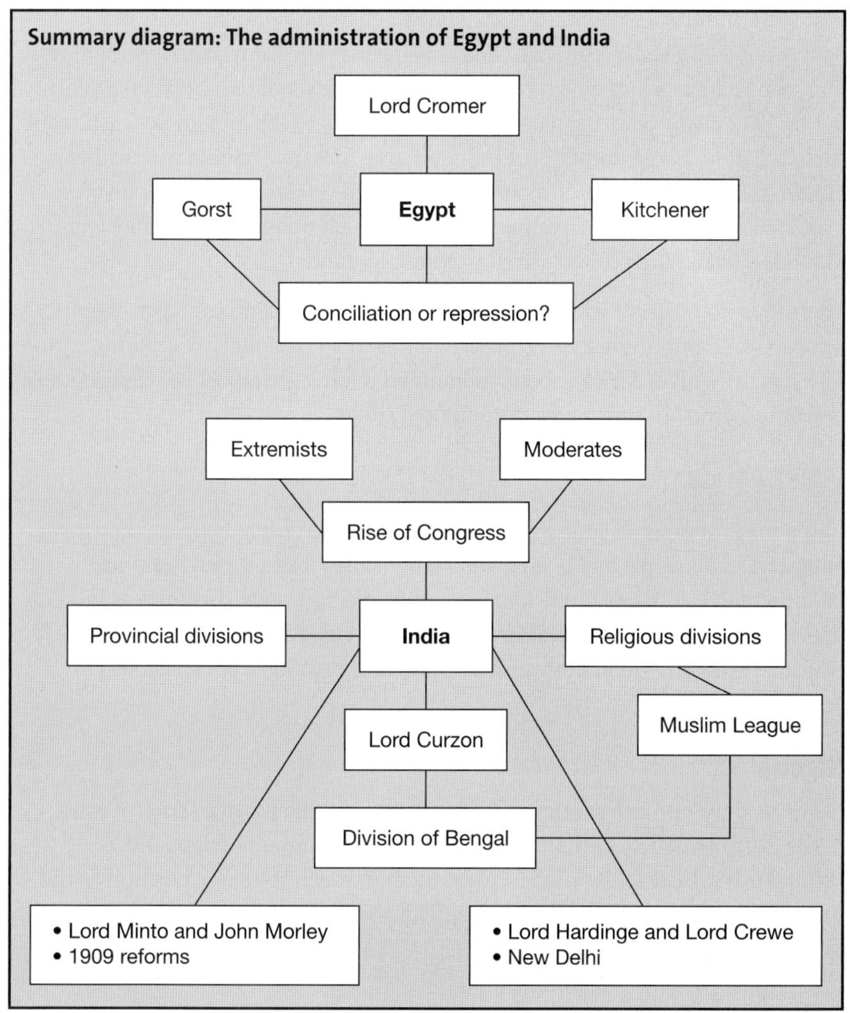

3 The consolidation of British rule in Africa

How effectively did Britain administer its African colonies in the period 1902–14?

The boundaries of British rule in Africa had been set by 1902. After 1902, British rule was not efficient or humane.

East Africa

After 1902, rich Britons were attracted to the idea of settling the highland areas along the equator in Kenya. The hope was that Kenya would become a 'white-man's country'. But by 1914, fewer than 5000 Britons had moved into Kenya. White people – less than one per cent of the population – held a fifth of Kenya's best land. In return for working for half the year for a nominal wage, black people were allowed to cultivate their own farms. The Kenyan government ran for some years at a loss which cost the British taxpayer about £100,000 a year, but by 1912 it was covering its costs, thanks largely to the growing of cash crops such as coffee. Large numbers of Indians came to Kenya to help with railway building. By 1914 they outnumbered white people by six to one and played a major role in the country's commercial life. Denied political rights, they were forbidden to acquire property in the 'white highlands'.

There was no influx of white settlers into Uganda. It had no stretches of empty territory to tempt Britons. Its economy managed well enough by growing cotton. The structure of its African society remained relatively untouched. Considerable power remained in the hands of traditional rulers.

West Africa

In the mid-nineteenth century, given the shortage of white people, some educated local people had been given responsible jobs in the civil service or appointed as officers in the local armed forces. However, as progress in preventing malaria made it easier for Britons to survive in jobs in west Africa, educated Africans were rarely given responsible positions, which caused resentment.

Nigeria

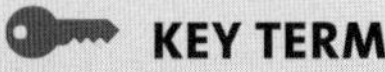

KEY TERM

Emir A North African chieftain.

Nigeria's development was moulded by Frederick Lugard. In a series of wars in the north between 1901 and 1903, he defeated but did not depose the ruling **emirs**. Instead, he tried to place them in much the same position as the Indian princes occupied under the Raj. This system of indirect rule had several advantages:

- It reduced the dislocation that British expansion was bound to cause in African society.
- It enabled Britain to rule the north with the minimum of friction. District commissioners gave their views to African rulers and accepted the fact that sometimes, on minor matters, the rulers had to be allowed to ignore the advice they had been given.
- It kept down the level of government spending.

Leaving power in the hands of traditional rulers held back the process of modernisation. But Lugard's support for gradual change was reasonably successful. Slavery, for example, which still existed in parts of Nigeria recently annexed by Britain, was ended by stages – with relatively little conflict. Lugard's methods meant that he was able to 'rule' a vast area with a white civilian staff totalling 104 and a military force of 2000–3000 Africans under 200 British officers and non-commissioned officers.

The Gold Coast (modern Ghana)

The Gold Coast benefited from the growing demand for cocoa, used for chocolate or as a drink. It became one of the richest areas in Africa.

Southern Africa

In Rhodesia, British rule resulted in the seizure of land, Africans being forced into **reservations**, and **conscription** of black labour. High taxes forced African men to seek work on farms or in mines. Conditions in the mines were harsh: arduous physical labour, prison-like compounds and a brutal work discipline. Beatings were common and sometimes resulted in death. White juries usually attributed such deaths to the 'enlarged spleens' of Africans: the few white people who were brought to trial were invariably acquitted.

KEY TERMS

Reservations Areas of land set aside for use by particular groups.

Conscription Compulsory enrolment for service, either in the armed forces or in particular areas of work.

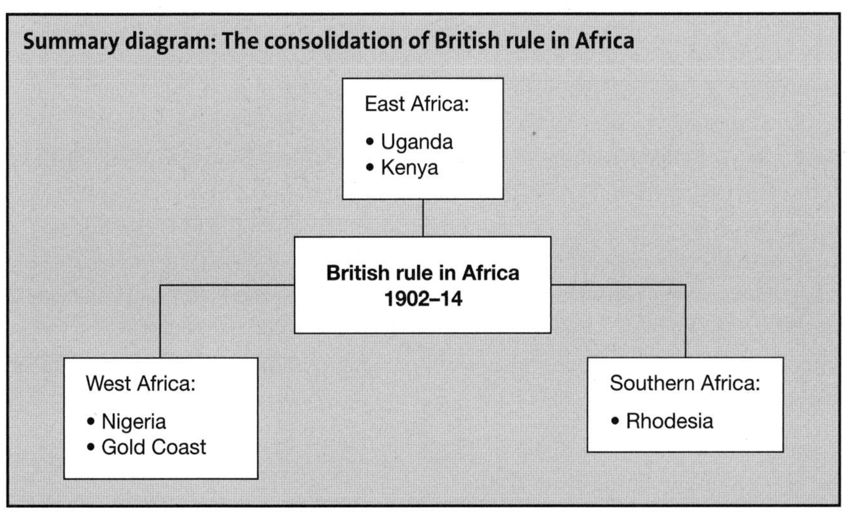

4 Trade and commerce

Why did Britain not end free trade in the period 1902–14?

Britain's economic situation, 1902–14

KEY TERMS

Deficit A shortfall of revenue, as compared with expenditure.

Protectionism The introduction of high import duties to protect a nation's industries from foreign competition.

In 1900, Britain imported £523 million worth of goods – double its annual average in the 1860s. The country had no trouble paying for them: in no year before 1914 did Britain have a balance of payments **deficit**. Usually the account was substantially in the black. While Britain's manufacturing supremacy was being challenged by the USA and Germany, its income from commercial services, such as shipping and insurance, increased by some 70 per cent in the two decades before 1913. Given that British investments abroad doubled between 1900 and 1913, Britain still held a powerful place in the global economy.

Nevertheless, the fact that Britain depended on its interest on foreign investment suggested that it was living off its past achievements. To some contemporaries, this was a matter for concern. Britain, they claimed, needed to extend its overseas markets. But the high protective tariffs of its main competitors made this difficult. By 1900, open markets were hard to find. British products were thus sold increasingly to its own imperial territories. In the 1890s, Canada, Australia and India accounted for over a third of British exports. However, these markets were not closed to foreign competitors, so Britain might soon face challenges on 'home' territory. Since most of its rivals had imposed heavy tariffs on British goods, some Britons supported the introduction of imperial **protectionism**. The most important politician to do so was Joseph Chamberlain.

Chamberlain and tariff reform

Chamberlain had long pressed for closer imperial union. He seized on the lessons of the Boer War to argue that Britain needed help with its world-wide commitments and that some co-ordinating machinery should be created to plan a unified policy. He put forward his ideas to the heads of the self-governing colonies when they met for Edward VII's coronation in 1902. But they were not really concerned about foreign policy consultation. They were far more interested in gaining a preferential tariff position in the British market. Chamberlain was impressed by what he heard. In 1903, he called for closer imperial economic unity: he called it tariff reform. He proposed that protective duties should be levied on goods from abroad. Given his main concern – imperial unity – there would be no tariffs on imperial imports. In Chamberlain's view, tariff reform would:

- raise money
- strengthen the Empire

Joseph Chamberlain

1836	Born in London, son of a successful manufacturer
1854	Moved to Birmingham to join his uncle's screw-making business
1866	Became actively involved in Liberal politics
1873	Became mayor of Birmingham, promoting many civic improvements
1876	Elected Liberal MP for Birmingham
1880	Became president of the Board of Trade
1886	Resigned from the Cabinet over the issue of Irish Home Rule
1892	Became leader of the Liberal Unionists
1895	Appointed colonial secretary in the Conservative/Unionist government
1900	Played a crucial role in the Conservative/Unionist election campaign
1903	Resigned from government to support the cause of tariff reform
1906	Suffered a serious stroke that ended his political career
1914	Died

Chamberlain has the distinction of being the only individual to have divided two major British political parties in the course of his career. He split the Liberal Party over the issue of Irish Home Rule. Less than twenty years later, his campaign for tariff reform divided the Conservatives. Churchill called Chamberlain 'a splendid piebald [black and white in patches]: first black, then white, or in political terms, first fiery red, then true blue'. This is the conventional opinion of Chamberlain's politics: the view that he began to the left of the Liberals and ended up to the right of the Conservatives. But arguably he was always a radical in home affairs and an imperialist in foreign affairs. Arguably, too, these views were not in conflict. Essentially, he rejected ***laissez-faire*** capitalism in favour of government intervention. His enthusiasm for Empire and his support for stronger imperial union are not in doubt. Given the growing challenges from Germany and the USA, he believed that imperial unity was vital if Britain was to remain a great power.

- protect British industry from foreign competition and from unfair practices like **dumping**
- safeguard British jobs
- pay for much-needed social reform, without resorting to other forms of taxation
- check the growth of socialism.

Chamberlain's support for tariff reform split the Conservative/Unionist coalition (see page 30) wide open because many Conservatives remained committed to free trade. Balfour did his best to preserve unity. But when Chamberlain announced his desire to leave the government to campaign in support of tariff reform, Balfour encouraged him to do so. The Tariff Reform League was created in July 1903. Most of its members were businessmen, attracted by its commitment to 'the defence and development of the industrial interests of the British Empire'.

KEY TERMS

Laissez-faire The principle that governments should not interfere in social and economic matters.

Dumping Exporting commodities for sale at below the cost of production to ruin overseas competition.

Support for free trade

Free traders, some within but most outside the Conservative Party, fought back. Traditional anti-protectionist arguments such as the below still carried weight:

- Duties on corn would raise food prices.
- Britain exported twice as much to foreign countries as it exported to its colonies. Britain sold more to Belgium than it did to the whole of Africa in the 1890s.
- High duties might simply protect inefficient British industries.
- Free trade helped to lower labour costs (by keeping food costs low). Thus, many industries derived a competitive edge over their foreign rivals.

In the 1906 general election, the Liberal Party, which supported free trade, won a landslide victory. The British electorate had shown it opposed protectionism – although not necessarily Empire.

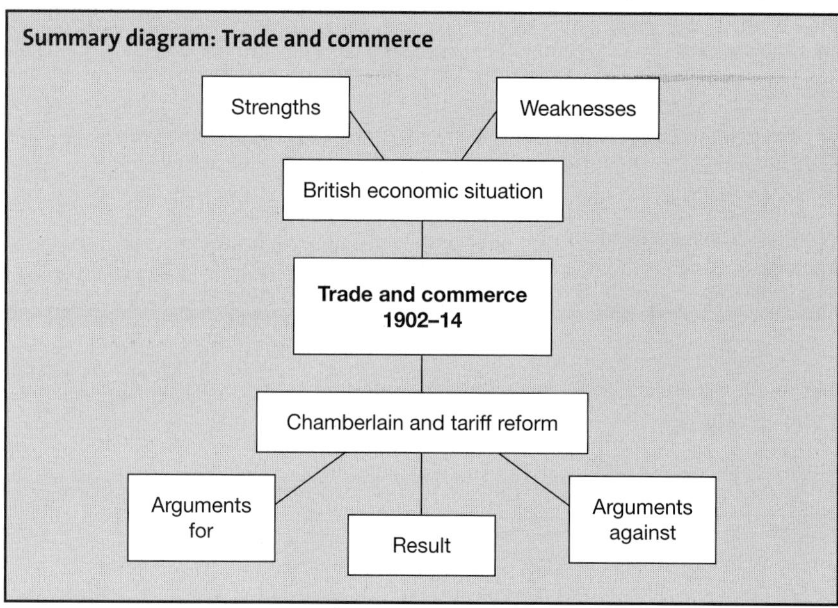

5 Key debate

▶ *To what extent did the Boer War lead to a decline of imperial sentiment in Britain?*

Historians disagree about the extent to which the Boer War led to a decline in imperial sentiment in Britain.

EXTRACT 1

From Frank McDonough, *The British Empire 1815–1914*, Hodder Education, 1994, pp. 101–2.

The Boer War was clearly one of those rare turning points in the history of the Empire between 1815 and 1914. It cast a giant shadow over British attitudes towards the Empire and imperial defence in the period from 1902 to the outbreak of the First World War in 1914. … After the Boer War the British never believed as strongly as they had before it that the British Empire was one on which the sun would never set.

Which of these two extracts provides the more convincing interpretation? ?

EXTRACT 2

From Nicholas Owen, 'Critics of Empire in Britain' in *The Oxford History of the British Empire, The Twentieth Century*, edited by Judith M. Brown and W.M. Roger Louis, Oxford University Press, 1999, p. 192.

Distaste for certain features of the Edwardian Empire should not be equated with anti-imperialism … Nor can the failure of the 'constructive imperialism' proposed by Joseph Chamberlain in 1903 be taken to indicate the unpopularity of imperialism. Rather, it illustrated the lack of widespread support for a particular, insular, and exclusive conception of Empire. Provided imperialism could recast itself in a form which avoided these unpopular implications, there seemed little reason why it should not brush off the attacks of its critics.

Decline of imperial sentiment?

A case can be made to the effect that the Boer War marked the dividing line between the passionate imperialism of late Victorian Britain and the loss of confidence in Empire thereafter:

- Pre-1902, imperialism had generally been seen as a 'positive mission' designed to bring 'civilisation' to underdeveloped societies. After 1902, imperialism in the eyes of many left-wing politicians became synonymous with 'capitalist cliques' and 'methods of barbarism'.
- Before the Boer War, imperialism had attracted supporters from both major political parties. After 1902, it was associated mainly with the Conservative/ Unionist coalition: a coalition which was heavily defeated by the Liberals in the 1906 and 1910 elections.

SOURCE A

? How did the advert in Source A try to use imperial imagery to sell its product?

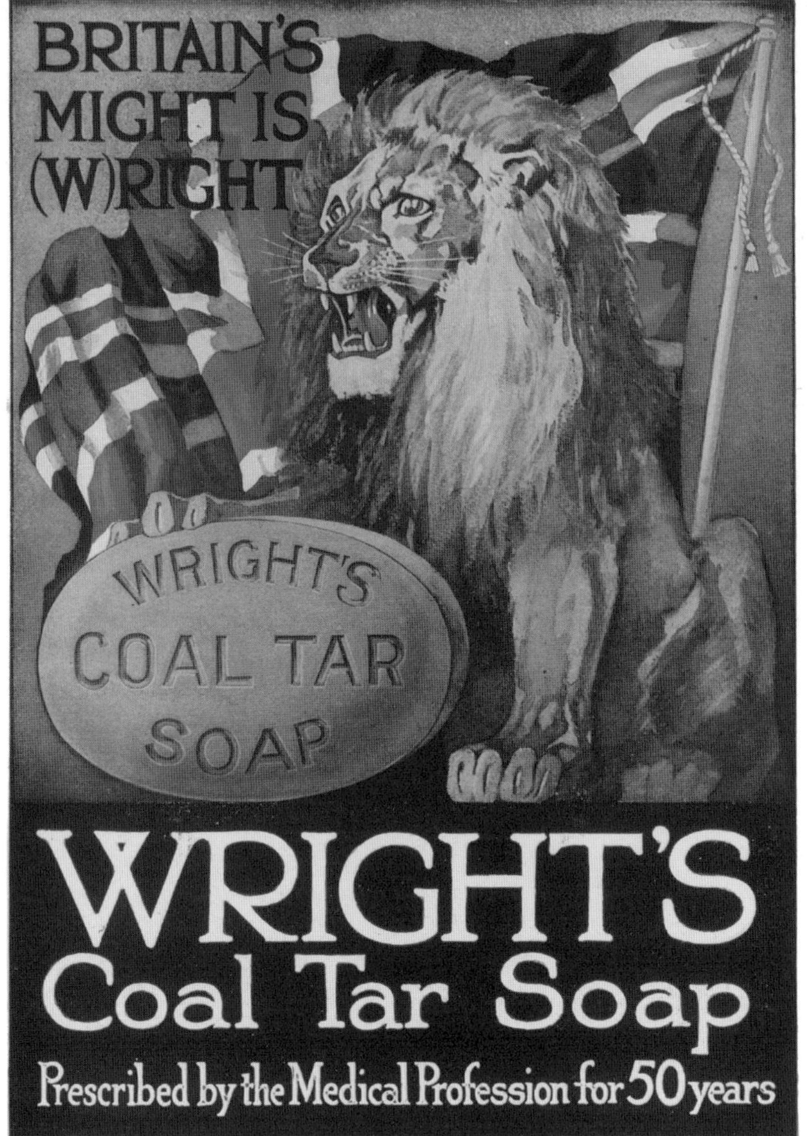

An advertisement from 1917 promoting soap using imperial imagery.

- Chamberlain failed to persuade the majority of the British public to support his schemes for tariff reform and imperial unity (see pages 51–3).
- Between 1900 and 1913, the overall share of Britain's exports going to the Empire fell slightly. Non-imperial markets remained far more important than all the British territories combined, providing 75 per cent of all imports and taking two-thirds of exports.

- Most colonial subjects had no love of the Empire. Even the self-governing colonies, which were most committed to the Empire, contained minority groups who were hostile, for example, French-speaking Canadians and Irish communities in Australia.
- The Liberal governments of Campbell-Bannerman (1905–8) and Asquith (1908–16) accorded low priority to imperial affairs. Not interested in closer imperial unity, the Liberals were also sceptical about the advantages of acquiring new territory. The years from 1905 to 1914 thus saw a process of muddling through in colonial matters.
- By 1914, even the Conservatives had backed down from grandiose schemes of Empire. In 1913, the party jettisoned support for import duties on food: an essential component of any system of imperial preference.
- In 1908, to loud Liberal, Irish and Labour cheers, the Commons rejected the idea of officially recognising Empire Day.
- Imperialists failed on many fronts. They failed to introduce imperial preference. They also failed to create a federated Empire. Colonial Conferences in 1902, 1907 and 1911, which aimed at ensuring a greater degree of unity, came to nothing.

Continuing strength of imperial sentiment?

There is plenty of evidence to suggest that imperial sentiment remained strong:

- Although there was little territorial expansion of the Empire after 1902, there was no suggestion of imperial withdrawal. The Liberal governments may have had no great schemes for Empire but they showed no desire to abandon it.
- The most popular newspapers, like the *Daily Mail* and the *Daily Express,* continued to adopt a pro-imperial tone.
- Britons continued to be bombarded with imperial imagery, from newspaper advertisements, hoardings and commercial packaging. Presumably businesses would not have marketed their wares in this way had the Empire been unpopular.
- Millions of Britons were directly involved in the imperial process, emigrating to Canada, Australia, New Zealand and South Africa. (Some 1.5 million Britons emigrated to the colonies between 1909 and 1914.) First-generation emigrants retained close links with Britain, the new cheap postal service linking them to their homeland. This helped to keep alive the sense that Britain was the centre of a 'Greater Britain' which reached out to all corners of the globe.
- Tens of thousands of Britons serving in the armed forces were based in various parts of the Empire. Most soldiers and sailors came from working-class families which, as a result, often had an interest in – and commitment to – Britain's imperial position.

- British patriotism, strong in the Boer War, remained strong thereafter. Pride in Empire was an important element of British patriotism. A number of patriotic leagues continued to be influential. The Navy League, for example, had 100,000 members in 1913, holding exhibitions and encouraging observance of Trafalgar and Empire Days.
- Young Britons were inculcated with imperial pride. Public schools continued to prepare their pupils for careers as colonial administrators or army officers. School textbooks stressed the achievements of Britons who helped to establish the Empire.
- The greatest imperial enthusiasts came from the public schools, as well as army and naval officers and colonial administrators. But many middle- and working-class Britons also supported imperialism.
- The success of the scout and guide movements, fostered by Baden-Powell, the hero of Mafeking, stressed the obligations and rewards of imperial citizenship.
- Britain and its imperial possessions were closely bound economically. India was Britain's second largest market after Germany. Between 1903 and 1914 British exports to – and imports from – the Empire increased by a third.
- The Empire remained an inspiration to popular writers such as Rudyard Kipling and H. Rider Haggard.
- The fact that so many Britons volunteered for service in 1914 at the start of the First World War suggests that patriotic sentiments were strong.
- The fact that so many men from the Empire volunteered to fight for Britain suggests that imperial sentiment was as strong in the **Dominions**/colonies as in Britain itself.

KEY TERM

Dominions Britain's self-governing colonies (for example, Australia and Canada).

Chapter summary

The Boer War resulted in the formation of a Boer-dominated South Africa. In Britain, the war led to the end of splendid isolation and concern over national efficiency. Chamberlain's efforts to introduce tariff reform were rejected by the electorate. In 1905, the Liberals came to power. The Liberal governments were less committed to Empire than the Conservatives. In Egypt and India there was increasing opposition to British rule. British rule in Africa was not particularly efficient or humane. While there may have been a decline in imperial sentiment in the period, there is evidence indicating that support for Empire remained strong.

Refresher questions

Use these questions to remind yourself of the key material covered in this chapter.

1 What were the main consequences of the Boer War for South Africa?
2 What were the main consequences of the Boer War for Britain?
3 Why was there concern about national efficiency in Britain?
4 What problems did Britain face in Egypt?
5 To what extent did Britain face increasing problems in India?
6 How effective was British rule in Africa?
7 What were the main arguments in favour of tariff reform?
8 Why did the British electorate reject tariff reform?
9 What evidence is there for a decline of imperial sentiment?
10 What evidence suggests that imperial sentiment remained strong?

Question practice

ESSAY QUESTIONS

1 'The Boer War had a greater impact on Britain than on southern Africa in the years 1899–1914.' Explain why you agree or disagree with this view.
2 'Britain tried to rule both Egypt and India by conciliatory means in the period 1882–1914.' Assess the validity of this statement.
3 'Those who supported tariff reform between 1902 and 1914 had a very good case'. Explain why you agree or disagree with this view.
4 'Imperial sentiment declined in Britain in the period 1902–14.' Assess the validity of this statement.

INTERPRETATION QUESTIONS (AS LEVEL AND A LEVEL)

1 With reference to Extracts A and B and your understanding of the historical context, which of these two extracts provides the more convincing interpretation of Lord Curzon's rule as Viceroy of India from 1898 to 1905?

2 Using your understanding of the historical context, assess how convincing the arguments in these three extracts are in relation to assessing Lord Curzon's rule as viceroy of India.

EXTRACT A

From Martin Kitchen, *The British Empire and Commonwealth: A Short History*, Macmillan Press, 1996, pp. 44–5.

Lord Curzon, who served as viceroy from 1898 to 1905, regarded virtually all of humanity as inferior and put the Indians near the bottom of the scale. He told Balfour in 1901 that there was not one Indian in the entire subcontinent capable of serving on the executive council and reminded him that the British position in India, which he believed was the key to Britain's greatness as a nation, rested on the 'extraordinary inferiority, in character, honesty and capacity of the [natives]'. Curzon encouraged the improvement of an educational system, though it did little but produce clerks for the vast bureaucracy. Only one Indian boy in five and one girl in forty attended primary school, and very little effort was made to train Indians in the sciences … Curzon did not set out to modernise India but to ensure that British administration was efficient and fair so that the superiority of the British way of life could be daily manifested. He did not intend to begin a new era but to reach the zenith of the old.

EXTRACT B

From Piers Brendon, *The Decline and Fall of the British Empire 1781–1997*, Vintage Books, 2008, pp. 240–1.

If toil was the criterion, Curzon's administration lived up to his exalted aspirations. His Viceregal existence was 'an endless typhoon of duty'. To paraphrase The Times, *he took to government as other men take to drink. He laboured with indefatigable zeal (and interminable, self-pitying complaint) to give India measures of justice, reform and public welfare. In his efforts to foster commerce, improve communications, develop irrigation, relieve famine, spread education, strengthen defence, increase security and promote efficiency, Curzon virtually reconstructed the Raj. He made himself almost as unpopular as Ripon with the white community (and initially popular with Indians) by condemning instances of racial violence on the part of British soldiers and civilians. He resisted Britain's 'Shylock' exploitation of India, writing to Whitehall as though he were the ruler of a foreign power … Incapable of delegation, he dissipated his energies in minutiae. He kept his own household accounts. He criticised his subordinates' punctuation and wardrobe. He complained about pigeon droppings in Calcutta's Public Library and the state of the lion's cage at the Zoo.*

EXTRACT C

From David Dilks, 'A Most Superior Person' in *British Empire Magazine*, Volume 60, Orbis/TimeLife/BBC, 1973, page 1629.

All predictions that he [Curzon] would soon be swamped in paper were false. He probed into questions relentlessly; settling issues which had been dragging about the offices for years, in some instances for decades. In short, he had a highly distinctive style as a ruler, compounded of meticulous attention to detail, very rapid judgement, boldness in conception, persistence in following through reforms, capacity to kindle enthusiasm among those who were not sure of themselves and to arouse resentment among those overborne by his personality or tactless language. He never dealt with a case of importance without scrutinizing its history and asking himself what would be the results of all the alternative courses. He made it his business not only to know the machine as it was, but to fettle it up. To his disappointment, he found the Indian Civil Service, although generally honest and incorruptible, deficient in initiative and ideas at the senior levels … What India needed, he judged, was stimulus, encouragement, example and incentive from the top instead of a respectable presidency.

Imperialism challenged, 1914–39

In 1914, Britain went to war with Germany and Austria-Hungary. In 1918, Britain emerged victorious from the First World War with its Empire greater in size than ever before. Yet in many ways Britain was weakened by the war and faced increasing imperial problems thereafter. This chapter will consider the impact of the First World War on the Empire by exploring the following themes:

★ The British Empire and the First World War
★ The Dominions
★ India
★ The Middle East
★ British colonial rule
★ Development of trade and commerce
★ British attitudes to Empire

The key debate on pages 113–15 of this chapter asks the question: To what extent was the British Empire in retreat by 1939?

Key dates

1914	Start of First World War
1917	Imperial War Cabinet established Balfour Declaration
1918	End of First World War
1919	Amritsar massacre
1920	British mandates established in Iraq, Transjordan and Palestine
1922	Founding of the Irish Free State Declaration of Egyptian independence
1923	Southern Rhodesia granted self-government
1926	Balfour Report defined Dominion status
1931	Statute of Westminster
1932	Establishment of Imperial Preference tariff system
1935	Government of India Act
1936	Arab rebellion in Palestine
1939	Start of Second World War

The British Empire and the First World War

▶ *To what extent did the Empire contribute to Allied victory in the First World War?*

The Empire was vital to Allied success in the First World War for a number of reasons.

Imperial unity

In 1914, large numbers of Australians, Canadians, New Zealanders and South Africans volunteered to fight because they felt great affinity with Britain. The Crown colonies too were generally loyal. Indians, Africans, West Indians and Asians volunteered for service in the imperial forces.

In 1917, Prime Minister Lloyd George called together a conference of Dominion prime ministers and established an Imperial War Cabinet, in which South African Jan Smuts played an important role.

The Empire's contribution to the war effort

The Empire provided Britain and its European allies with men and resources:

- Dominion troops fought bravely in Europe, the Middle East and Africa, and made a major contribution on the Western Front in 1917–18.
- The legislation to raise the armies, the taxation to pay for them and the administration to run them were all provided by the Dominion governments. In 1916, New Zealand adopted conscription, as did Canada in 1918. Although the Australian electorate rejected conscription, some 413,000 Australians enlisted – 30 per cent of all eligible males.
- In total, the Dominions provided some 1.3 million men to the Allied cause. For this they paid a high price. Australia lost 58,500 dead, Canada 56,500 and New Zealand 16,000.
- Over 1.4 million Indian troops – all volunteers – were mobilised. Some fought on the Western Front in 1914–15. Far more fought in the Middle East and Africa. Over 48,000 died.
- 70,000 British-African troops fought in Africa.
- Africans, Indians, West Indians and Chinese participated on the Western Front as members of the labour corps.
- The Empire's economic resources greatly assisted the Allied war effort.

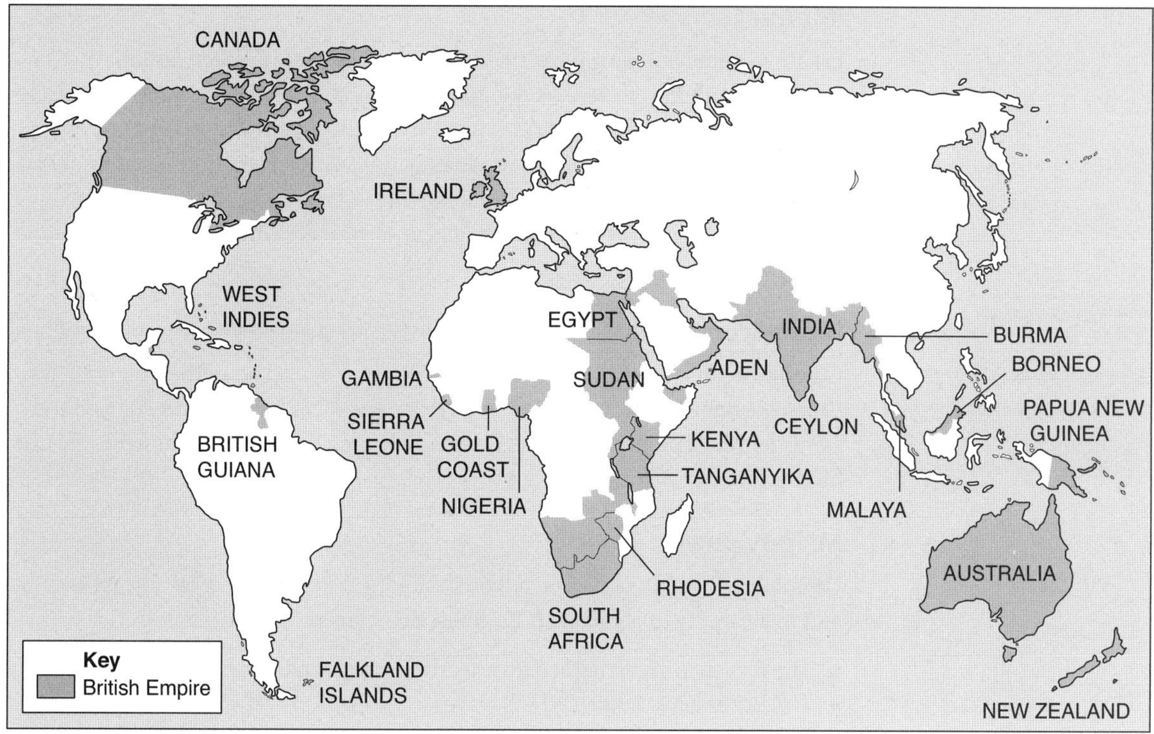

Figure 5.1 The British Empire c1922.

Imperial strengths in 1919

At the end of the First World War, the British Empire seemed to be at its peak. In November 1918, Lord Curzon declared, 'The British flag has never flown over a more powerful and united empire … Never did our voice count more in the councils of nations; or in the determining of the future destinies of mankind.'

Expansion of the Empire

The peace settlements with Germany and Turkey after 1918 resulted in Britain acquiring a variety of new territories including Tanganyika, most of Togoland and the Cameroons in Africa, and Palestine, Transjordan and Iraq in the Middle East. It was not just Britain which acquired new lands. Australia was given German New Guinea, New Zealand was given Samoa, while South Africa was given German South West Africa. The fact that these territories were to be ruled as **mandates**, and the countries administering them (and preparing them for self-rule) should be responsible to the **League of Nations**, seemed to be irrelevant. In theory, Britain was committed to granting self-government to all its colonies when they were perceived to be ready: mandates thus appeared to be no different from the rest of its colonies. What appeared to matter more was that 2 million square miles were added to the Empire, which now amounted to a quarter of the world's land surface.

KEY TERMS

Mandate The power conferred upon a state by the League of Nations to govern and protect a region.

League of Nations An organisation, similar to the present-day United Nations, established in 1919 to help preserve world peace.

Informal empire

Britain's influence was not confined to its 'formal' empire of territorial possessions and protectorates. It had long been able to exert its will over regions by means other than direct rule. After 1918, it effectively controlled a large number of strategically important states in the Middle East. It also had financial and commercial pre-eminence in other areas (for example, Argentina). Britain regarded its position in these 'client' states as of no less importance than its authority in its colonial territories.

KEY TERM

USSR The Union of Soviet Socialist Republics, formed in 1922.

Lack of competition

Chiefly, because the USA and the **USSR** were so bound up in their own affairs, Britain seemed to be the world's sole great power. No other nation enjoyed the same degree of global influence. Germany was shattered by defeat while France had suffered grievous casualties.

Military power

Ultimately, Britain's power rested on its ability to keep order in its formal empire and in its ability to persuade or frighten client states into cooperation:

- The British army remained an effective force in colonial conflicts.
- The Royal Navy still ruled the waves.
- Britain could now use its air force. Air power, which could involve indiscriminate bombing of rebel villages, was cheaper than sending in troops. Winston Churchill, for example, was prepared to use poison gas against troublesome subjects in Iraq and elsewhere.

Support for Empire

Britons were still proud of their Empire. Most saw it as a benevolent system which brought peace, prosperity and happiness to less fortunate areas until such time as the peoples of those areas could manage their own affairs.

Imperial weaknesses in 1919

The Empire was less strong than it appeared.

The impact of war

Britain had won the First World War, but in winning had suffered a terrible haemorrhage of blood and wealth. Some 725,000 Britons were killed. The war had cost billions of pounds, increasing Britain's national debt fourteen-fold.

The Empire's structure

The Empire was far from the political union that the expression the 'British Empire' implied. Britain did not rule over an ordered array of colonial governments. Indeed, there was little system in the Empire's constitutional structure:

- The Dominions were essentially self-governing.
- The status of some of the other hundred or so other territories (excluding the 565 princely states in India) varied enormously and they were at different stages of political development. Most colonies or dependencies had a governor who relied on local elites for support.
- There was no single departmental voice on imperial affairs.
- The Foreign Office supervised Britain's relations with client states and semi-colonies.
- The Dominion Office dealt with the Dominions.
- The Indian viceroy was supervised by the India Office. But the viceroy also managed British interests in the Persian Gulf and Afghanistan and administered both Aden and Burma.
- The other colonies were overseen by the Colonial Office.
- External defence was the sphere of the Admiralty and the War Office.
- The Treasury had huge financial power.
- The officials who administered the vast imperial concern were astonishingly few. The Indian Civil Service was only 1250 strong. Its Ceylonese equivalent numbered 100. Britain ruled all of its African possessions with 1200 administrators and 200 judges and legal officers.

The threat of nationalism

After 1919, the Empire was to be subject to various strains, both internal and external. Until the late 1930s, the spread of nationalism was the most direct threat:

- Most Dominions sought to assert their autonomy and independence from Britain.
- In Africa and Asia, new educated elites resented British rule.
- The growing force of nationalism was reflected in episodes such as disturbances in India in 1919–20 (see pages 99–100) and anti-British riots in Egypt in 1919.
- The Easter Rising in Ireland (see below) and the Bolshevik Revolution in Russia in 1917 inspired independence movements throughout the Empire.

Economic weakness

Britain was economically weakened by the war and its industrial power was eclipsed by the USA. Moreover, it had been forced to sell many of its overseas investments, for example those in the USA, on which it had depended to balance the books.

Military weakness

Declining economic power lessened Britain's ability to sustain its military commitments. The cost of defending such a mixed collection of territories was a major problem. With the exception of the Indian army, local military units in the colonies were of modest strength and, if left unsupported by British troops, could not be relied on to suppress an insurrection. In consequence, the British army (soon under 200,000 strong) was posted round the world in relatively small numbers. In the early 1920s, British forces were stretched near to breaking point as they struggled to keep control in Ireland, Egypt, Iraq and India.

The Irish Free State

In 1916, Irish nationalists rose in rebellion in Dublin. The 'Easter Rising' was quickly defeated, but troubles continued and Sinn Féin, an extreme nationalist party, won increasing support. After success in the 1918 general election, Sinn Féin MPs set up an Irish Parliament in Dublin and declared independence. The Irish Republican Army (IRA) waged a guerrilla war against British rule. The hostilities were sporadic: the total number of lives lost in the struggle amounted to no more than 1500 – an average day's casualties for the British army during the First World War. By late 1920, British security forces were gaining the upper hand, but many Britons had lost confidence in the justice of their cause. Lloyd George and Irish nationalist leaders finally agreed that a new Irish Free State should be granted 'home rule', although it would remain as a Dominion within the Empire. Six of nine counties in Ulster remained part of the United Kingdom and became Northern Ireland.

If Britain could not retain control of most of Ireland, it seemed unlikely it could hold on to India. Certainly, Irish independence inspired nationalists everywhere, especially in India.

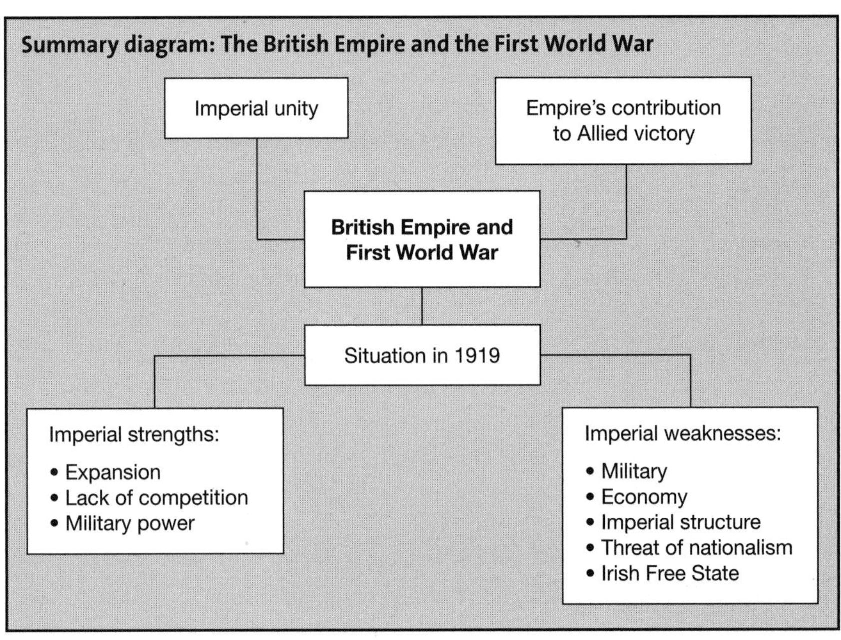

2 The Dominions

▶ *To what extent were the bonds between Britain and the Dominions weakened in the period 1919–39?*

By 1919, the Dominions – Canada, Newfoundland, Australia, New Zealand, and South Africa – were essentially self-governing. Nevertheless, Britain still controlled their foreign policies. The decision to commit the Dominions to war in 1914 had been taken by the British Cabinet alone. But as the war progressed, the Dominions increasingly saw themselves as equal partners with Britain. After 1918 they were represented separately at the Paris Peace Conference and in the League of Nations (Newfoundland apart).

Disunity

In general, Britain and the Dominions had cooperated well during the war. It was assumed that diplomatic cooperation would continue after 1918. The Imperial War Cabinet (see page 90) agreed that in future British prime ministers would work out an imperial foreign policy by a process of 'continuous consultation' with Dominion leaders. Unfortunately, Britain and the Dominions had separate and divergent national interests. Discussions on the renewal of the Anglo-Japanese treaty (see page 72) in 1920–1 showed that it was difficult to please everyone: Australia and New Zealand favoured renewal, Canada opposed it. It also soon became clear that it was difficult to consult the Dominions on every issue. Britain had interests in many parts of the world and was not prepared to accept the limits on its freedom of action that 'continuous consultation' would have involved.

The 1922 **Chanak crisis** showed that Britain could not expect automatic backing from the Dominions. Britain allowed the crisis with Turkey to develop without consultation with the Dominions. When Lloyd George appealed to the Dominions to send troops to Turkey, he met with varied responses. While New Zealand offered support, Australia was less enthusiastic and Canada flatly refused. The South African government prudently said nothing. In the event, no military assistance was needed, but the crisis proved that the diplomatic unity of Britain and its Dominions was a fiction. The policy of 'continuous consultation' was allowed to drop. Britain pursued its own policy, and some Dominions were soon pursuing theirs. Canada led the way in establishing its own diplomatic missions abroad.

KEY TERM

Chanak crisis
An international crisis which almost resulted in a war between Britain and Turkey in 1922.

However, there was some effort at maintaining the pretence of unity. Imperial conferences, attended by the Dominion leaders, were held in London but at increasingly irregular intervals: 1921, 1923, 1926, 1930 and 1937. There was also a Committee of Imperial Defence but few Dominion representatives attended its meetings. The Dominions were far from eager to share the burden of imperial defence. They relied on Britain to bear the lion's share of spending on the military forces necessary to ensure their security.

The Balfour Declaration and the Statute of Westminster

KEY TERM

Commonwealth A group of states united by a common interest or joint history.

Although the Dominions were, for most practical purposes, independent countries, that independence was established by custom rather than by formal definition. In the 1920s, Britain was pressurised by South Africa, Ireland and Canada to define Dominion status more precisely. The 1926 **Commonwealth** Conference agreed on the Balfour Declaration. This stated that the Dominions were 'autonomous communities within the Empire, equal in status, in no way subordinate to one to another in any aspect of their domestic or external affairs, though united by a common allegiance to the Crown'.

The Statute of Westminster (1931) put the finishing touches to the process by which an Empire based on central authority was transformed into a Commonwealth of independent states. Dominions now had the right to change their own constitutions and even withdraw from the Commonwealth if they so wished. Common allegiance to the Crown was the only formal link between the Dominions.

Britain's relations with the Dominions

Britain's relations with the Dominions varied.

Ireland

For ten years after the 1922 settlement, the Irish Free State generally cooperated with Britain. But, in 1932, Fianna Fáil became the largest party in the Irish Parliament. Éamon de Valera, Fianna Fáil's leader, made no secret of the fact that he wanted to create a united and independent Ireland. By late 1932, Britain and Ireland were locked in a 'trade war', both countries increasing duties against goods from the other. In 1937, a new Irish constitution laid claim to all 32 counties of Ireland and described Southern Ireland – or Éire – as 'a sovereign, independent, democratic state'. Éire remained a Commonwealth member in name only.

South Africa

In South Africa, the coming to power of the Afrikaner Nationalist Party in 1924 caused problems for Britain. Many Boers were anti-British and anxious to assert their independence. Relations between Britain and South Africa were uneasy throughout the interwar years.

Canada

Canadian loyalties were affected by divisions between the French- and English-speaking communities. Mackenzie King, Canadian prime minister for most of the interwar period, depended on the support of the French-Canadians and was less pro-British than previous Canadian leaders.

Newfoundland, a large island with few people, governed itself throughout the 1920s. But, unable to cope with the Great Depression of the early 1930s, it returned to being a colony ruled from London.

Australia and New Zealand

Most Australians and New Zealanders remained loyal to the Empire. The growing threat from Japan in the 1930s served to strengthen Australian and New Zealand friendship with Britain.

Loyalty to Britain

Although the formal bonds of Empire disappeared, many people in the Dominions felt attached to Britain by ties of sentiment – a shared past, a common language, similar institutions and loyalty to the Royal family. Most British emigrants still went to the Dominions – although in the 1930s, the flow of population of the English-speaking world was into Britain rather than away from it as depression hit the Commonwealth. Many British families had relatives and friends in the Dominions. The Dominions were also bound to Britain by ties of self-interest. Britain remained a vital market and an important source of capital.

Proof of the continuing importance of the Commonwealth came in 1939. When Britain declared war on Germany; Australia, New Zealand and Canada all did the same. In South Africa, the Afrikaner Nationalist Party supported a policy of neutrality. But General Smuts forced a debate in the House of Assembly and secured a majority for war by 80 votes to 67. Only Éire remained neutral.

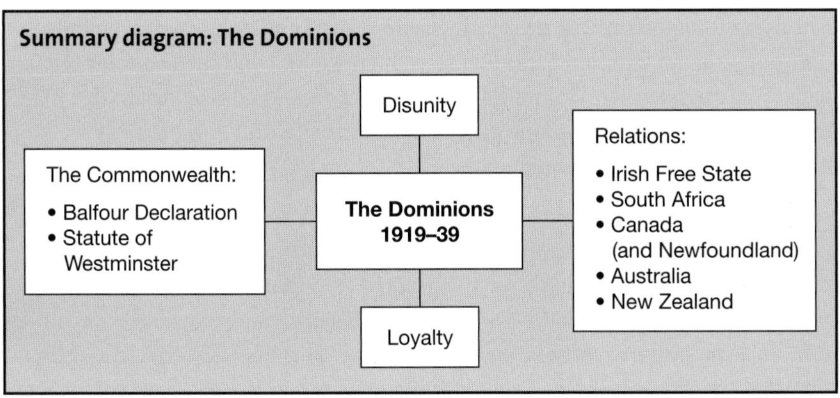

3 India

To what extent had India achieved self-government by 1939?

The main imperial struggle between 1919 and 1939 was in India. Indian demands for independence were opposed by the British government, which realised that the loss of India would have far-reaching effects on Britain's prestige and power.

The situation in 1919

The Raj, with its large army and magnificent state pageantry, was outwardly impressive, yet throughout India the problems of acute poverty and ignorance were massive.

The Raj was ruled by just over 1000 British civil servants, supported by thousands of Indian bureaucrats. The Indian police force was 200,000 strong. Ultimately, British authority rested on the Indian army, which was commanded by British officers and supported by British troops. The army had two main concerns: to defend India from the threats of invasion and to maintain internal security. The main external threats came from Afghanistan and Russia. This did not amount to much in the interwar period: an Afghan invasion in 1919 was easily defeated, and Russian (communist) ideas were a greater danger than Russian soldiers. Growing unrest in India was a greater problem than the external threat. By 1919, Congress, once a minority pressure group, had become a large organisation with some claims to be a national movement.

The Montagu Declaration

In 1914, India had entered the First World War as a loyal member of the British Empire. Large numbers of Indians volunteered to serve the King-Emperor. But as the war dragged on, imperial enthusiasm waned and political concessions were demanded by Indian nationalists as the price for continued support. Tilak, leader of Congress after Gokhale's death, and Mohammad Ali Jinnah, the president of the Muslim League (see page 76), made a pact to fight for self-government by constitutional means.

In 1917, Edwin Montagu, secretary of state for India, aware of rising opposition, announced that Britain accepted 'the increasing association of Indians in every branch of the administration' and 'the gradual development of self-governing institutions, with a view to the progressive realisation of responsible government in India as an integral part of the British Empire'. The 1919 Government of India Act was framed to give substance to Montagu's declaration. Elected Indians were allowed some power to determine policy at provincial level, but only on non-contentious issues (such as health and education). The viceroy was left in control of important matters, such as defence, and was given authority to legislate by

Mohandos Karamchand Gandhi

1869	Born, son of the chief minister of the small princely state of Porbandar
1882	Married a child-bride chosen for him by his father
1888–93	Educated in Britain; qualified as a barrister
1893	Began work as a lawyer in South Africa; led a successful passive resistance campaign against measures which discriminated against Indians
1915	Returned to India to help the Congress Party; he quickly became its main guide, campaigning actively for Indian rights by means of civil disobedience
1922	Imprisoned for encouraging rebellion
1924	Released: continued to work for a non-violent route to independence
1930	Led the 'Salt March' (see page 102); arrested
1931	Released from prison; took part in London Round Table Conference, arriving at meetings dressed only in a loincloth
1942	Launched 'Quit India' campaign against Britain; arrested
1944	Released
1948	Assassinated by a Hindu fanatic

Gandhi never wavered in his devotion to the cause of Indian independence. He was equally committed to non-violent protest, devising and instigating new methods of civil disobedience to disrupt British rule. There was sometimes a strong element of coercion in his tactics and they could, and often did, spill over into violence. Accordingly, Gandhi was often seen as a hypocrite by British officials. He was an inspired and inspiring leader for many Hindus. However, his influence on events has probably been exaggerated. The history of Indian independence is too complex to be explained by the ideas and activities of a single leader. Gandhi's influence, even in Congress, was far from paramount. He was more a moralist and religious leader than a politician. His greatest importance was his appeal to the Hindu masses who called him Mahatma (Holy One).

decree for six months in the case of an emergency. This did not satisfy Indian nationalists who wanted nothing less than full-scale independence. Congress leaders advocated a policy of **passive resistance** as a way of putting pressure on Britain.

KEY TERM

Passive resistance
Deliberate refusal to do what law or regulation demands and submission to the consequent penalties.

The Amritsar massacre

In 1918–19, India was far from calm. There were economic problems and a world-wide influenza epidemic killed millions of Indians. Faced with the threat of disorder, the Indian government passed the Rowlatt Act, allowing provincial governors to imprison without trial anyone suspected of subversion. This led to more protests. The most serious disturbances were in the Punjab region, especially in the city of Amritsar where several Europeans were killed in serious rioting.

The governor of the Punjab, fearing that the region was on the verge of a major revolt, called on the army to restore order. On 13 April 1919, in defiance of a ban on public meetings, a large crowd assembled near the Golden Temple in Amritsar. General Dyer, who had been sent to restore order, ordered his troops to open fire; 379 people were killed and 1200 wounded. Dyer went on to punish those he thought responsible for the disturbances: eighteen were executed and hundreds flogged. An embarrassed British government set up an official inquiry which criticised Dyer for ordering the firing without warning and for allowing the shooting to continue longer than was necessary. Dyer was relieved of his command and sent home on sick leave, even though the governor of the Punjab maintained that Dyer's action had averted much worse disorder. While the Commons approved the government's treatment of Dyer, a House of Lords motion deplored the injustice shown to him. Many saw him as the 'saviour of India' and a fund to pay his defence costs raised £26,000.

Gandhi and civil disobedience

The Amritsar massacre damaged Britain's reputation as a civilising influence. Congress's campaign of civil disobedience gathered momentum. Gandhi was regarded as the campaign's leader. His techniques included days of fasting and prayer when all work and trade ceased, refusal to pay taxes, the boycotting of British goods and the deliberate flounting of the law. He temporarily united Congress and Muslims in common cause. Although never encompassing the whole of India, the civil disobedience campaign put British authorities under considerable pressure.

KEY FIGURE

Jawaharlal Nehru (1889–1964)

Educated in England, he returned to India in 1912 to practise law but soon left his profession to follow Gandhi. In 1929, he was elected president of the Indian National Congress in succession to his father. Between 1921 and 1945 he served nine prison sentences for participating in the civil disobedience movement against the British. After 1945, he was a central in the negotiations for the creation of an independent India. He became the first prime minister of independent India (1947–64).

Gandhi, Motilal Nehru and Jawaharlal Nehru

After the Amritsar massacre, India's struggle for independence was dominated by Motilal Nehru, **Jawaharlal Nehru** and Mahatma Gandhi – sometimes termed Father, Son and Holy Ghost:

- Gandhi's moral stature gave him unique authority both within and outside Congress.
- Motilal, Nehru's father, a successful lawyer, was converted to nationalism by his son after the Amritsar massacre.
- Jawaharlal Nehru, like Gandhi, had been educated in Britain and qualified as a lawyer. On returning to India, he became a follower of Gandhi.

All three men were imprisoned for their support for civil disobedience in the early 1920s.

Failure of the civil disobedience campaign

In 1922, Gandhi called off the campaign because he claimed that it was leading to bloodshed. In reality, the campaign was running out of steam. It failed to mobilise the whole of India, and the alliance that Congress had forged with the Muslims had begun to collapse. While passive and violent resistance continued throughout the 1920s, order was slowly re-established.

Diarchy

The 1919 Act allowed Indians some control over their own affairs. **Diarchy** worked after a fashion. In 1923, 5 million Indians elected representatives to the expanded provincial councils and to the National Legislative Assembly. Indian politicians used their new fiscal powers to begin establishing a system of protective tariffs to encourage India's textile and iron and steel industries.

KEY TERM

Diarchy A form of government in which two bodies are vested with power.

Congress's problems

By the 1920s, Congress was a nation-wide movement, its new leaders having links with the mass of people in a way that the first leaders did not. Nevertheless, its leadership was divided, particularly over the issue of participation in India's new constitutional bodies:

- Gandhi had no time for the new councils. Instead, he worked to win the support and trust of Indian peasants, especially those of the lowest caste.
- Motilal believed that Congress should exploit the new councils and put the case for Dominion status.
- Nehru wanted to adopt more violent tactics towards the Raj's institutions.

It was not just Congress's leadership which was divided. By the late 1920s, most Muslims had left Congress because they regarded it as a party for Hindu interests.

Sir John Simon's Commission

Lord Birkenhead, the new secretary of state for India, had no faith in the Indians' capacity for self-government. He wanted to devise a constitutional framework that would preserve British supremacy. That was also the aim of the new viceroy, Lord Irwin. In 1927, Birkenhead ordered a review of the 1919 Act. This task was entrusted to a commission led by Sir John Simon. The commission had no Indian members, which provoked widespread protest. The commission finally recommended responsible government for India, but only at provincial level.

Talk of reform

Lord Irwin, a moderate Conservative, believed that Indian self-determination could not be opposed indefinitely. Communal violence had increased during the 1920s and Irwin feared a catastrophic social breakdown. In 1929, after consulting the newly elected Labour government in Britain, Irwin decided that a conciliatory gesture was needed. He announced that Dominion status was the 'natural issue of India's constitutional progress' and proposed a Round Table Conference (see below), with Indian and British members, to discuss India's future. Winston Churchill and other right-wing Conservatives were highly critical of the pledge of Dominion status. Churchill, at odds with Baldwin, the Conservative leader, resigned from the shadow Cabinet over the issue.

Congress also had little confidence in Irwin's proposals. Its leaders boycotted the Round Table talks and embarked on a new campaign of civil disobedience. Gandhi's 241-mile march to the sea in 1930 to make salt (without paying the unpopular salt tax) attracted great attention. Many Congress supporters determined to break the salt laws. Soon 60,000 were in prison. Gandhi's arrest in May simply prompted more civil disobedience and serious outbreaks of violence.

The Round Table Conferences

In 1930, the first session of the Round Table Conference opened in London but made little headway. In January 1931, Gandhi, freed from prison, began discussions with Irwin. He eventually agreed to try to end the civil disobedience campaign and to attend the next Round Table session. In return, the viceroy would release non-violent prisoners and relax repression. Many Conservatives opposed Irwin's 'deal' with Gandhi. Churchill described British policy as 'a hideous act of self-mutilation'. Indian radicals were also critical, denouncing the pact as a betrayal. Nehru, while deploring the compromise, persuaded Congress to ratify it out of loyalty to Gandhi.

Little was achieved at the second session of the Round Table Conference (September 1931). Gandhi returned to India to find a new and less sympathetic viceroy, Lord Willingdon. He was soon involved in another civil disobedience campaign and re-arrested. Firm government action, including the arrest of 80,000 Congress supporters, resulted in the campaign's collapse.

The 1935 Government of India Act

The British government determined that some progress should be made towards India's Dominion status. After four years of bitter right-wing Conservative opposition in Parliament, the Government of India Act finally passed in 1935:

- The new act, which separated Burma from India, envisaged an all-India federation which would include the princely states.
- A national legislature would come into operation when over half the 565 Indian princes joined the federation.
- There would be an elected Indian Parliament. A third of the members of this assembly would be appointed by the Indian princes, the rest elected from the provinces, where a third of the seats would be reserved for Muslims.
- The British Viceroy would continue to be head of state, retaining powers over finance, defence and foreign affairs, and the right to act on his own initiative in an emergency with the authority to veto laws and suspend the constitution.
- The Act gave significant powers to Indian politicians by establishing provincial governments, elected by a much wider franchise than before, in which ministers responsible to the legislature controlled all aspects of the administration.

The 1935 Act was attacked in Britain for going too far and in India for not going far enough. In Churchill's view, it marked 'the definite decline and even disappearance of our authority in India'. The Indian nationalist Subhas Chandra Bose, by contrast, said, 'It was a scheme not for self-government, but for maintaining British rule'. Gandhi was similarly critical: 'India is still a prison, but the superintendent allows the prisoners to elect the officers who run the jail'.

The provincial elections

Congress, although critical of the Act, allowed party members to contest elections to the eleven provincial legislatures in 1936–7. Congress ministries were formed in most provinces. The Muslim League, by contrast, secured less than a quarter of the seats reserved for Muslims. Senior British officials accepted the results of the elections. Instead of trying to divide the nationalists, they started working with them in the provincial governments. Both parties soon found they were content with this collaboration: the British because provincial Congress politicians were less radical than expected; the Congressmen because they finally had considerable power.

The situation in 1939

While it now seemed certain that India would move on steadily to Dominion status, serious problems remained:

- Muslims resented Hindu dominance.
- No progress had been made towards the creation of a legislature at the centre because the princes could not agree terms on which to join the federation.
- By 1939, Britain had still not resigned itself to Indian independence. Indeed, in the late 1930s it seemed essential that India remain under British control to help counter the threat from Germany and Japan.

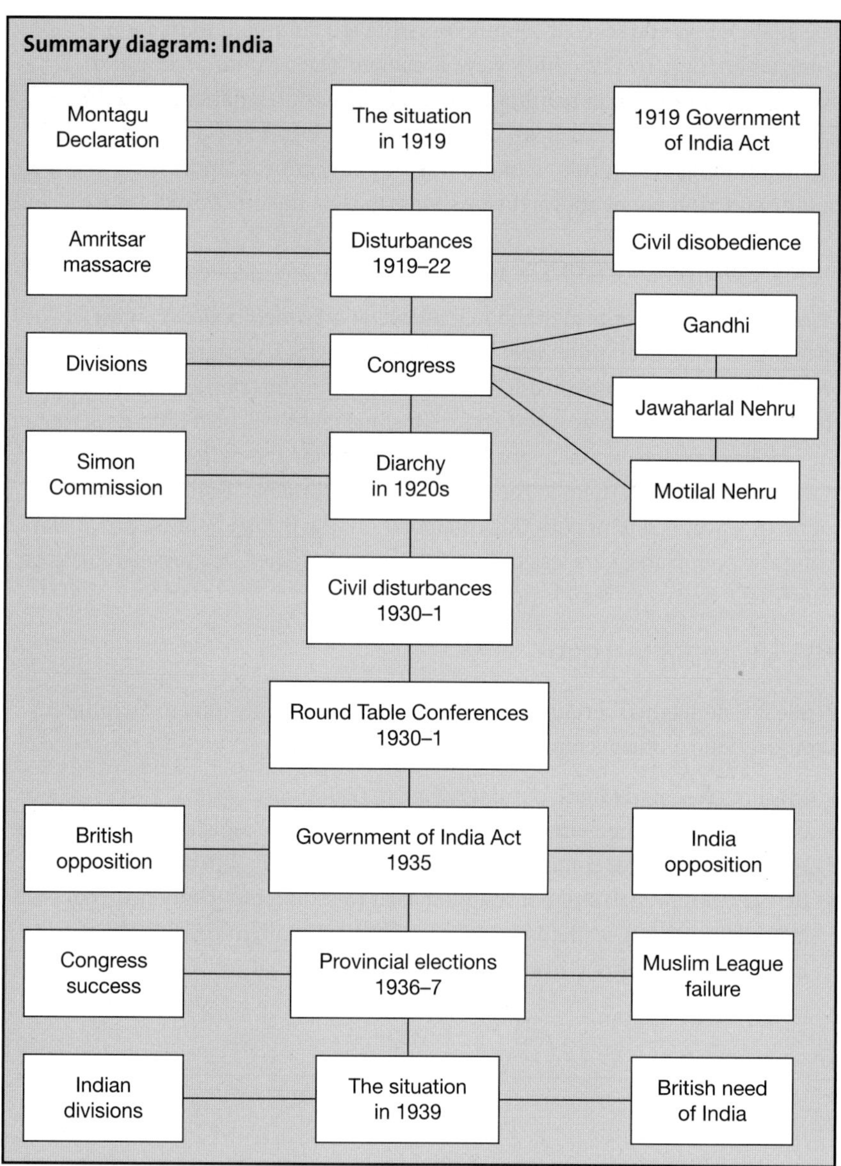
Summary diagram: India
Montagu Declaration
The situation in 1919
1919 Government of India Act
Amritsar massacre
Disturbances 1919–22
Civil disobedience
Gandhi
Divisions
Congress
Jawaharlal Nehru
Simon Commission
Diarchy in 1920s
Motilal Nehru
Civil disturbances 1930–1
Round Table Conferences 1930–1
British opposition
Government of India Act 1935
India opposition
Congress success
Provincial elections 1936–7
Muslim League failure
Indian divisions
The situation in 1939
British need of India

The Middle East

▶ *To what extent did Britain face serious challenges in the Middle East in the period 1919–39?*

The situation in 1919

By 1914, Britain controlled Aden and had considerable influence over Egypt and many sheikdoms and sultanates along the Persian Gulf. The First World War greatly extended British interests. In 1919, Britain took over the administration of Palestine, Transjordan and Mesopotamia. The security of the Suez Canal was a fundamental objective of British policy while the discovery of oil made the region increasingly important economically. Britain's dominant position depended on the careful management of Anglo-Arab relations. Interference with local society was generally kept to a minimum, for Britain was anxious not to arouse a full-scale Arab revolt. Control was exerted through friendly local rulers who depended for their survival on Britain's military assistance.

Egypt

Serious demonstrations in 1919 convinced British officials that Britain's 1914 annexation of Egypt should not be made permanent. In 1922, Britain recognised Egypt's independence, but still controlled Egypt's foreign and defence policies and kept an army in the country to guard the Suez Canal. A treaty in 1936 allowed the presence of 10,000 British troops in the Suez Canal zone and unlimited numbers of British troops in Egypt in an emergency.

Iraq

A revolt in Mesopotamia (Iraq) in 1920 was suppressed only with difficulty. Winston Churchill, colonial secretary in 1921, determined to find a ruler, acceptable to Iraqis and friendly to Britain. He supported Feisal, son of Sherif Hussein, a trusted Arab leader. Although Feisal had no previous connection with the area, he was duly 'elected' King of Iraq. In 1922, a treaty was signed under which Iraq became an independent state bound to Britain during the period of the mandate. The mandate ended in 1930 but Iraq accepted the presence of British military bases thereafter.

Palestine

Palestine posed enormous problems for Britain in the interwar period.

The Balfour Declaration

In 1917, the Balfour Declaration promised Britain's support for the 'establishment in Palestine of a national home for the Jewish people'. The Declaration was issued with the interests of Jews in mind, but with the particular object of

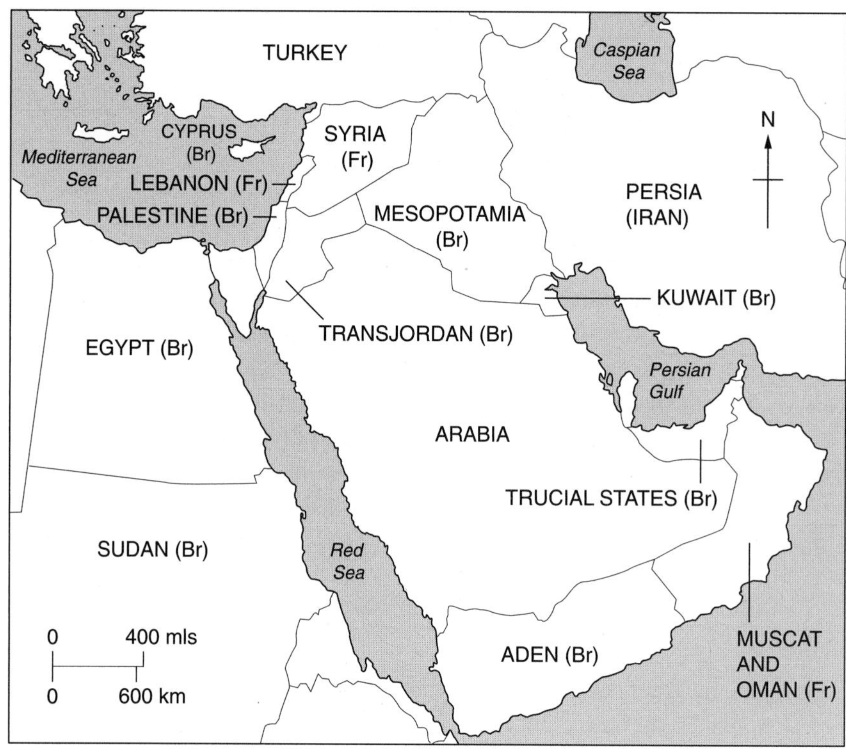

Figure 5.2 The Middle East after 1919.

winning support from American Jewish opinion for the Allied war effort. It was deliberately vague. What was to be the exact status of a national home? What were to be its frontiers? A further and greater problem was how to reconcile Jewish immigration into an area where the greater number of people were Arabs. Balfour saw no reason for a British presence in Palestine and would have preferred the USA to have become the mandatory power. However, most British politicians, recognising the strategic importance of the area, supported British control of Palestine.

Jewish immigration

Large-scale Jewish immigration caused increasing native Arab resentment. British politicians tended to sympathise with the Jewish desire to have a country of their own and some even envisaged a Jewish-colonised Palestine becoming a 'cornerstone' of the British Empire. However, most British officials in the Middle East sympathised with the native Palestinians who opposed Jewish immigration. The Jews and their supporters won the day. By 1925, there had been considerable Jewish immigration into Palestine and many Jews made no secret of their intention to turn the 'national home' into a Jewish nation-state. In 1929, there were serious anti-Jewish riots across Palestine. A 1930 White Paper proposed a limit on future Jewish immigration. This aroused so much opposition in pro-Jewish circles in Britain and the USA that no action was taken on its recommendations.

Jewish–Palestinian conflict

With the coming to power of Hitler in 1933 and the persecution of European Jews that followed, there was added pressure to increase Jewish immigration. Palestine was now seen as a Jewish sanctuary as well as a homeland. But increased immigration provoked increasing Arab opposition. In 1936, an Arab revolt broke out, directed against Jews, the British and moderate Arab leaders. Britain had to send troops to Palestine to maintain control.

The situation by 1939

In 1937, the Peel Commission recommended the partition of Palestine into an Arab state and a Jewish state (with a British buffer zone). However, it proved impossible to devise a workable plan of partition. In 1939, Britain abandoned the idea of partition, which was unpopular with Palestinians. Instead, it considered establishing an independent federated Palestinian state. Meanwhile, Jewish immigration was to be limited to 10,000 people a year for five years, with an additional 25,000 in the first year. Thereafter no further immigration would be allowed without Arab approval. This would preserve an Arab majority in Palestine for the foreseeable future. With war in Europe looming, Britain was anxious not to alienate Arab opinion.

Summary diagram: The Middle East

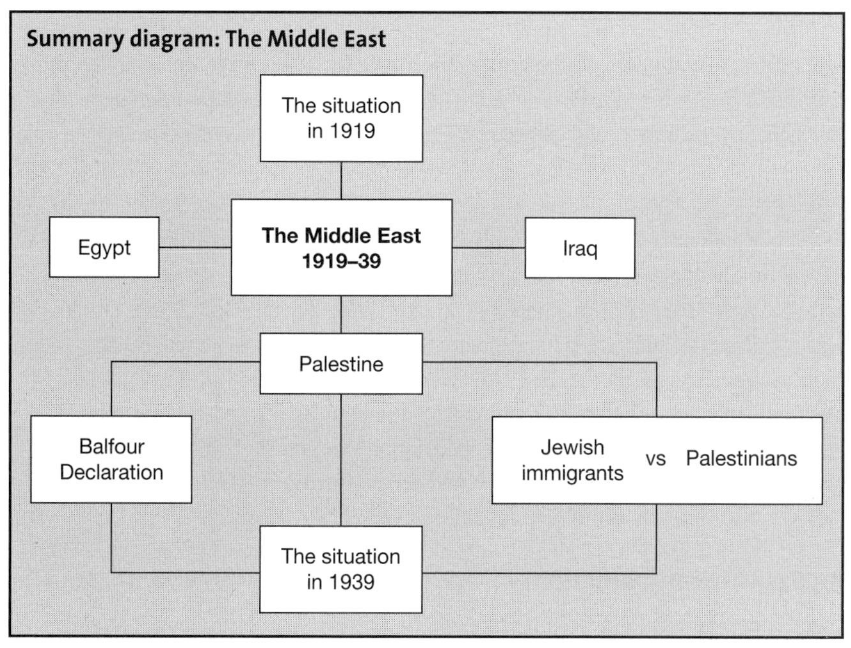

British colonial rule

To what extent was British rule beneficial to the colonies in the period 1919–39?

Most Britons assumed that the colonies would one day evolve into independent members of a multiracial Commonwealth. However, little progress was made in this direction between the wars. In most colonies there seemed little pressure for 'home rule'. Without pressure from below, it was unlikely that Britain would grant independence. The colonies were considered too valuable to be voluntarily given up. Moreover, racial prejudice and the habit of authority made it difficult for colonial officials to take seriously the idea of non-Europeans governing themselves successfully. Even a few Labour MPs believed that the aim of **self-determination** was not realistic in most dependencies for a long time to come.

KEY TERM

Self-determination
The power of people (of a particular group/nation) to choose their own form of government.

The West Indies

The West Indies remained a backwater. Britain made few concessions to democracy. By 1930, 175,000 West Indians, a tenth of the population, were employed in the sugar industry. Trade unions were prohibited and pay was low. The impact of the Depression in the 1930s led to serious disturbances on some islands. Britain recognised that the troubles were the result of past neglect and a Royal Commission recommended more subsidies to improve social conditions.

Africa

The only colonial people to be granted self-rule (in 1923) were the 30,000 white settlers in Southern Rhodesia who ruled over a million black people. Elsewhere in Africa, the situation was mixed.

Kenya

In 1919, Kenya received representative government in the form of an assembly for a white electorate. Between 1919 and 1923, Kenyan white settlers passed a series of measures to strengthen their control over black people. More labour was required of them, their wages were reduced, their taxes increased and their movements restricted. In 1923, the new colonial secretary, the Duke of Devonshire, declared that 'the interests of the [Kenyan] African natives must be paramount'. The Devonshire Declaration prevented the white settlers establishing a self-governing colony within the Commonwealth. By 1939, there were 21,000 Kenyan white people: one to every 175 Africans.

An East African Dominion?

Leo Amery, appointed colonial secretary in 1925, was an enthusiastic advocate of Empire. He dreamed of creating an East African Dominion, dominated by white people, comprising Kenya, Uganda, Tanganyika, Northern and Southern

Rhodesia and Nyasaland. The Conservative Cabinet was less enthusiastic and Amery's dreams came to nothing. A 1929 Royal Commission argued that African interests had to be paramount and white settlers were not the best trustees of those interests. There should be no responsible government for Kenya and no 'closer union' of Kenya, Uganda and Tanganyika until ways had been developed to consult African opinion.

West Africa

In the 1920s, black people were brought into the Gold Coast's higher civil service by Governor Guggisberg. Nigeria, larger and with more disparate elements than the Gold Coast, was harder to unite and modernise. Here, as in Sierra Leone and the Gambia, there was a division between coastal and inland areas. Along the coast, at least in the capital cities, there were groups of educated Africans who would have liked greater political power for themselves but were uneasily aware that the great majority of the population who lived further inland were much less sophisticated and would be certain to gain most of the political power by any withdrawal of British authority.

Conclusion

Britain's record in Africa between the wars was not good, albeit it was probably better in most respects than that of other European states. In the main, Britain ruled through local collaborators, relying on white prestige and the threat of force. A governor of Nigeria said that 'The great merit of British rule is that there is so little of it.' Undoubtedly, the British squeezed where they could. In the copper belt of Northern Rhodesia between 1930 and 1940, they took £2.4 million in taxes and gave only £136,000 in development grants. So little money was spent on Nyasaland that workers emigrated to the more racially hostile environments of Rhodesia and South Africa.

The general character of British rule

The 1920s and 1930s were the heyday of the **Colonial Service**, which took much of the 'cream' of Britain's public schools and universities. The character of British rule in the dependencies is often seen as despotism exercised by pompous and bigoted men in shorts and pith helmets. Or (less fashionably) it is depicted as a selfless struggle against the poverty and ignorance of the primitive masses. In reality, the number of British officials was so small and the financial resources of most colonies so slim that colonial rule had to rely on locally recruited subordinates to staff both its bureaucracies and its security forces.

KEY TERM

Colonial Service
The people who worked for the British Colonial Office.

Relatively little money was spent on colonial economic development, education or public health. It had long been government policy that colonies should be financially self-supporting. Not much was done, therefore, to fulfil what Britain claimed was its 'positive trust' to its colonial subjects. In most African colonies fewer than ten per cent of black children went to school (most of which were substandard). A governor of Tanganyika described his colony as 'lying in mothballs' between the wars. This is an apt description of what happened in most dependencies. Few experienced much in the way of economic prosperity and most suffered severely from the Depression of the 1930s.

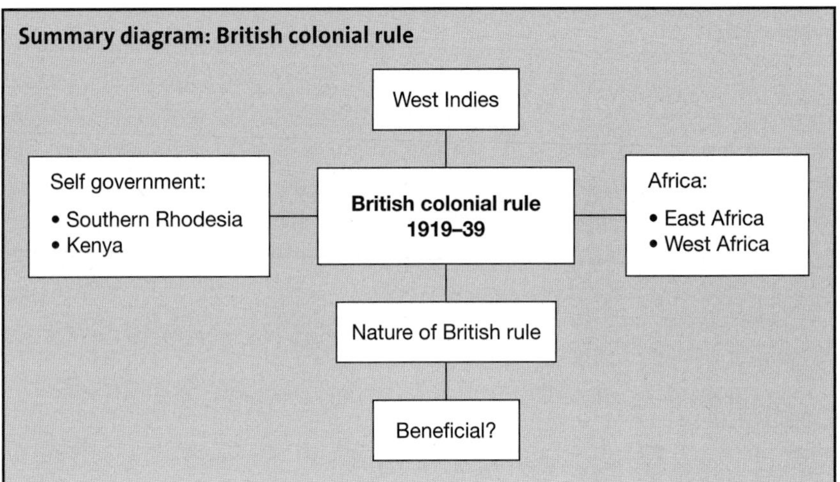

6 Development of trade and commerce

▶ *To what extent did increased trade with the Empire/ Commonwealth help Britain through difficult economic times in the period 1919–39?*

Post-1919, the Empire was increasingly important to Britain's trading position. In the 1920s, many Conservative MPs hoped to introduce some kind of imperial tariff protection which would obstruct foreign imports, encourage inter-imperial trade and make the Empire economically self-sufficient – just as Joseph Chamberlain had envisaged. In 1926, an Empire Marketing Board was set up to promote the sale of imperial goods. However, arguments for imperial protection never carried total conviction because Britain still conducted most of its trade with countries which were not part of the Empire.

Imperial preference

The Great Depression of the early 1930s had a major impact on Britain's economic relations with the Empire. In 1932, Britain abandoned free trade and introduced the Import Duties Act which imposed a ten per cent tariff on most imports. An Imperial Economic Conference at Ottawa (1932) accepted the principle of imperial preference. The conference resulted in a series of agreements over details of preferential trade between Britain and the Dominions and between the Dominions themselves.

Although imperial preference did not fulfil the hopes of those who had been pressing for complete Empire free trade, it had some positive effects. Britain's trade with the Empire/Commonwealth increased considerably after 1932. Between 1935 and 1939, nearly 40 per cent of its imports came from – and 49 per cent of its exports went to – the Empire/Commonwealth. The trade agreements increased imperial cohesion. The British government arranged bulk purchases of particular crops. For example, by 1939, Britain bought the entire cocoa crop of British West Africa. However, there was a downside. Dependence on imperial markets possibly made British industry less competitive in the rest of the world. Britain possibly paid more than it needed to for food and other raw materials. Dominion farmers, rather than British consumers, benefited most directly from preferential tariffs.

The sterling area

In 1931, the British government gave up the gold standard by ceasing to keep the value of the pound equal to a fixed weight of gold. The pound could now fluctuate in a way that was alarming for countries whose economic activity was closely linked to Britain. All Commonwealth countries, except Canada, which was more closely linked to the USA, formed an economic unit whose currencies remained fixed in value against one another. The British government acted as a banker to the sterling area, holding the free reserves of the other members, trying to smooth the fluctuations of sterling, and allowing members of the group opportunities to raise loans in London that were denied to non-members. These arrangements ensured that Commonwealth countries were sheltered somewhat from the world-wide depression.

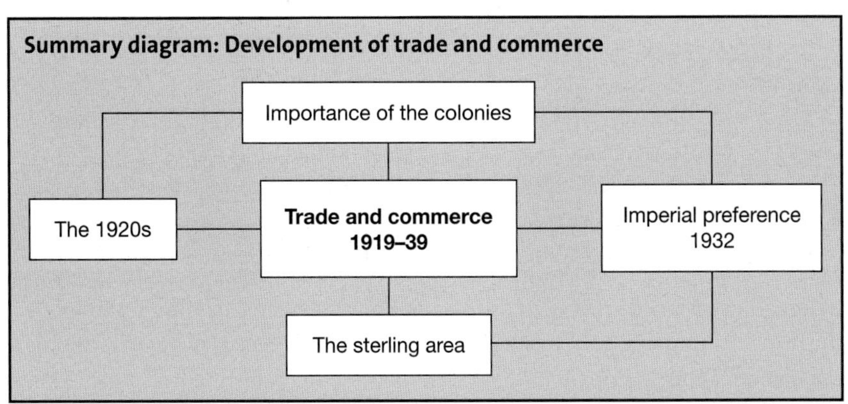

 British attitudes to Empire

▶ *Was the Empire an asset or a burden to Britain in the 1920s and 1930s?*

Most interwar British politicians regarded the Empire as a major asset. So did most Britons.

Support for Empire

There is plenty of evidence to suggest that support for Empire in Britain remained strong:

- Throughout the 1920s and 1930s, imperialist supporters, like Lord Beaverbrook, owner of the influential *Daily Express*, tried to sell the idea of Empire.
- Imperialist groups, such as the British Empire Union, were established.
- Imperial enthusiasts supported two enormous Empire exhibitions – at Wembley in 1924 and Glasgow in 1938. They attracted millions of visitors.
- Lord Reith, head of the BBC, saw radio as a force which might help to unite the Empire. The BBC usually portrayed the Empire as a 'good thing'. Empire Day (24 May, Queen Victoria's birthday) was given prominence on the radio. The King's Christmas Day broadcasts had a strong imperial flavour. In 1932, the BBC began an Empire Service which broadcast to all the countries of the Empire.
- The martial virtues of imperial heroes were popularised by children's authors and by many adult thriller writers. The courage of the men who defended the Empire was a theme that was also exploited by British and American film-makers. Popular feature films (such as *The Drum* and *The Four Feathers*), which gave a positive image of the British imperial system, were influential in forming people's attitudes.
- Portrayal of the adventurous aspects of the Empire was recognised by the armed services as a useful way to attract recruits.
- Traditional methods of advertising Greater Britain flourished in the 1920s and 1930s.
- Scouting continued to flourish.
- The Empire remained an important element of British national identity.

Opposition to Empire

Many Britons, raised to believe in the virtues of parliamentary democracy, found it difficult to reconcile this with the idea of Empire. There were doubts about the justice of imperial rule, particularly when violence was used against colonial opposition. There was increasing concern about the rights of indigenous peoples.

Many Britons were not convinced that expenditure on imperial defence (rather than on welfare) was in Britain's best interest. The Labour Party, which formed two short-lived governments in the interwar period, was especially critical of the Empire.

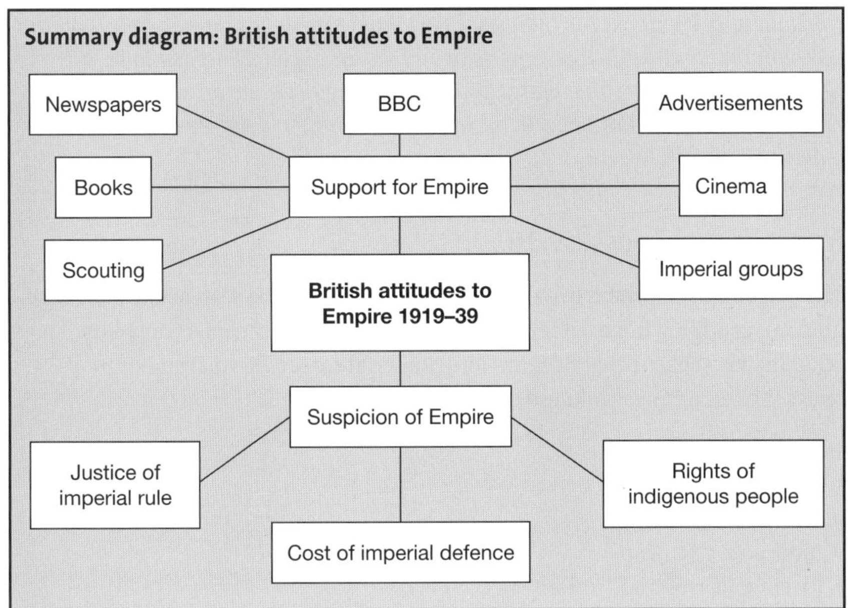

8 Key debate

▶ *To what extent was the British Empire in retreat by 1939?*

Historians have different views about the Empire in 1939. Some claim that Britain's imperial power was played out. Others claim that the Empire was not in irreversible decline or even in retreat.

EXTRACT 1

From Martin Kitchen, *The British Empire and Commonwealth: A Short History*, Macmillan Press, 1996, pp. 82–3.

Looking back at the Empire on the eve of World War II, it seems clearly to have been on the brink of collapse. The white Dominions were independent nations, India was soon to be a sovereign state, other colonies in Africa, Asia and the Caribbean were to follow suit.

Extracts 1 and 2 differ in emphasis. Which provides the more convincing explanation? ?

EXTRACT 2

From Bernard Porter, *The Lion's Share: A Short History of British Imperialism 1850–2004*, Pearson, 2004, p. 288.

Over the whole field of policy between the wars almost nothing was done by any government to prepare the colonies to live without Britain or to prepare Britain to live without the colonies. Everything was done – or not done – on the assumption that the British empire would, as far ahead as needed to be foreseen, continue as an empire. Or as something not quite an empire, and so the more likely to buck the general trend of empires, which was – of course – to 'decline and fall'.

Imperial weakness by 1939?

The establishment of the Irish Free State in 1921–2 can be seen as the start of a gradual, grudging imperial retreat which characterised the interwar years. Those scholars who believe that Britain's long imperial career was played out by 1939 stress the increasing weakness of the British economy:

- poor management
- an inability to exploit new ideas
- outdated technology
- poor salesmanship
- over-powerful trade unions
- shoddy workmanship
- poor labour relations.

By the 1930s, Britain started to have a balance of payments deficit, reflecting its weakening competitive position. Britain was also weak militarily. In the 1930s, Britain was threatened by the growing strength and ambitions of Germany, Italy and Japan. Britain's economic difficulties reduced its capacity to increase its armaments and sustain large forces all over the globe.

It is possible to see the writing on the wall in India and elsewhere. Arguably, the British people, if not their governments, lacked the resolution to hold down the growing resistance to imperial rule. Possibly, changes in the Dominions were squeezing out British influence. Perhaps British politicians were deluding themselves in believing that by shrewd tactics, artful concessions and ingenious constitutional arrangements they could prolong their Empire indefinitely. How could a nation with two per cent of the world's population continue to control over twenty per cent of its population?

Imperial strengths by 1939?

Few people in 1939 predicted the rapid decline of the Empire. Despite its economic difficulties, Britain was quite capable of sustaining its imperial commitments. Indeed, the economic situation, in particular Britain's dependence on imported food and need for export markets, seemed an excellent reason for the Empire's maintenance. It is also possible to overstate Britain's economic decline. Protectionist policies and preferential trade with the Dominions helped to sustain British industry through the harsh economic climate of the 1930s. Britain remained the world's greatest trader and the world's largest investor.

There was still enthusiasm in Britain for colonial rule. Politicians, like Churchill, proclaimed the strength and solidarity of the Empire and doubted that Asiatics and Africans would ever be capable of governing themselves. Most politicians and newspapers represented the Empire as a vital national interest from which all groups gained. The Dominions continued in many respects to be **satellite states**. Britain found it relatively easy to contain colonial nationalism by working with local collaborators and by displaying military power in an emergency. As long as Britain remained a great world power, separation – a complete break with Britain – appealed only to a fringe of extremists in Africa and Asia. Arguably, therefore, the evolution of Britain's imperial system would have been very different but for the impact of the Second World War.

KEY TERM

Satellite states Countries which rely on and obey the dictates of a more powerful state.

Chapter summary

The Empire helped Britain to win the First World War. By 1919, the Empire was at its most extensive territorially. However, its huge size tended to mask its weaknesses. The fact that Ireland and Egypt both won independence in 1922 suggested that Britain lacked the will to maintain its Empire. In India, British rule was challenged by Congress and the Muslim League. Congress, led by Gandhi, waged campaigns of mass disobedience. In 1935, the Government of India Act gave India self-rule at provincial level, albeit with the viceroy remaining in command nationally. Britain maintained its pre-eminent position in the Middle East, despite problems in Palestine. Nor was British rule challenged in Africa, where the only people granted home rule were white settlers in Southern Rhodesia. Britain spent little on its colonies, most of which remained sunk in poverty. The Balfour Declaration and the Statute of Westminster ensured that the Dominions were essentially independent countries. However, most remained loyal to Britain. The introduction of imperial preference in 1932 helped to maintain colonial loyalty. Most British politicians and ordinary Britons seem to have regarded the Empire as 'good thing'. Historians debate the extent to which the Empire was in retreat by 1939.

Refresher questions

Use these questions to remind yourself of the key material covered in this chapter.

1 How did the Empire assist Britain in the First World War?
2 To what extent did Britain's imperial strengths outweigh its weaknesses after 1919?
3 How strong were Britain's relations with its Dominions in the interwar years?
4 What role did Gandhi play in India?
5 Why was the 1935 Government of India Act attacked by both the Conservative right and supporters of Congress?
6 What challenges did Britain face in the Middle East in the years 1919–39?
7 How well did Britain rule Africa and its other colonies between the wars?
8 Why did Britain introduce imperial preference in 1932?
9 How strong was British support for the Empire by 1939?
10 Was the Empire on the point of collapse by 1939?

Question practice

ESSAY QUESTIONS

1 'In the context of the period 1918–45, it was clear that the British Empire was on the point of collapse by the end of the Second World War.' To what extent do you agree with this view?
2 'The long withdrawal from India was conducted with considerable skill by Britain in the period 1918–47.' Assess the validity of this statement.
3 'Britain's handling of the Palestinian situation was far from glorious in the period 1923–48.' To what extent do you agree with this statement?
4 'Britain gave the appearance of being a great world power in the years 1918–47.' Assess the validity of this statement.
5 'The British Empire was greatly weakened by the impact of the First World War in the period 1914–39'. Assess the validity of this statement.
6 'The bonds between Britain and the Dominions were greatly weakened in the period 1918–39.' Assess the validity of this statement.
7 'Britain conceded considerable ground to Indian nationalists in the period 1919–39.' Assess the validity of this statement.
8 'Given it put so little in, not surprisingly Britain got little out of most of its colonial dependencies in the period 1914–39.' Assess the validity of this statement.

CHAPTER 6

Imperialism challenged, 1939–47

In 1940, at the height of the Battle of Britain, Prime Minister Winston Churchill talked of the British Empire lasting a thousand years. The Battle of Britain ensured that Britain survived. It ultimately emerged victorious from the Second World War. But the Empire did not survive a thousand years. This chapter will consider the war's impact on the Empire by examining the following themes:

★ The impact of the Second World War

★ The situation in 1945

★ Indian independence

★ British withdrawal from Palestine

Key dates

1939	Start of Second World War
1942	Japanese forces occupied much of South-East Asia
	Quit India movement
1945	End of Second World War
1947	Independence and partition of India and Pakistan
1948	State of Israel created

1 The impact of the Second World War

▸ *To what extent did the Empire support Britain in the Second World War?*

In September 1939, Britain went to war with Germany. The war initially did not go well. By 1940 Britain faced a German-dominated Europe. However, it was not alone. As in 1914, it could rely on assistance from its Dominions (except Éire) and dependencies.

The situation in India

In September 1939, the Viceroy Lord Linlithgow, without consulting Indian leaders, announced that India was at war. Many Indians contributed to the British war effort. The princes supported Britain, and so did India's military officers, while 2.5 million Indians volunteered to fight in the armed forces. Opposition Indian leaders were divided on how to respond to the war:

- Gandhi, a pacifist, opposed any support for the British war effort. Nevertheless, he refused to sanction a mass campaign of civil disobedience.
- Some Indian nationalists (for example, Subhas Chandra Bose), believing that Britain's plight was India's opportunity, were prepared to work with Germany and (later) Japan.
- The Congress Party, now dominated by Nehru, refused support for the war effort unless India was first granted independence. When this was refused, Congress called on provincial governments to resign office. They did so – many reluctantly.

Britain thus had to set up non-Congress provincial governments. Mohammed Ali Jinnah, leader of the Muslim League, pledged a degree of support for Britain. By so doing, he hoped to win British support for a separate Muslim state of Pakistan.

Egypt and the Middle East

The war enabled Britain to assert itself in Egypt and the Middle East:

- Britain effectively took over Egypt in 1939.
- The Shah of Iran failed to convince Britain of his support and was deposed.
- When the prime minister of Iraq tried to negotiate with Germany, he was driven into exile.

The Atlantic Charter

Hoping to win US support, Churchill, in August 1941, met US President Franklin D. Roosevelt at Placentia Bay, Newfoundland. The outcome of their meeting was the Atlantic Charter. This was a high-sounding declaration of Anglo-American principles. It included a pledge to 'respect the right of all peoples to choose the form of government under which they will live'. Back in Britain, Churchill declared that the Charter's promise of self-determination did not apply to the Empire. Indian nationalists were outraged.

The Japanese threat

In December 1941, Japan attacked the US naval base at Pearl Harbor and British bases in the Pacific. The good news (for Britain) was that the attack brought the USA into the Second World War. The bad news was that by mid-1942 Japanese forces had captured Malaya, Singapore (a vital fortress), Burma and Hong Kong. Even Australia and India seemed to be in danger.

'Quit India'

In 1942, as the Japanese army advanced towards India's borders, there was serious disorder within India. The USA urged Churchill to give India such measures of freedom and democracy as would rally its people to fight for those ideals in the global conflict. Labour members of Churchill's government argued that Linlithgow's 'crude imperialism' was impeding India's war effort. Under considerable pressure, Churchill agreed to send Sir Stafford Cripps, a left-wing member of the Labour Party, to India to negotiate. Churchill reluctantly agreed that Cripps could offer India independence after the war in return for support during it. Congress leaders, settling for nothing short of immediate full independence, turned down the offer. Gandhi refused to accept a 'post-dated cheque' from (a journalist added) 'a failing bank'. Cripps' mission thus failed.

Congress now embarked on another mass disobedience campaign: 'Quit India'. British authorities took firm action, arresting Congress's leaders. Congress rank and file supporters did their best to dislocate the war effort, sabotaging railways, cutting telephone lines and attacking government buildings. Troops and aircraft helped the police to quell the disturbances. Several thousand Indians were killed and wounded and 100,000 arrested. By November 1942, the authorities had the situation under control. Significantly, the Indian army remained loyal to Britain. The main beneficiary of 'Quit India' was the Muslim League. Given Congress was unable to function, Muslim League leaders formed governments in four northern provinces.

Americans continued to insist they were not fighting the war to preserve the Raj, but Churchill declared: 'We mean to hold our own. I have not become the King's First Minister in order to preside over the liquidation of the British Empire.'

India 1943–5

In the last two years of the war, India's grievances grew:

- Inflation rose.
- Bengal suffered a severe famine in 1943 which may have killed 3 million people: the provincial administration was unprepared for the catastrophe. Linlithgow professed concern but did not even visit Bengal. However, his successor, Field-Marshal Lord Wavell, did visit Bengal and galvanised the relief work.

Despite these problems, India made a considerable contribution to the Allied war effort: the Indian army fought well in 1944, holding the Japanese at bay in north-east India, and India helped to pay for the war. By 1945, Britain owed India £1375 million.

Churchill was determined to hang on to India. Britain was slipping from its position as a great power as the USA and the USSR came to dominate the wartime alliance. Wavell took a different view. He feared that a disaffected India might become 'a running sore' which would sap Britain's strength. British public opinion, he believed, would not allow him to hold down India by force. The only alternative was to reach a settlement in line with the interwar reforms by which India could become a friendly partner within the Commonwealth.

Allied victory

Alliance with the USSR and the USA ensured British victory in the Second World War. Japan's surrender in August 1945 enabled British forces to regain lost territories in South-East Asia. One-quarter of the world's land surface, therefore, remained part of the British Empire or Commonwealth, as it was now commonly called. Victory in 1945, as in 1918, seemed proof of the Empire/Commonwealth's strength and solidarity. During the war, it had provided Britain with 5 million servicemen and essential food and raw materials.

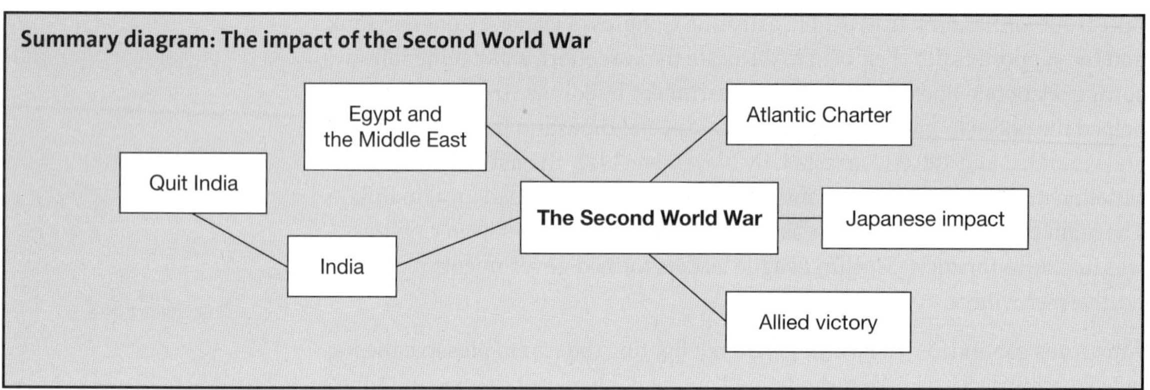

2 The situation in 1945

▶ *To what extent did Britain emerge from the Second World War as a great power?*

Britain emerged from the war victorious. Although it had lost about 400,000 people, this was only about one-fiftieth of the USSR's dead. The scale of destruction in British cities bore no comparison with Germany. Britain had escaped the rigours of enemy occupation and its economy seemed far ahead of the war-shattered economies of Europe. British forces had played a major part in Allied victory. Those forces, which in 1945 numbered 5 million men, were stationed all over the globe – in Germany, Austria, Italy, Greece, Palestine, Iran, Iraq, Syria, north Africa, Indo-China and the Dutch East Indies, as well as many parts of the Empire.

British weakness

Britain's position in 1945 was far weaker than it appeared.

The USSR and the USA

Britain could not compare in size and strength with the USA and the USSR:

- The USSR had done most of the hard fighting against Germany and in 1945 possessed enormous conventional forces. In 1945 there were deep fears in Britain about the USSR's aims. It already controlled most of eastern Europe. Greece, Turkey, Iran, Iraq and even Italy seemed vulnerable to Soviet pressure. It seemed likely, therefore, that Britain would need to maintain a massive military presence in Europe in order to deter any Soviet threat.
- The USA emerged from the war as easily the richest country on earth. Subject to neither bombing nor invasion, the American economy had thrived under the stimulus of war. By 1945, the USA produced half the world's manufactured goods. It was also a great military power. As well as possessing large, well-equipped conventional forces, the USA was the only country with the ability to manufacture nuclear bombs.

British economic problems

Britain's main problem was that it lacked the economic resources to match the two superpowers. The war had exacerbated Britain's economic problems:

- The destruction of houses, factories and shipping had cost Britain a quarter of its wealth.
- Most foreign assets had been sold to pay for wartime imports, significantly reducing the income from abroad that had previously contributed to Britain's economic strength.
- In 1945, British exports totalled £350 million – 40 per cent of the pre-war figure – while imports had reached £2000 million. This massive trade deficit would not be easy to remedy. Valuable markets had been lost, mainly to American competitors, and it was likely to take Britain many years to restructure its industries for peacetime production.
- Britain was in debt to the tune of £3500 million. (Some £2500 million was owed to its colonies.) Repayment of this debt seemed impossible. Indeed, in 1945 it seemed likely that Britain would run out of hard currency and be unable to import the raw materials on which its economy depended. American assistance was vital. But many British officials were troubled by the extent of Britain's dependence on the USA, wondering how far dependence on American loans was compatible with Britain's existence as an independent great power.

The weakening of imperial ties

In many respects, the war had weakened imperial ties.

The economic situation

Before 1939, Britain's economic strength had helped bind the colonies to the British imperial system. But in 1945 Britain was in dire economic straits. If it was too poor to buy what the Dominions and colonies produced, too poor to invest in their economic development and unable to provide the manufactured goods they needed, some of the most significant factors holding the Empire together would be lost.

Britain and the Dominions

The war had emphasised the difference of interests between Britain and each of the Dominions. Éire had not even fought on Britain's side and many South Africans had not wished to fight. By 1945, Canada, Australia and New Zealand had all slipped into the USA's orbit:

- In 1940, Canada had set up a Joint Defence Board with the USA, the first alliance contracted between a Dominion and a foreign power.
- The fall of Singapore and the subsequent collapse of British power in South-East Asia had made obvious Britain's inability to defend Australia and New Zealand. They turned instead to the USA. With Australia threatened by Japanese invasion in 1942, Australian Prime Minister John Curtin declared, 'Australia looks to America, free of any pangs as to our traditional links with the United Kingdom'.

Other problems

The war had undermined the foundations of British imperial power in other ways:

- During the war, Britain had mobilised the Empire's resources to an unprecedented degree. Colonial economies were regulated by controls over output, prices, marketing and labour. Opposition to British rule in India and Egypt had been forcibly suppressed. Regimentation and suppression led to increased opposition to British rule.
- Japanese success in 1941–4 shattered the myth of white superiority, a myth on which colonial rule had depended. Even though Britain, with American backing, had ultimately triumphed, Japan's wartime victories were a stimulus to Asian independence.
- The ideological struggle against Hitler had made assertion of pre-war colonial principles unfashionable. Although many British politicians (probably) still believed that the white race was superior, it was less easy to openly claim it.
- The USA and the USSR were ideologically anti-colonial in outlook and their opposition to empire was likely to influence the hopes of colonial peoples.

- The creation of the United Nations was another anti-imperialist step. Most of its members opposed imperial rule.
- Europe's other imperial powers – France, Belgium and the Netherlands – emerged physically weakened by the war. By 1945, it was clear that many peoples of the world no longer regarded empires as possessing the same sort of political legitimacy as nations.

In short, the terms on which Britain had built and guarded a world-wide Empire had changed. A new world order had come about, with new institutions, new ideologies and a new balance of power.

Attlee's Labour government

In July 1945, the British electorate voted Churchill out of office and elected a Labour government, led by **Clement Attlee**. Attlee, a tenacious politician and an excellent team leader, led an experienced Cabinet, many of whose members had served in Churchill's wartime National Government. Labour's success was mainly the result of its proposed domestic policy. Imperial issues attracted little attention during the election campaign. Nevertheless, many pundits predicted that there would be a major shift in imperial policy. Certainly, there were some important differences between Labour and Conservative imperialist attitudes. The Labour Party had a long-standing aversion to imperialism and was more committed to promoting self-government within the Empire, starting with Indian independence.

However, Attlee's government had no intention of jettisoning the Empire. Most ministers recognised that without its colonies (and their resources), Britain would no longer be a great power. Moreover, its economic prosperity would be threatened. Attlee and his tough foreign secretary, Ernest Bevin, were determined to defend Britain's interests. Neither wished to be seen as the liquidator of the Empire. Only in regard to India was Attlee committed to granting independence.

KEY FIGURE

Clement Attlee (1883–1967)

Attlee became leader of the Labour Party in 1935. He was deputy prime minister in Churchill's wartime coalition government and in 1945 won the general election and became prime minister. He presided over the establishment of the welfare state, nationalising major industries and introducing the National Health Service. His government also granted independence to India and Pakistan in 1947.

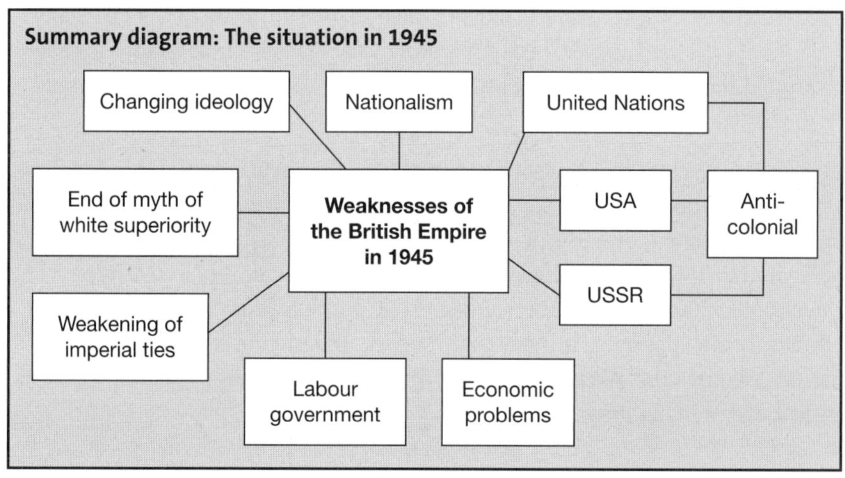

 Indian independence

▶ *To what extent did Britain withdraw from India with honour and dignity?*

In 1945, Churchill believed that Britain could and must hold on to India, as it was vital economically and militarily. But Attlee's government, and particularly Attlee himself, was committed to Indian independence. The mounting costs of the Raj reinforced Attlee in his view that the time had come to leave India and to leave quickly before what remained of British power was overwhelmed by events. There was also a fear of adverse international, especially American, opinion if Britain tried to cling to power. Britain, desperately in need of American dollars, dare not alienate its ally.

The situation in 1945–6

Attlee hoped that an independent India would remain united and within the Commonwealth, looking to Britain for guidance and leadership out of free choice, not out of compulsion. In this way, Britain might actually benefit from Indian independence. It would no longer have the burden of having to keep large numbers of troops in India and yet might be able to rely on the Indian army to safeguard its interests in the rest of Asia. Attlee's aims were likely to be difficult to achieve:

- Far from pledging friendship within the Commonwealth, most Congress leaders talked of a mass insurrection which would expel Britain from India 'lock, stock and barrel'.
- Worsening relations between Congress and the Muslim League seemed to offer little hope of achieving a united India. Rising prices and delays in demobilisation aggravated unrest, which became acute during the national and provincial elections of 1945–6. The Muslim League, which had enormously strengthened its position during the war, won the vast majority of Muslim seats. Congress won most of the non-Muslim seats in the Legislative Assembly as well as control of eight provinces. The Muslim's League's leaders argued that a continuation of British rule would be preferable to a Congress monopoly of power.

By 1946, it was clear that Britain had to reach a settlement acceptable to Muslims as well as Hindus or risk civil war. The task became more urgent as Britain's hold on India slackened. By early 1946, there were only 64,000 British servicemen compared to 389,000 Indian soldiers. More Indian officials replaced Europeans, leaving only 500 British civil servants and 500 police officers. Muslims and Hindus formed opposing armed bands and the situation became toxic with hatred. Viceroy Lord Wavell feared that the Indian government might be unable to deal with a major insurrection.

Discussions, 1946–7

Attlee wanted the Indians to work out their own solution to Indian independence. This was easier said than done. In 1945, Wavell had held a conference of India's main politicians but Congress and Muslim League leaders could not agree. In March 1946, a Cabinet mission was sent to India. It quickly concluded that the Indians were unlikely to reach agreement without British assistance. In May 1946, the British mission, therefore, produced its own plan. This envisaged the Indian provinces forming themselves into groups, enabling Muslim provinces to cluster together into a kind of Pakistan without full sovereignty. An all-India federal government would control foreign policy, defence and communications, but provincial governments would deal with all other matters. For a time, it seemed that this scheme might be accepted by both Congress and the Muslim League.

But, in July, Nehru denounced the scheme because it deprived India of a strong central authority. The Muslim League also withdrew its support for the plan and called for 'direct action' to achieve a united Pakistan. Serious violence by Muslim mobs had already broken out in the Punjab where the forces of authority did little to help panic-stricken Hindus. Jinnah's 'Direct Action Day' on 16 August 1946 increased the number of Hindu victims. Hindus and Sikhs retaliated as inter-communal massacres spread across northern India. Thousands of people died in Calcutta.

In December 1946, Wavell returned to Britain. He told the Cabinet that civil war between India's 255 million Hindus and 92 million Muslims might break out at any time and that Britain could not maintain control beyond March 1948, if indeed until then. He suggested that the position might prove different if Britain declared its intention to remain in India for a further fifteen years and reinforced its army by a further four or five divisions. Given the promises of the Labour government, this was out of the question.

The worsening economic situation in Britain in 1946–7 encouraged Attlee's government to force the pace. Attlee favoured issuing an announcement to the effect that Britain proposed to transfer power in India not later than June 1948. This was strongly opposed by Wavell. There was also disagreement about the manner in which British withdrawal should take place. Wavell thought it should be organised on the lines of a military evacuation from hostile territory. The Cabinet was convinced that the results of such a policy would be appalling for India and Britain alike. Attlee, certain that power could be transferred in an orderly manner, now took two initiatives: in February 1947, he announced that Britain would leave India no later than June 1948, and Wavell was replaced as viceroy by **Lord Mountbatten**, formerly supreme Allied commander in South-East Asia.

KEY FIGURE

Lord Mountbatten of Burma (1900–79)

Son of Prince Louis of Battenberg and Princess Victoria of Hesse-Darmstadt (Queen Victoria's granddaughter), he entered the Royal Navy in 1913. In the Second World War, he became supreme Allied commander in South-East Asia (1943–5), retaking Burma. As viceroy in India in 1947, he presided over the transfer of power to India and Pakistan. He died in Ireland, the victim of an IRA bomb.

The end of the Raj

Mountbatten, according to historian Piers Brendon (2007) was 'reckless, flamboyant, egotistical, outspoken, ingratiating, vain, shallow, flagrantly handsome and pathologically ambitious'. But Brendon acknowledges that he also possessed the flair and dynamism to win what he could for Britain in the circumstances of 1947.

Prior to accepting the post of viceroy, Mountbatten asked for and received authority to make his own decisions on the spot. He arrived in India in March 1947, still hopeful that that a settlement might be achieved which would preserve Indian unity. He soon concluded that partition was the only way to prevent civil war. Nehru, with whom Mountbatten had established a close rapport, gave his reluctant consent. This was perhaps Mountbatten's main achievement – although some historians consider that it was more the achievement of his wife, who established intimate relations with the Congress leader. In June 1947, Congress and Muslim League leaders approved Mountbatten's plan. Mountbatten, believing there was nothing to be said for further delay, determined to push the agreed plan through by mid-August 1947, abandoning in the process all hopes of an Anglo-Indian defence treaty. According to the plan:

- There were to be two Dominions – India and Pakistan.
- Each Indian province would be free to join the Dominion of its choice.
- Nothing was said about how the 565 princely states were to be integrated into the two Dominions.
- It was unclear how the frontiers in the border areas were to be determined. What was certain was that partition would leave large religious minorities within both India and Pakistan.

The princely states had to be cajoled into acceding into one country or the other. Again, Mountbatten displayed his powers of persuasion. However, he failed in Hyderabad (which India seized in 1948) and Kashmir, whose Hindu ruler eventually took his largely Muslim subjects into India – a source of bitter conflict. The Indian Independence Bill was rushed through Parliament, receiving royal assent on 15 August 1947. The Raj was over and the future of India and Pakistan passed out of British control. The Labour government hailed the emancipation of a fifth of the world's population, stressing the continuity and amity of relations with India and Pakistan. It claimed that everything had gone according to plan and that nothing became the Raj like the leaving of it.

Conclusion

Most historians, echoing most contemporaries, think Britain had little option but to quit India, and many commend the speed at which the withdrawal occurred. The alternative would have been an intolerable burden on Britain, the possibility of civil war, and the endangering of Britain's relationship with the USA and the Muslim world. Given Hindu–Muslim antagonism, there was no alternative to partition. The fact that India and Pakistan remained within the Commonwealth was a symbol of British success.

However, critics of Attlee's policy had, and have, a case. Attlee can be accused of leaving India with little honour. Tens of millions of people found that new boundaries had turned them into religious minorities. Britain's precipitate withdrawal probably contributed to the terrible inter-communal violence – ethnic cleansing on a huge scale – in which a million people died and 13 million became refugees. Thousands of villages were reduced to ashes. A Punjabi magistrate remarked, 'You British believe in fair play. You have left India in the same condition of chaos as you found it.'

From Britain's point of view, Attlee had achieved none of his initial aims. India was divided and Britain had no defence agreement with India or Pakistan. Britain hoped that partnership would succeed trusteeship and that there would be commercial cooperation. But none of this came to pass. Partition alienated Pakistan and India from Britain and entrenched enmity between the two new states.

Burma and Ceylon

With the loss of India, Britain had little further strategic interest in Burma and Ceylon.

Burma

Much of Burma had been occupied by Japan in the Second World War and an embarrassing number of Burmese had collaborated with the Japanese. British rule had always been resented in Burma. Even positive British efforts – railway building, public health work, agricultural improvements – gained little favour. In truth, Britain spent very little on Burma. The capital, Rangoon, had only one public library, which spent £10 a year on books. Attlee, appreciating the prohibitive cost of keeping Burma under imperial control without Indian troops, concluded that it was better to come to terms with the strong Burmese nationalist movement. Thus, by January 1948 Burma had been granted independence. It opted to leave the Commonwealth.

Ceylon

The Ceylonese, rather than attempting to resist British rule by violence, had sought independence by means of cooperation – with some success. In 1931, a Commission, led by Lord Donoughmore, had recommended a constitution by which the governor would rule with the aid of a Ceylonese-dominated State Council. This council was to be elected by universal suffrage, the first Asian colonial nation to obtain such a franchise. In 1942, ministers became, in effect, the governor's Cabinet. The following year, Britain undertook to introduce full internal self-government when the war ended. Ceylon was finally given independence in February 1948. The country (which later changed its name to Sri Lanka) remained within the Commonwealth and agreed to a defence treaty with Britain.

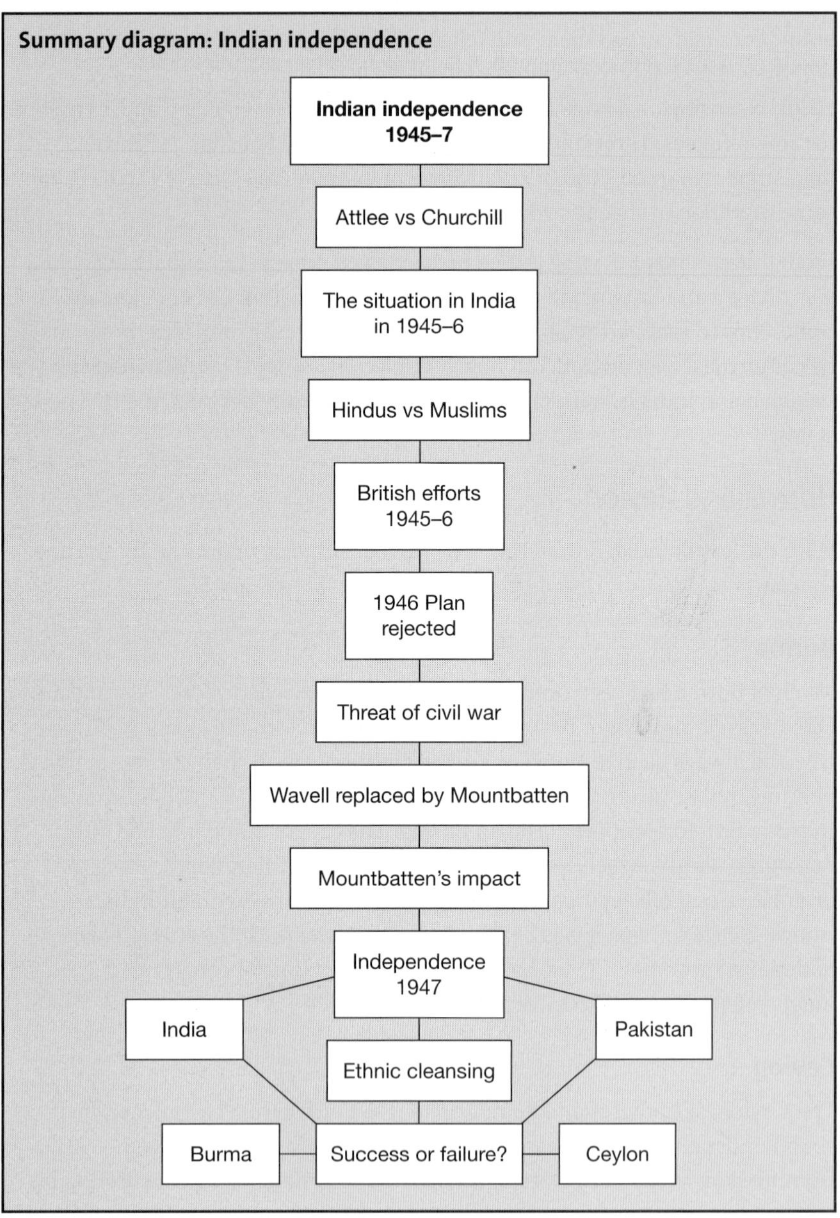

British withdrawal from Palestine

 *Why was Britain so unsuccessful in Palestine in the years 1945–8?*

Palestine had been a problem throughout the interwar period. By 1939, Jews made up a third of its population, a fact resented by the indigenous Arab population. Jews opposed British limits on Jewish immigration and Britain's avowed intention to create an Arab-dominated Palestine (see page 107).

The situation in 1945

The Second World War made the Palestine problem more insoluble:

- By mid-1945 there were 200,000 displaced Jews in Europe, many of whom wished to settle in Palestine.
- There was huge sympathy for the **Holocaust** survivors, especially in the USA.
- Within Palestine, Britain faced a well-organised Jewish militia – the Haganah, spearheaded by two terrorist organisations, the Stern Gang and the Irgun. The Stern Gang had actually favoured an alliance with Hitler against Britain. Jewish attacks on British officials had occurred throughout the war and continued in 1945.
- Palestinians opposed Jewish immigration and the establishment of a Jewish state.
- The Palestinian cause was supported by all Arab states.
- Britain had its own interests to protect. Given the uncertainty over the future of the Suez Canal, military chiefs argued that Palestine was important strategically and that Britain should continue to maintain a military presence there.

 **KEY TERMS**

Holocaust Hitler's attempt to eliminate all the Jews in Europe after 1941.

Zionists Jews who wished to establish a national home in Palestine.

British policy in 1945

In 1945, it was generally expected that Attlee's government would support the **Zionist** cause. A Labour policy statement in 1944 had suggested that Jews should be allowed to become the majority in Palestine. However, once in office, Foreign Secretary Bevin expressed doubts about large-scale Jewish immigration. Given the importance of Middle East oil, he feared alienating the Arabs. Bevin's main aim, similar to that of British pre-war governments, was to find a compromise that would satisfy Jews and Arabs alike. He declared that he would stake his political future on negotiating a settlement. However, the hopes of finding a compromise were never high.

British problems in 1945

In September 1945, a Cabinet committee, supporting Bevin, recommended a monthly quota of 1500 Jewish immigrants to Palestine. This did not satisfy various Jewish agencies which demanded the immediate entry of 100,000 Jews. Within Palestine, Zionists resorted to more acts of terrorism and the British authorities found it difficult to maintain order. US President Truman, courting the Jewish vote in America but also genuinely sympathetic to the Jewish cause, demanded large-scale immigration and the creation of an independent Jewish state. Attlee tried to persuade Truman that there were other places capable of receiving large numbers of Jews – without effect.

The Anglo-American Committee

Bevin secured the appointment of an Anglo-American Committee to make recommendations on Palestine's future (November 1945). Britain hoped that the two issues – the future of Palestine and the settlement of European Jews – could both be studied. But the Americans would only agree to consider the problem of Jewish settlement within the specific context of Palestine.

The Anglo-American Committee, reporting in May 1946, opposed the idea of partition but recommended the immediate admission of 100,000 Jewish immigrants. The report was immediately rejected by Jewish and Arab leaders. While Britain disapproved of the immigrant recommendations, Truman announced his support for the admittance of 100,000 immigrants. Attlee's Cabinet decided that it would only agree to this figure if illegal Jewish military organisations in Palestine were disbanded and if the USA would accept the responsibility with Britain for implementing the Committee's recommendations. Neither of these conditions was satisfied.

Jewish terror

Acts of terror increased, forcing Britain to send more troops to Palestine. Several thousand Jewish terrorist suspects were arrested. The cycle of provocation and reprisal became more vicious. In July 1946, the King David Hotel in Jerusalem was blown up by Jewish terrorists, killing 91 people. The violence strengthened Britain's determination to oppose concessions to Jewish immigrants.

Britain versus the USA

Britain's main plan in mid-1946 was for Palestine to be divided into Arab and Jewish provinces under a central administration presided over by a British high commissioner. But this was opposed by Truman, Arabs and Jews. In January 1947, a new round of talks began. By now, Truman accepted the idea of partition, but Bevin, aware that Arab leaders were totally opposed to a Jewish state in Palestine and aware that neither side would accept boundaries agreeable to the other, opposed the idea. There seemed no room for compromise and Bevin admitted to being 'at the end of my tether'.

United Nations' action

By early 1947, 100,000 British troops occupied Palestine (a territory the size of Wales), the equivalent of one soldier for every eighteen inhabitants – at an annual cost of £40 million. But the British authorities were still unable to keep order in the face of Jewish resistance. Even Churchill could see no merit in hanging on in Palestine. The conscript soldiers who were there 'might well be at home strengthening our depleted industry', he declared. 'What are they doing there? What good are we getting out of it?'

In February 1947, as the economic situation in Britain worsened, with bread rationing and fuel shortages, Bevin referred the Palestine problem to the United Nations. This was a gamble as much as an admission of defeat. Bevin believed that the United Nations would create a single state in Palestine with Britain as the overseer. This would strengthen Britain's hand and reduce, if not end, American and other international criticism.

Meanwhile, Britain continued to lose the propaganda war. In July 1947, the ship *Exodus*, carrying 4500 illegal Jewish refugees, was boarded by the Royal Navy off Palestine. Britain sent the refugees to Hamburg, part of the British zone in Germany, an insensitive decision which provided the Zionist cause with a propaganda coup.

In September 1947, a United Nations special committee finally reported. Against Bevin's expectations, it proposed that:

- independence should be granted to Palestine as soon as possible
- Palestine should be partitioned
- Jerusalem was to remain under United Nations' control
- the proposed Jewish state was to cover 55 per cent of Palestine (although Jews only numbered one-third of the population)
- 150,000 Jewish immigrants were to be admitted over the two years, during which British responsibility as a mandatory power would continue to be exercised.

The creation of Israel

Bevin, outraged by the United Nations' proposals, claimed they were 'manifestly unjust to the Arabs' and predicted an Arab rising in Palestine. When they were passed in November 1947, the British government declared that it had no intention of implementing a settlement with which it so strongly disagreed. It announced that Britain would quit Palestine in mid-May 1948.

Despite American pressure to stay, Bevin adhered to his determination to leave Palestine. As Jewish–Arab hostilities intensified, Britain washed its hands of the conflict. At the village of Dir Yassin, on 9 April 1948, the Irgun and Stern Gang killed more than 250 Arabs. This and other massacres were part of an ethnic cleansing operation which resulted in some 750,000 Arabs fleeing or being expelled from what was to become Israel.

The new state of Israel was proclaimed in May 1948 and immediately recognised by the USA. It was soon invaded by neighbouring Arab states: Egypt, Transjordan, Lebanon, Syria and Iraq. However, by January 1949, against the odds and British expectancy, the Israelis had defeated the invaders and gained territory. Thereafter, the United Nations' partition plan did not come into effect and many Palestinians found themselves within Israel. Britain belatedly recognised Israel in January 1949.

British policy in Palestine: conclusion

It is possible to attribute the tragedy of the Palestine situation to British misrule. Many Arabs blame Britain for allowing Jewish immigrants into Palestine in the first place. Jews, on the other hand, have accused Bevin of being anti-Semitic and opposing the creation of Israel. It is certainly possible to make out a strong case against the 1917 Balfour Declaration which encouraged Jews to settle in Palestine. But this was a decision made many years before Attlee's government came to power. Arguably, Attlee and Bevin inherited an impossible situation. Bevin did his best to reconcile the irreconcilable, but given the intransigence of both sides, compromise proved to be an impossible goal. Britain can be accused of abdicating its responsibilities in 1948, but by then over 300 British lives had been lost and £100 million spent in a vain attempt to quell the forces of Jewish and Arab nationalism. It is possibly fairer to blame the USA (as Bevin himself did) for promoting the Zionist cause and not accepting more responsibility in Palestine. To charge Bevin with being anti-Semitic is also unfair. He hoped to treat Arab and Jew alike. But he was also determined to preserve Britain's influence in the Middle East. A pro-Jewish policy in Palestine would have seriously damaged Britain's standing among all Arabs.

Although Britain emerged with little credit from the Palestine debacle, at least Bevin managed to isolate Palestine from the overall development of Anglo-American relations, and Britain continued to dominate the Middle East and retain alliances with many Arab states.

Labour policy: conclusion

Attlee's government had hoped to preserve Britain's world power status. By 1948, this hope had been shattered. It was clear that Britain was no longer in the same superpower league as the USA and the USSR. Given the situation, it was – and still is – easy to criticise Labour's external policy-making. 'It is with deep grief I watch the clattering down of the British Empire with all its glories', Churchill told the Commons in March 1947. 'Scuttle everywhere is the order of the day.' Many on the left were more critical of Britain's increasingly subservient relationship to the USA and were disappointed that Britain had failed to offer a distinctive ideology to the world, a middle way between Soviet communism and American capitalism. Modern historians, of both left- and right-wing views, tend to criticise Labour for not cutting Britain's overseas commitments.

However, given the massive problems Britain faced, Attlee and Bevin perhaps deserve more praise than blame. Churchill's accusation of 'scuttle' can be seen as unfair. Britain had little option but to accept Indian independence and even Churchill supported withdrawal from Palestine. Given its economic position, the notion that Britain might become a 'third force' was a pipe dream. The idea that Britain could or should stand between the USA and USSR and play off one against the other was similarly unrealistic. Britain was far closer to the democratic USA than to the totalitarian USSR. Finally, the Labour government had little option but to accept Britain's world-wide commitments. For any British government to have embarked on a policy of precipitate withdrawal everywhere would have been regarded as a premature act of abdication which would almost certainly have resulted in regional chaos, communist gains and disastrous economic consequences for Britain.

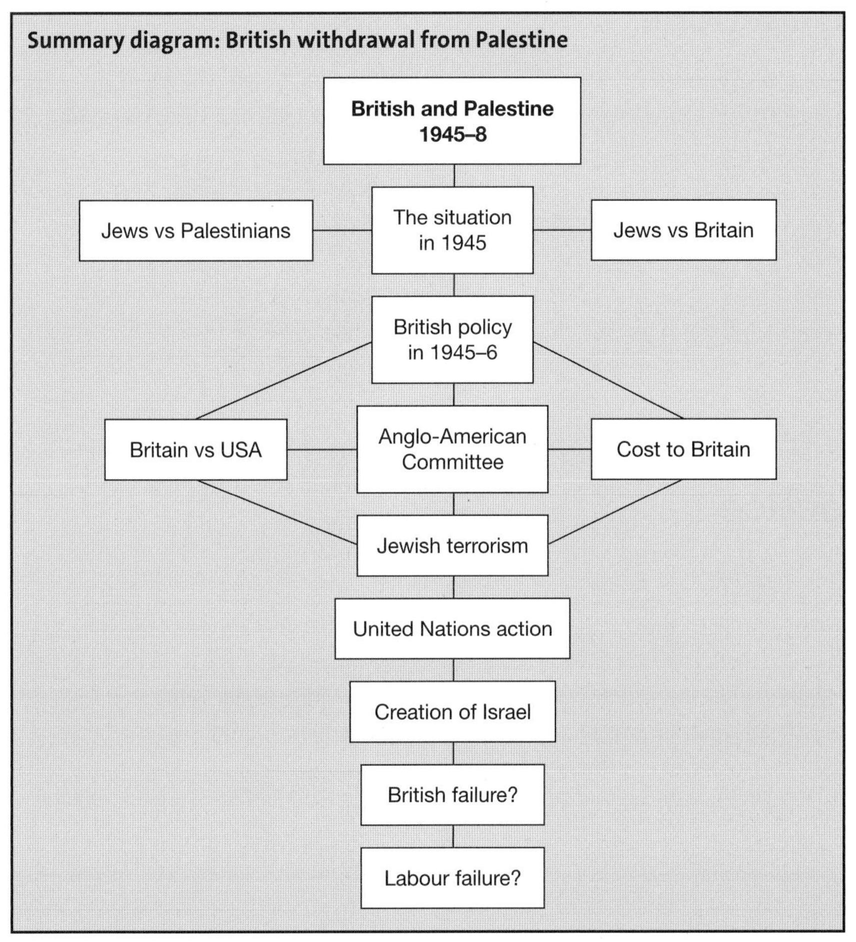

Chapter summary

Britain, with the help of the Dominions (except Éire), emerged victorious from the Second World War, its Empire seemingly intact. However, it did not have the military power of the USA and the USSR and faced huge economic and financial problems in 1945. Attlee's Labour government, more supportive of the Empire than expected, was committed to granting independence to India, which had been restive throughout the war. After tortuous negotiations, independence came about in 1947 but not in the way Britain intended. Two countries emerged – India and Pakistan. Although both joined the Commonwealth, neither showed any intention of becoming a British satellite state. With India gone, Britain also granted independence to Burma and Ceylon. Britain faced severe problems in Palestine, where Jewish settlers (supported by the USA) demanded their own independent state. After two years of internal strife, Britain washed its hands of Palestine. The Jewish state of Israel came into being in 1948.

Refresher questions

Use these questions to remind yourself of the key material covered in this chapter.

1 What problems did Britain face in India in the Second World War?

2 Why did the Second World War weaken imperial ties?

3 What problems did Britain face in 1945?

4 Why was Attlee committed to granting Indian independence?

5 What were Britain's aims in India in 1945–6?

6 To what extent were British aims in India realised in 1947?

7 Why was Palestine a problem in 1945?

8 What efforts did Britain make to find a solution to the Palestinian problem?

9 Does Britain deserve any credit for its handling of the Palestinian situation in the years 1945–8?

Question practice

ESSAY QUESTIONS

1 'Despite all its problems, Britain acted as a great imperial power in the period 1918–48.' Assess the validity of this view.

2 'Britain achieved few of its goals in India in the period 1914–47.' Assess the validity of this view.

3 'Britain's handling of the Palestinian situation was far from glorious in the period 1923–48.' Assess the validity of this statement.

4 'Britain's handling of the situation in India was remarkably skilful in the period 1919–47.' Assess the validity of this statement.

CHAPTER 7

The winds of change, 1947–57

The granting of independence to India, Pakistan, Burma and Ceylon and the abandonment of Palestine in 1947–8 were not seen by the Labour government as the start of a general decolonisation process. Attlee's government was acutely aware that Britain's prosperity and its continued position as a great power depended on the Empire/Commonwealth. The Conservatives, who came to power in 1951, believed much the same. British policy-makers still hoped that the Commonwealth would become a third force, balancing the power of the USA and the USSR. This was not to happen. Instead, Britain soon faced fresh international challenges. This chapter will consider those challenges by examining the following themes:

★ Developing the Empire/Commonwealth, 1947–51

★ Conservative imperialism, 1951–5

★ Anthony Eden and the Suez Crisis

Key dates

1951	Churchill became prime minister
1952	Start of Mau Mau rebellion in Kenya
1953	Establishment of Central African Federation
1954	Britain agreed to withdraw forces from Suez Canal zone
1955	Eden became prime minister
1956	Suez Crisis
	End of Mau Mau rebellion

1 Developing the Empire/Commonwealth, 1947–51

▶ *To what extent was Britain successful in developing the Empire/Commonwealth in the years 1947–51?*

Attlee's Labour government made a number of efforts to develop the Empire/Commonwealth.

The old Dominions

Of all the various territories that made up the Empire/Commonwealth, the 'old' Dominions of Canada, Australia, New Zealand and South Africa were regarded as Britain's most reliable friends, tied to Britain not just by common interests but by bonds of kith and kin. But hopes that the partnership between Britain and the old Dominions could become a much closer grouping with common foreign and defence policies soon collapsed. The Dominions had their own interests and were prepared to assert their separate identities.

Britain's decline in power was evident with the formation of the ANZUS military pact between Australia, New Zealand and the USA in 1951; significantly, Britain was excluded. Although Attlee claimed that the pact was in line with the notion that individual countries should take the lead on behalf of the whole Commonwealth in areas where they were especially concerned, the ANZUS pact implied that the USA had taken over Britain's responsibilities in the Pacific.

The new Commonwealth

Attlee's government was hopeful of building a 'new' Commonwealth, an association of free, independent states which would transcend race, colour and creed (belief). It envisaged the new Commonwealth serving as an effective vehicle of British influence. However, India, Pakistan and Ceylon did not share the enthusiasm of the white Dominions for the great power pretensions of Britain, still less their support for British colonial rule elsewhere. The new Commonwealth was thus far less a club than the old. It enjoyed no natural unity and its members had little in common with each other.

There were other problems:

- Britain, anxious to lead the Commonwealth, could not offer enough reward for association in the form of trade, investment and defence.
- Talk of racial partnership as a central purpose of the Commonwealth had little appeal to white South Africans. The Nationalist Party which came to power in 1948 supported a policy of **apartheid**. Given South Africa's strategic and economic importance (it was a major source of uranium and gold), Attlee's government toned down its criticism of Nationalist policies. Even so, South Africa's policies remained an embarrassment for Britain and at odds with the idea of the new Commonwealth.

KEY TERM

Apartheid Segregation and separate development of races.

In 1948–9, it seemed that the new Commonwealth might collapse almost before it had begun. Before 1948, Dominions had been required to recognise the British Crown as their head of state. In 1947–8, Britain had made no effort to bend the rules to allow Éire or Burma to become republics and stay within the Commonwealth. India's determination to become a republic in 1948, however, was a cause of major concern. India, a potentially vast trading partner and a seemingly vital ally in a continent where communist influence was advancing rapidly, was more important than Burma or Éire. A compromise was finally worked out whereby republican India would remain within the Commonwealth, accepting the British monarch as 'Head of the Commonwealth' rather than as head of India.

The sterling area

The Second World War greatly weakened Britain's power as a trading nation and by 1945 Britain no longer had an abundance of capital. There was thus a likelihood that the countries within the British imperial system which were free to do so would look to the USA for economic partnership. But, strangely, Britain's post-war economic weakness served to reinforce Commonwealth solidarity in trade and finance. Almost all the Dominions and several independent countries (such as Iraq) used the British pound sterling as the basis of their currency, banking their overseas earnings in London. The danger of the collapse of the pound in 1947 threatened them all with bankruptcy. Britain, moreover, remained the most important market for most members of the sterling area (see page 111). They seemed, therefore, to have little option but to sink or swim with Britain.

Various measures, agreed to in 1947, tied sterling area members far more closely than before 1939 to a common trade policy, obliging them to purchase more of their imports from Britain. The sterling area thus became a closed economic bloc in a way that the Empire had never been. With a quarter of the world's population and trade, it exceeded its main rival, the dollar area. The perpetuation of this closely integrated trading and currency bloc was a central aim of British policy.

Developing the colonies

After 1947, Britain still controlled a host of colonial territories, particularly in Africa. British leaders were optimistic about the stability of their African possessions. Indeed, some hoped that Africa might become a new Raj – a vast tropical plantation, a bottomless pit of mineral wealth and a source of men for its armed forces. Before 1939, relatively little had been done in most colonies to promote economic or social reform or to encourage political independence.

Labour politicians had long talked in vague terms of 'developing' the colonies. But most had little idea of what development should take place or how it should be done. Nevertheless, Arthur Creech-Jones, Attlee's colonial secretary, was determined to aid Britain's colonies. He regarded colonial economic and social development as the crucial precondition for progress to self-government:

- A Colonial Development and Welfare Act (1945) allocated £120 million over ten years to assist the colonies' development.
- A 1948 Act established the Colonial Development Corporation and the Overseas Food Corporation to improve living standards in the colonies.

The second colonial occupation

In much of Africa, Britain embarked on what has been called a 'second colonial occupation'. Anxious to develop colonial economies as rapidly as possible to provide Britain with urgently needed raw materials, colonial governments interfered in all areas of economic life and scores of British 'experts' descended on Africa with schemes for agricultural improvement. The East African Groundnut Scheme, for example, was launched in 1948 in an attempt to reduce the deficit of oils and fats in Britain. The scheme (which cost Britain £36 million) failed, providing neither margarine for Britain nor employment for Africans. This example of spectacular economic mismanagement was far from being an isolated one. To make matters worse, the British government's enthusiasm for change upset many of the local vested interests on whose support British colonial rule depended.

By 1950, the Labour government claimed that it had abolished the old type of capitalist imperialism. However, the truth was somewhat different. Far from helping the colonies' economic development, Britain actually exploited its colonies for all they were worth, restricting investment, controlling their trade and the prices of their main commodities, and also rationing the goods they could purchase from Britain. Between 1945 and 1951, the colonies were forced to lend Britain more money than Britain actually invested in the colonies. For all its fine words, Attlee's government allowed the British dependencies to be exploited more than at any time since colonies were established.

The Gold Coast

Riots in Accra (1948) convinced British officials that the Gold Coast was near to revolution. Attlee's government therefore decided to give Gold Coast Africans more say in decision-making. A system of universal suffrage to elect an assembly was introduced but British authorities continued to control finance, the police and the civil service. Kwame Nkrumah, leader of the Convention People's Party, denounced the changes as inadequate. Educated in the USA, Nkrumah had returned to the Gold Coast in 1947. His mission was simple: to throw the Europeans out of Africa. In 1950, he urged civil disobedience and helped to cause a general strike. Briefly imprisoned, this served to strengthen his appeal. His party won more seats than any other in the first election under the new constitution. Accordingly, he soon became chief minister in the Executive Council.

Nigeria

If power was devolved to Africans in one colony, there was no reason why this should not happen elsewhere. Nigerians, aware of developments in the Gold Coast, pressed (successfully) for more political participation. Attlee's government believed that the Gold Coast and Nigeria were special cases: both were well-populated countries with educated elites capable of taking on governmental responsibility. In neither country were matters complicated by large numbers of white settlers.

Labour responsibility?

Britain's deliberate encouragement of democratic politics presented African politicians with opportunities they could use to good effect. Whether intentionally or unintentionally, Attlee's government helped to create the conditions in which colonial politicians would have the means to organise on a large scale and ultimately drive out British rule. It should be said in Labour's defence that the move towards African independence was gathering momentum and there was little any British government could – or should – have done to prevent it.

Malaya

Even after 1947, Britain still had some interests in South-East Asia, especially in Malaya. In 1945, the Malayan peninsula consisted of nine states, each ruled by a sultan but under British protection, two British settlements, and Singapore. Essentially Britain had allied itself with the Malayan elite. Colonial officials ruled while local royalty reigned. The population was multiracial, mostly Malays and Chinese in roughly equal numbers. The area was vital economically because it produced one-third of the world's tin and huge amounts of rubber, the bulk of both products being sold to the USA. Malaya was the most important source of dollars in the Empire. Its rubber alone earned more hard currency than all Britain's domestic exports to the USA in the late 1940s.

In 1948, Britain, aiming to provide a stronger, more viable political unit, decided to group the states and settlements into the Federation of Malaya. Malayan Chinese feared that the Malays would dominate the new Federation. Malayan communists, exploiting the Chinese community's disaffection and encouraged by communist success in China itself, stirred up strikes and violence. The situation became so serious that a state of emergency was declared and thousands of British troops were sent to Malaya. The worst year of the emergency was 1951. More than 1000 civilians and members of the security forces were killed. The guerrilla war dragged on until the late 1950s. Helped by the fact that the majority of the Malayan population remained pro-British, Britain dealt with the situation successfully, resettling hundreds of thousands of Chinese in specially guarded villages and winning the battle for Malayan 'hearts and minds'.

The Middle East

In the late 1940s, despite the loss of Palestine, Britain had a dominant presence in the Middle East. It had the right to keep troops in the Suez Canal zone and shared responsibility with Egypt for the Sudan. It held Aden and effectively controlled most of the sheikhdoms along the southern coast of the Arabian peninsula and in the Persian Gulf. It had military bases in Iraq and close ties with Jordan, whose army was commanded by a British officer.

Bevin regarded the Middle East as of cardinal importance, first because of its oil reserves, most of which were controlled by British companies, and second because of the Suez Canal. He was determined that the area should remain a British sphere of influence and was particularly determined to keep Russian influence out. Generally, Bevin tried to maintain British hegemony by cooperating with the Arab states in the region.

British attitudes to Empire

Between 1947 and 1957, there was little public pressure to jettison Britain's remaining colonies:

- There was an awareness of the Empire/Commonwealth's economic importance. In 1951, it supplied 49 per cent of British imports and took 54 per cent of British exports – a greater percentage than at any time in its history. British jobs were thus at stake if the Empire/Commonwealth was abandoned.
- The Empire/Commonwealth seemed vital if Britain was to remain a world power.

However, some Britons:

- queried the expense of the military campaigns in Kenya (see pages 143–4) and Malaya (see page 139) which together cost about £100 million: such spending seemed pointless if the two areas were soon to win independence
- resented the cost of Britain's large overseas garrisons
- were uneasy about the authoritarian nature of many colonial governments, which contrasted sharply with Britain's domestic liberalism.

Nevertheless, most people, like most politicians, seem to have believed it would take decades before most colonies were ready for independence:

- In many colonies, the population seemed too small to permit easy development towards independence. Federation was a possibility but often the proposed units of a federation (for example in the West Indies) were hundreds of miles apart and had little in common.
- In much of Africa, the proportion of educated people seemed too low to permit independence.
- Within several territories, there was a problem of ethnic/tribal division which could lead to bloodshed if Britain pulled out too quickly.

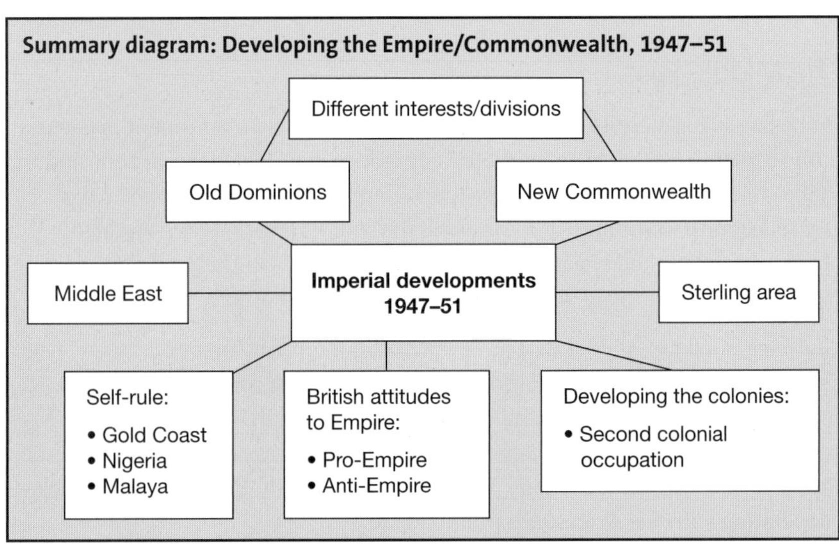

2 Conservative imperialism, 1951–5

▸ *To what extent did British imperial policy change under Winston Churchill in the years 1951–5?*

In the October 1951 general election, the Conservatives won a majority of seats and Churchill returned as prime minister. It was expected that the new government would assert more authority in world affairs than Attlee's government. This was certainly Churchill's intention.

Winston Churchill's government

By 1951, Churchill was far from the towering presence he had been during the Second World War. He was 77, had already suffered two strokes, and was to suffer two more in the course of his premiership. He said in 1954: 'I feel like an aeroplane at the end of its flight, in the dusk, with the petrol running out, in search of a safe landing.' He coped with day-to-day business but perhaps lacked the drive to follow up ideas. However, his mental and physical failings can be exaggerated. He still had a fine brain and remained an impressive performer in Parliament and in Cabinet.

Anthony Eden

Anthony Eden was easily the most important member of Churchill's Cabinet. Most people at the time assumed that the two men had virtually identical aims and worked closely together. The truth was not so simple. There was some personal suspicion, if not animosity, between the two of them. Nevertheless, to a large extent Churchill relied on Eden's judgement and gave him a remarkably free hand.

Eden seemed the 'glamour boy' of British politics, holding an exciting job in which he showed tremendous skill. In reality, both the job and Eden were less impressive. Overworked and unwilling to delegate, he found himself under considerable stress, not eased by constant travelling and ill-health. Despite his shortcomings, Eden was a first-class negotiator and it seemed to many at the time as though Britain was again represented with style and assurance abroad.

 **KEY FIGURE**

Anthony Eden (1897–1977)

A successful foreign secretary in the Second World War and under Churchill from 1951 to 1955, Eden became Conservative prime minister in 1955. He was forced to resign in 1957 after the failure of British intervention in Egypt in 1956 – the so-called Suez Crisis.

Churchill's aims

Churchill was convinced that Britain's presence at the 'top table' was essential for the benefit of Britain and the world. In 1951, Britain was still the world's third greatest power, a long way behind the USA and the USSR, but well ahead of all other competitors. Churchill had promised that he would do his utmost to preserve the Commonwealth and Empire 'as an independent factor in world affairs'.

Winston Churchill

1874	Born, the son of Lord Randolph Churchill and his American wife Jenny
1893–4	Trained as a cavalry officer at Sandhurst
1897	Campaigned on the north-west frontier of India; wrote articles for newspapers
1898	Fought in the Sudan (at Omdurman); also worked as a war correspondent for the *Morning Post*
1899–1900	Became a hero in the Boer War
1900	Elected Conservative MP for Oldham
1904	Joined the Liberal Party because he opposed tariff reform
1908–10	President of the Board of Trade
1911	Home secretary
1911–15	First Lord of the Admiralty
1917	Minister of munitions
1924–9	Conservative chancellor of the exchequer
1940–5	Prime minister
1951–5	Returned as prime minister
1965	Died

Churchill, at the forefront of the political scene for over 50 years, is best known for his leadership during the Second World War. Throughout his life, he was an ardent patriot and imperialist. The Boer War was an important step in his rise to political power. Working as a war correspondent for the *Morning Post*, he was captured by the Boers. Escaping from a prisoner-of-war camp in Pretoria, he managed to make his way to Portuguese Mozambique. This exploit made him a national hero. Returning to Britain, he was elected as a Conservative MP in 1900. Thereafter, he was rarely out of the news.

Churchill's problems

It was soon obvious that Churchill and Eden faced exactly the same problems as those which had faced Attlee and Bevin. 'The problems I now face are much greater in number and complexity than they used to be', moaned Churchill. In many respects the chief problem facing Churchill's government was the state of the British economy. Although it was recovering, it faced competition from Germany, France and Japan, whose economies were improving far more rapidly than Britain's. The Treasury continually warned the government that Britain was carrying too many foreign responsibilities in relation to its resources. While Eden accepted the logic of the Treasury's case more than Churchill, he similarly was opposed to Britain jettisoning its overseas commitments, arguing that this would do untold damage to both its international status and its economy.

Churchill's advantages

- After the substantial decolonisation in Asia in the late 1940s, the USA was much more concerned about keeping its European allies devoted to the struggle against communism. This was more important than encouraging Britain, France, Belgium and Portugal to give up more colonies.
- The USSR was not yet deeply involved in the world outside Europe. This allowed Britain to maintain its imperial position free from external pressure.
- By 1951, Britain's economy had improved somewhat. The devaluation of the pound in 1949 – from \$4 to \$2.80 – had helped British exports.

- In Africa, traditional leaders were still powerful and they displayed little interest in promoting nationalist mass movements that they could not control.

Imperial concerns, 1951–5

What is striking about Britain's relations with its colonies in the early 1950s is the wide variation in attitudes and policy between one region and another, especially in Africa.

West Africa

By 1955, Churchill's Cabinet accepted that the Gold Coast and Nigeria should soon become independent. Most experts thought this would make little difference to Britain's economic or strategic interests.

East Africa

In Tanganyika, Uganda and Kenya, there were few educated Africans, serious tribal divisions and quite large numbers of Asians, brought into the area by Britain earlier in the century. In Kenya, there were also thousands of white settlers, accustomed to holding local political power, as well as social and economic privilege, and determined to resist black rule. The white people had the support of many British Conservatives who hoped that Kenya would remain a 'white man's country'.

Britain's main plan was to create an East African Federation, harnessing Tanganyika (where there was one European for every 430 Africans) and Uganda (where there were even fewer white people) to white-led Kenya. Encountering African opposition, the plan was soon abandoned.

The Mau Mau emergency

The Kikuyu tribe, the largest in Kenya, protested against rising prices, the fact that Europeans held the best land, and other aspects of racial discrimination. The failure of peaceful protest led to violence. From 1952 to 1956 what became known as the Mau Mau emergency took place. Part Kikuyu conspiracy, part peasant revolt and part criminal gang action, it espoused revolutionary terror. Its supporters killed 95 Europeans and 13,000 black people (many of whom worked for white employers). Only after Britain sent thousands of troops to Kenya was the rebellion suppressed. Throughout its imperial history, the British generally paid lip service to legality – a concept which they had introduced in many areas. This was not the case in Kenya, which became a police state, dispensing racist terror. British security forces formed 'strike squads' to carry out assassinations, shot civilians in cold blood and massacred the innocent with the guilty. Between 1952 and 1958, 1090 Africans were hanged, some on a travelling gallows built at the governor's bequest. Mau Mau suspects were routinely tortured to extract information. Tens of thousands of the Kikuyu population were resettled in hundreds of gaol-villages where there was a regime of searches, curfews, restrictions and forced labour. These were effective, destroying much of the Mau Mau organisation. Over 20,000 Mau Mau fighters were killed during the emergency. Britain was fortunate that many black Kenyans showed little desire to help a movement which would replace British supremacy with Kikuyu supremacy. Meanwhile, Britain sponsored welfare programmes to help the ethnic groups who remained loyal.

Central Africa

In central Africa, especially in Southern Rhodesia, there were growing numbers of white settlers, who had a great deal of local autonomy and who, like the Kenyan white settlers, believed they represented a superior civilisation. They had no intention of sacrificing power to the black majority. Attlee and Churchill both supported the establishment of a Central African Federation comprising Northern and Southern Rhodesia and Nyasaland. Finally formed in 1953, the Federation, which was entirely controlled by whites people, had almost complete powers of self-government. But the British government maintained a veto over any legislation that might worsen the position of black people.

Egypt and the Suez Canal

In 1951, Britain continued to control the Suez Canal zone in Egypt, a complex of bases in which some 40,000 troops were located. This was highly unpopular in Egypt but Egyptian government's efforts to force Britain out failed. Churchill regarded the Suez base as of vital importance. However, the Anglo-Egyptian Treaty of 1936 was due to expire in 1956. Thereafter, Britain could not lawfully maintain troops in any part of Egypt without the assent of the Egyptian government – assent which would certainly not be given.

In early 1952, Anglo-Egyptian relations, bad at the best of times, deteriorated further. Riots occurred in Cairo and large numbers of British business premises were destroyed. Churchill was confident that British troops in the canal zone could hold the military situation. But Britain could not hold the political situation. In 1952, a group of Egyptian army officers seized power, forcing King Farouk into exile.

Discussions between the new Egyptian government and Britain on the Sudan and the canal zone continued. Somewhat surprisingly, given the ardently nationalist nature of the new regime, there seemed to be a more conciliatory atmosphere. In 1953, Britain and Egypt reached agreement on the Sudan. The country would have a three-year period of virtual home rule. Thereafter, it would be allowed to choose between complete independence or union with Egypt. Britain and Egypt did all they could to influence the elections of a Sudanese Constituent Assembly in whose hands the eventual decision would lie. The Sudanese, to Britain's satisfaction, chose independence, commencing in 1956.

The Suez Canal proved more difficult. Britain suggested numerous compromises but since all involved British troops remaining in the canal zone, all were rejected by the Egyptians. In 1953, Eden determined to change tack. He was helped by the fact that Britain's military leaders now agreed that the Suez base was no longer essential. Churchill's conviction that the thermonuclear age had made large bases obsolete, helped to reconcile him to the loss of Suez. So did the crippling cost of remaining in the canal zone – over £50 million a year. Although a third of the ships passing through Suez were still British, the canal was no longer the vital imperial artery it had been in the days of the Raj.

In July 1954, agreement was reached. British troops would be withdrawn from the canal zone within twenty months. In the event of an attack on Egypt, Britain could reoccupy the base. Eden's conciliatory diplomacy seemed to have at last resolved Anglo-Egyptian differences. However, in November 1954, **Gamal Nasser**, a nationalist army officer who was determined to throw off all vestiges of British imperialism, won power in Egypt. This boded ill for future relations.

KEY FIGURE

Gamal Nasser (1918–70)

An army officer, Nasser helped to establish the nationalist Free Officers group, which overthrew the Egyptian monarchy in 1952. He became prime minister and then president of Egypt. His nationalisation of the Suez Canal led to an unsuccessful Anglo-French attack on Egypt (1956), after which he was established as a leader of the Arab world.

Cyprus

Churchill and Eden hoped that Cyprus (British since 1878) would become a suitable alternative base from which Britain could sustain its dominance in the Middle East. However, by 1954 it was evident that most Greek Cypriots (80 per cent of the island's population) wanted union with Greece, a move strongly opposed by the Turkish minority. The Foreign Office made it clear that the island was to remain British. Greek Cypriots, led by Archbishop Makarios, pressed their demands and a guerrilla organisation (EOKA), led by Colonel Grivas, waged a terrorist campaign, resulting in some 200 deaths. Britain declared a state of emergency and ultimately 25,000 British troops were sent to maintain order. By 1957, British forces had the upper hand and Grivas announced a truce.

Churchill: conclusion

In 1955, Churchill, aged 80, decided to resign. Some historians are critical of his peacetime administration, claiming that he lacked drive and energy and had exaggerated ideas about Britain's position in the world. However, it is also possible to claim that Churchill provided a lead and sense of purpose, then stood back and let others, like Eden, handle the actual detail. Nor did Churchill overestimate Britain's strength. Far from trying to cling on to Empire, he accepted Britain's withdrawal from Sudan and Suez and moves towards independence in the Gold Coast and Nigeria. Arguably, Churchill pursued pragmatic colonial policies, not dissimilar to those of Attlee.

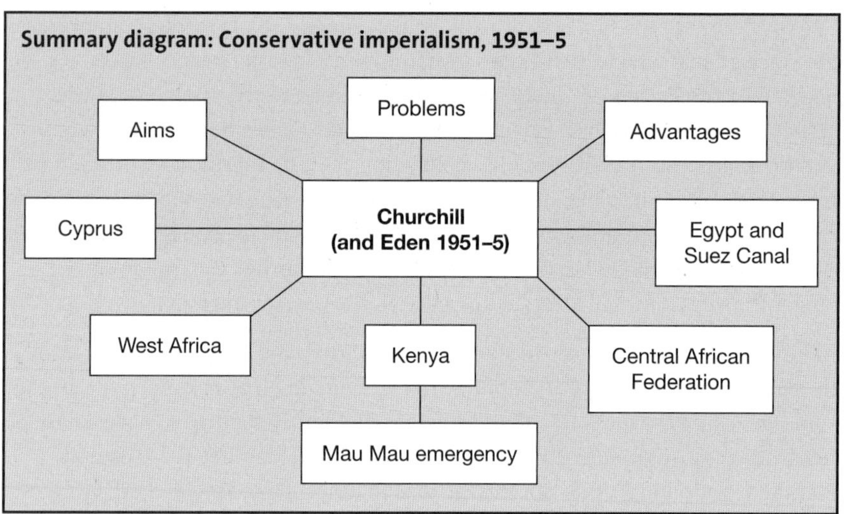

3 Anthony Eden and the Suez Crisis

▶ *To what extent did the Suez Crisis prove that Britain was no longer a great world power?*

In 1955, Anthony Eden became prime minister. Few prime ministers have entered office as popular or with such a great reputation as an international statesman. In his late fifties, he was a man of charm, intelligence, industry and good looks, respected by many on both left and right. However, Eden was far from a 'superman'. He could be bad-tempered and petty and was prone to ill-health. A workaholic, he found it hard to delegate, and tended to live on his nerves.

Eden's aims

On the surface, Eden's aims were not dissimilar to Churchill's. While accepting that Britain was probably attempting too much in too many areas, he was determined to maintain Britain's influence in the world. His travels had confirmed his sense of the Commonwealth's unity and he believed that this was the essential foundation of Britain's power. However, there were some important differences between Eden and Churchill. Churchill's belief in cooperation with the USA had been an article of faith. Eden, while accepting the importance of working with the Americans, was more dubious about their wisdom and integrity, and was confident that Britain had the power to act independently.

Eden was particularly determined to maintain Britain's position in the Middle East. That position seemed strong in 1955. Differences with Egypt appeared to have been settled in 1954. Turkey was linked to the West through NATO and Pakistan through **SEATO**, Iraq and Jordan had pro-British regimes and Britain continued to have considerable influence in parts of the Arabian peninsula. In February 1955, Turkey and Iraq (with British backing) concluded a military alliance known as the Baghdad Pact. Britain formally joined the Pact in April 1955 and was soon followed by Pakistan and Iran. The Baghdad Pact was designed largely to contain Soviet influence. However, its main effect was to antagonise the Egyptian leader Nasser.

KEY TERM

SEATO The South-East Asian Treaty Organisation was set up in 1954.

The threat of Nasser

Nasser was opposed to Western (particularly British) influence in the Middle East. Envisaging himself as leader of the Arab world, Nasser encouraged nationalist movements across north Africa and the Middle East. Initially, Eden hoped to appease Nasser. Thus:

- British troops left the Suez Canal zone according to the 1954 plan.
- Britain and the USA agreed to give Nasser financial aid, enabling him to build the Aswan Dam, a massive project which would provide Egypt with water and hydroelectric power from the River Nile.

But events seemed to indicate that Nasser could not be 'bought'. In March 1956, King Hussein of Jordan dismissed Glubb Pasha, the British commander of his army. Glubb had been the personification of British influence in the Middle East and his sacking was a serious blow to Britain's prestige. Eden blamed Nasser for Glubb's dismissal. To give Nasser vast loans looked like rewarding an enemy, particularly as Nasser recognised communist China and seemed prepared to ally with the USSR. In July, the Anglo-American Aswan loan offer was withdrawn. Nasser retaliated on 26 July 1956 by nationalising the Suez Canal Company, in which the British government and British and French financial interests had a major stake. Investors would receive the market value of their shares but henceforward the company would belong entirely to Egypt.

Eden's response

A great deal of British trade, especially oil, was dependent on the canal. Its seizure provided Nasser with future opportunities to blackmail Britain. Moreover, Nasser had clearly thrown down a challenge to Britain and the world order. If he was allowed to get away with his action, his standing throughout the Arab world would surge while British prestige would plummet.

Eden believed Nasser must be stopped sooner rather than later. Nasser's regime was developing the hallmarks of a totalitarian state: suppression of civil liberties, rabble-rousing speeches and organised subversion in other countries. Eden was not alone in wanting to bring about Nasser's downfall. Churchill said, 'We can't have this malicious swine sitting across our communications.' Labour leader Hugh Gaitskell condemned Nasser and a Commons debate on 2 August left the impression of a virtual consensus behind firm action.

Eden knew he could count on French support. The French, who also had a financial stake in the Suez Canal Company, held Nasser responsible for much of the trouble they were encountering in Algeria. They saw the Suez Crisis as a means of stopping him radiating his dangerous appeal across the Arab world. French leaders were quite prepared to use force.

British policy: July to October 1956

Immediate action was ruled out because British forces needed at least six weeks to prepare. Moreover, US President Eisenhower opposed armed intervention. Eisenhower, while agreeing that Nasser was a threat to Western interests, preferred more covert operations to overthrow him. The US government was reluctant to be associated with anything that smacked of colonialism and which might rebound to the benefit of communism.

While the slow build-up of British forces in the eastern Mediterranean continued, Eden made a virtue of necessity and agreed to negotiate. Britain's stated objective was not to restore the Suez Canal Company but instead to put the canal under some sort of international control. Eden's private aim, however, remained the toppling of Nasser, whether by force or as a result of a diplomatic defeat, which would so damage his prestige that he might well fall. The USA and the Labour Party hoped that a negotiated settlement could be worked out in the United Nations. In October, Britain put forward a number of resolutions but the USSR and Yugoslavia vetoed Britain's proposals.

Unfortunately, the longer negotiations continued, the less easy it became to justify military action. The USA still refused to support the use of force. By now the Labour Party had also made it clear that it would only support British action which had the consent of the United Nations. By October it was clear to Eden that negotiations with Nasser were getting nowhere. Aware that many members of his own party were pressing for strong action and that the British force in the eastern Mediterranean could not remain idle indefinitely, Eden was anxious to force the issue. However, if Britain was to attack Egypt, an excuse for action, acceptable to British and world opinion, seemed essential.

The Sèvres plan

Israel, like Britain and France, was alarmed by Nasser's growing prestige and the fact that he portrayed himself as the Arab champion who would lead them to victory against Israel. He ensured that Israeli ships were banned from the Suez Canal and Egyptian commandos mounted attacks on Israel. Israel was determined to take retaliatory action. However, the Israeli government wanted Britain as a military ally before mounting an operation against Egypt.

In mid-October, Britain agreed to a French–Israeli plan (the so-called Sèvres plan) whereby Israel would attack Egypt across the Sinai, giving Britain and France an excuse to occupy the canal on the pretext of saving it from damage. The Sèvres plan, while giving Britain an excuse for intervention, did have a number of major snags which should have been apparent with any degree of foresight:

- To imagine that the collusion between Britain, France and Israel could be kept secret was naïve in the extreme.
- Britain's Arab allies were hardly likely to look kindly on a British attack arranged in advance with Israel.
- The USA was still opposed to military intervention. This was serious because Eden had been warned by the Treasury that the strength of the pound sterling was too fragile for Britain to go it alone without American backing.

The Suez invasion

On 29 October, the Sèvres plan was put into operation. Israeli forces invaded the Sinai, quickly overrunning Egyptian forces. The next day, Britain and France issued ultimatums requiring Israel and Egypt to cease warlike action and withdraw to positions ten miles clear of the Suez Canal. Egypt was further required to allow Anglo-French forces to occupy positions along the canal. Egypt and Israel were given twelve hours to comply, otherwise Britain and France would intervene. Israel naturally agreed. As anticipated, Egypt refused. Consequently, the Royal Air Force bombed Egyptian airfields (on 31 October) and the Anglo-French invasion force, which had been assembled at Malta, sailed towards Egypt (which it would not reach until 6 November). In retaliation, Nasser blocked the Suez Canal.

The Anglo-French attack caused an enormous furore. In Britain, most Conservative MPs and most Britons (according to opinion polls) supported Eden's action. But Labour MPs condemned it; as did the USSR. Eisenhower's condemnation was far more important. His anger was understandable. He had made clear his opposition to the use of force and resented the fact that he had been deceived by his closest ally. In the United Nations, most countries, including several Commonwealth members, were similarly critical. An American resolution calling for an immediate ceasefire passed by 64 votes to five (Britain, France, Israel, Australia and New Zealand). Only by using its veto power on the Security Council was Britain able to block United Nations' calls for an immediate ceasefire.

On 5 November, Anglo-French paratroopers landed in Egypt. On the same day the USSR issued threats that it might launch missile attacks on London and Paris if the invasion was not called off. This probably had little effect. Eden's government guessed that the Russians were bluffing. More importantly, in early November, US financial pressure had led to a run on the pound and a rapid drain on Britain's gold and dollar reserves.

On 6 November, the Anglo-French seaborne forces landed in Egypt. From a military point of view the operation, involving 45,000 British troops, was a success. Twenty miles of the canal was quickly occupied and casualties were light. However, Egypt and Israel (bullied by the USA) now agreed a ceasefire, removing all pretext for the invasion. Convinced by Chancellor of the Exchequer Harold Macmillan that Britain faced financial ruin if the USA carried out its threat, Eden determined to abort the Suez operation. In an effort to save face, he announced that he was now ready to support a Canadian idea for a United Nations Emergency Force to garrison the canal and ordered a ceasefire. France had little alternative but to follow suit.

Eisenhower insisted on a complete Anglo-French withdrawal before the USA would offer Britain any financial support. American pressure had such a dramatic effect only because of Britain's determination not to devalue the pound. The fear was that this would lead to the destruction of sterling's international position. Eden's government decided, in effect, to sacrifice its Middle Eastern policy to its sterling policy. On 28–29 November, Macmillan persuaded a demoralised Cabinet (with Eden now absent ill) that Britain must withdraw – unconditionally – from Egypt.

The Suez failure

Eden, whose health had deteriorated, resigned in January 1957. Given the Suez debacle, his resignation was probably inevitable. Most contemporaries, like most historians, viewed Suez as an unqualified disaster. Michael Foot, a Labour MP at the time of Suez, wrote in 1975: 'Instead of opening the Canal, it was blocked; instead of saving British lives and property, they had been put at Nasser's mercy; instead of toppling Nasser, he was enthroned; instead of keeping the oil flowing, it was soon to be rationed; instead of winning friends, we had lost them … the expedition had achieved the exact opposite of the government's declared intention.' These charges are difficult to answer. Eden had overestimated Britain's power and fatally misjudged America's reaction to his military operation. As a result, he achieved none of his objectives. Nasser emerged from the crisis as the pre-eminent leader of Arab nationalism while Britain's prestige had been seriously damaged.

In Eden's defence, ill-health throughout the crisis might have impaired his judgement. Some historians have tried to shift the blame by spreading more widely the responsibility for the decisions to go ahead and then to stop. Macmillan, who strongly supported the operation at first but who then lost heart, would certainly seem to deserve some blame. In fairness to both Eden and Macmillan, few British politicians expected the intensity of the American reaction. The US government was blamed by many Conservatives at the time for letting down its closest ally. But the notion of 'American perfidy' should not be taken too far. Eisenhower had said all along that he opposed the use of force. In the end, the fatal errors were British, and most of them were Eden's.

It is possible to claim that if Eden had ignored American and United Nations' pressure, he might have been successful. However, exactly what Eden expected to do with the Suez Canal, if it had been secured, seems not to have been sufficiently thought through. It is unlikely that Nasser would have been overthrown by the Egyptians and replaced by a new pro-British Egyptian government. Nor does it seem likely that Britain or France could have held Egypt down by force.

The results of Suez

Suez can be seen as a major event – a watershed, separating the years in which Britain's survival as a world power seemed possible from the years after – years which saw the rapid end of Empire and the scaling down of Britain's global commitments. Certainly, the cost of Suez to British standing throughout the Middle East was high. Pro-British regimes in the region were seriously embarrassed and weakened. Jordan felt bound to denounce its treaty with Britain. British influence in Iraq faded and, in 1958, a government similar to that in Egypt came to power. Britain's international prestige also suffered. The Suez venture made it apparent that Britain was no longer a major world power, unless it acted in concert with the USA. The Commonwealth had shown itself to be less susceptible to British guidance than many had imagined. For an Egyptian leader to twist the lion's tail and get away with it was a hard blow to Britain's self-esteem. Nasser's success encouraged Arab nationalists and anti-colonial nationalists elsewhere.

However, other historians have viewed Suez as little more than a melodramatic episode, which merely exposed underlying and obvious trends in the decline of British power:

- Eden's departure apart, Suez had relatively little impact on British politics. The Conservative Party went on to win the 1959 election.
- Relations with the USA were quickly restored. Eisenhower (and later Kennedy) was anxious to employ Britain in the struggle with the USSR. This meant shoring up Britain's position in the Middle East. With American help, Britain continued to dominate a number of sheikhdoms on the fringe of the Arabian peninsula.
- Many Britons had begun to question the nature of Britain's world role long before Suez. It is too easy to see the accelerated colonial withdrawal after 1957 as the direct consequence of the humiliation of 1956. Arguably, Suez did not trigger an imperial explosion but at most simply gave a push to movements which were already in motion.
- Britain still aspired to be a great power after 1956. It had nuclear weapons and the Commonwealth remained a global body, albeit not one with teeth.

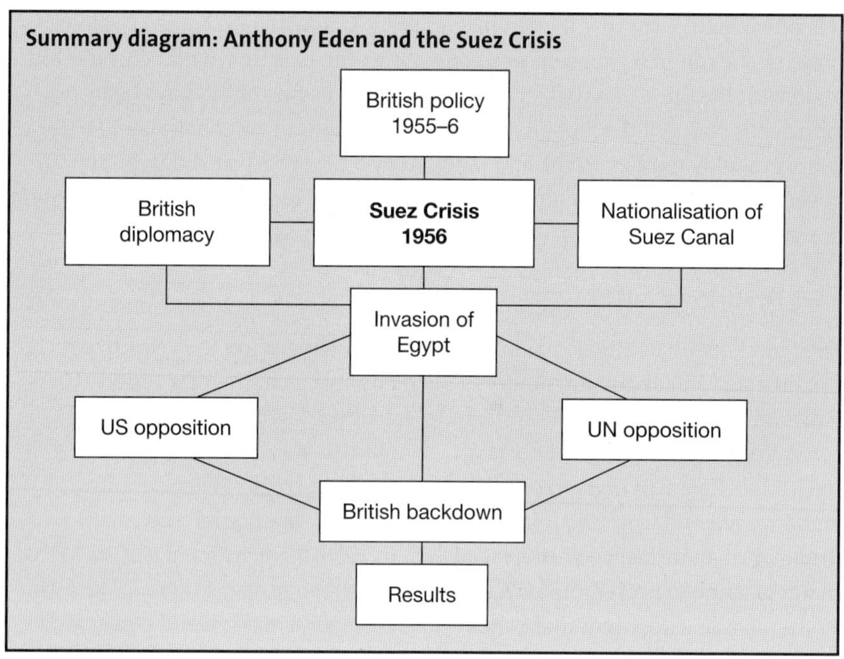

Chapter summary

In the 1951 election, Attlee was defeated by Churchill. The Conservatives remained in power until 1964. Conservative imperial policies were not very different from those of Labour. Neither party was eager to abandon Empire. Both hoped that the Commonwealth could become a major international force. These hopes were not realised. The new Asian Commonwealth members had little in common with the old. However, Britain and the Commonwealth countries remained important trading partners. Sterling area members were tied closely together financially and commercially. Attlee's government tried to develop the economy of the colonies, especially in Africa, but their policies tended to increase resentment rather than prosperity. By the mid-1950s, the Gold Coast and Nigeria were close to independence. The situation was different in east and central Africa. In Kenya, British forces helped defeat the Mau Mau emergency. Further south, Britain supported the Central African Federation, which was dominated by Southern Rhodesian white people. Britain continued to exert huge influence over the Middle East but found itself challenged in Egypt (over the Suez Canal) and in Cyprus. Eden, who replaced Churchill as prime minister in 1955, faced pressure from Egyptian leader Nasser. Nasser's nationalisation of the Suez Canal in 1956 led to Britain, France and Israel agreeing to a secret plan to seize the canal. An Anglo-French invasion of Egypt was opposed by the USA, forcing Eden to back down. Britain was humiliated and its international prestige weakened. Eden resigned in 1957.

Refresher questions

Use these questions to remind yourself of the key material covered in this chapter.

1. How did most Britons regard the Empire in the period 1947–57?
2. How did British governments regard the Empire?
3. Why did the Commonwealth not become a third force in international politics?
4. How successful were British governments in developing economic ties with the Dominions and dependencies in the years 1947–57?
5. How successful were Labour efforts to develop Britain's African colonies?
6. Why did Britain send forces to Malaya in the early 1950s?
7. How consistent were the African policies followed by British governments in the period 1947–57?
8. What problems did Britain face in Egypt in the period 1950–6?
9. Why did Eden send British forces to Suez in 1956?
10. What were the main results of the Suez Crisis?

Question practice

ESSAY QUESTIONS

1. 'All British governments pursued similar imperial policies in the years 1918–57.' Assess the validity of this statement.
2. 'There was little indication that the British Empire in Africa was about to collapse in the period 1918–57.' Assess the validity of this statement.
3. Britain achieved most of its imperial aims in the period 1918–55.' Assess the validity of this view.
4. 'The Suez Crisis was Britain's greatest imperial disaster in the period 1918–56.' Assess the validity of this statement.

CHAPTER 8

The winds of change, 1957–67

When Harold Macmillan replaced Anthony Eden as prime minister in 1957, Britain still controlled a vast Empire. Macmillan's avowed intention was to maintain that Empire. Yet when he left office in 1963, most of the Empire had gone. By 1967, even less of the Empire remained. This chapter will examine how decolonisation came about by considering the following themes:

- ★ Harold Macmillan and Empire
- ★ Decolonisation pressures
- ★ Decolonisation, 1957–63
- ★ The post-colonial situation, 1964–7

The key debate on pages 173–4 of this chapter asks the question: To what extent was the British Empire a force for good?

Key dates

1957	Ghana and Malaya became independent
1960	Nigeria and Cyprus became independent
	Macmillan's 'wind of change' speech
1961	Sierra Leone and Tanganyika gained independence
	South Africa withdrew from the Commonwealth
1962	Uganda, Trinidad and Tobago and Jamaica gained independence
1963	Kenya granted independence
	Creation of Federation of Malaysia
1964	Malawi, Northern Rhodesia and Malta became independent
1965	Southern Rhodesia declared independence
1966	Lesotho and Botswana gained independence
1967	Britain withdrew from Aden

Harold Macmillan and Empire

▶ *To what extent was Macmillan responsible for British decolonisation in the period 1957–63?*

In 1957, Britain still controlled important areas in Africa, Asia and the West Indies. Between 1948 and 1957, only three British colonies had become independent: Sudan (1956), Ghana (1957) and Malaya (1957). Between 1957 and 1967, however, and especially between 1960 and 1963, the British Empire effectively came to an end. Few Empires have disappeared so swiftly, so completely and with so little armed conflict. Historians continue to debate why this process occurred and to what extent Macmillan was responsible.

Harold Macmillan

Macmillan became prime minister in 1957. His main concern was to revive the flagging fortunes of both his country and his party after the humiliation of Suez. He succeeded in doing both. In the 1959 general election, the Conservatives increased their majority. This victory was essentially a testament to 'Super Mac's' perceived success on the home front. Many believed, as Macmillan boasted, that they had 'never had it so good'.

Macmillan's imperial aims

Macmillan was determined to play an important role on the world stage. 'We are a great world power,' he said in 1957, 'and we intend to remain so.' Consequently, he appears to have had no plans for an abrupt withdrawal from Empire, although he did wonder whether he was 'destined to be the re-modeller or the liquidator of Empire'. Like many British politicians, he wanted to hand over power only when colonies were ready and able to administer themselves. He was also reluctant to sacrifice kith and kin in Kenya, Rhodesia and elsewhere to 'natives'. Indeed, he privately denounced the treachery of Europeans who 'attacked the whites of Africa and championed the blacks'.

In public, Macmillan denied any intention of giving up the Empire. But behind the scenes he initiated a number of reviews to weigh up the Empire's advantages. A Cabinet Colonial Policy Committee, set up to review the Empire's costs, came up with mixed findings, judging that the overall economic considerations were evenly balanced with expenditure savings here being offset by reduced commercial advantage there. It concluded that: 'The United Kingdom has been too long connected with its colonial possessions to sever ties abruptly without creating a bewilderment which would be discreditable and dangerous.' By the end of 1959, however, Macmillan seems to have become convinced that the leisurely programme for the transfer of power envisaged by the Colonial Office would no longer do. The appointment of Iain Macleod as colonial

Harold Macmillan

1894	Born into the Macmillan publishing family
1914–18	After being educated at Eton and Oxford, he served (bravely) in the Grenadier Guards during the First World War
1919	Worked for the family publishing business
1924	Elected as a Conservative MP
1929	Lost his seat
1931	Re-elected as a Conservative; in the 1930s, he criticised his party for appeasement and for its failure to do more for the unemployed
1951	Became a successful minister of housing
1954	Became minister of defence
1955	Served as foreign secretary
1955	Became chancellor of the exchequer
1957	Succeeded Eden as prime minister
1959	Won the general election, telling the British people that they had 'never had it so good'
1963	Failed to join the European Economic Community (EEC)
1963	Resigned as prime minister because of ill-health
1984	Became first earl of Stockton
1986	Died

Macmillan was a complex personality: sensitive and cynical; compassionate and ruthless; privately shy but publicly self-confident; a mix of professional politician, country gentleman and great performer – particularly on television, which was fast developing as an essential means of communication. Although often nervous and highly strung, he had the gift of appearing cool and unflappable and, unlike Eden, was never overwhelmed by work, for which he had a great appetite. He quickly established his authority over his Cabinet colleagues and in Parliament and enjoyed the exercise of power.

It is difficult to decide whether Macmillan's successes in international affairs outweighed his failures. His critics accuse him of constant U-turns, of surrendering the Empire too quickly, of trying and failing to enter the EEC, and of failing to find Britain a viable world role. His supporters, on the other hand, can point to a number of successes including his special relationship with American Presidents Eisenhower and Kennedy and Britain's relatively painless withdrawal from Africa. Given Britain's weakness, retreat and redirection had to be the order of the day. He retreated – and tried to redirect British policy – and he did so with some panache.

secretary in October 1959 is often seen as an indication of a change of policy on Macmillan's part.

Macleod, unlike previous colonial secretaries, sympathised with African aspirations. Fearing terrible bloodshed, he favoured rapid decolonisation. However, it is still unclear whether Macleod acted largely on his own initiative or applied principles which had been laid down by Macmillan. (Macleod had taken very little interest in colonial affairs before he became secretary of state.) Those historians who see Macmillan as the puppeteer, planning and directing the change of colonial policy, usually regard the 1959 general election as a crucial factor. They claim that a host of younger, more liberal Conservative MPs entered Parliament, submerging more reactionary elements who had sentimental attachments to Empire. This is seen as having given Macmillan his opportunity.

Macmillan's role

Certainly, Macmillan had huge authority over all aspects of British external policy by the autumn of 1959. However, his impact on colonial policy should not be exaggerated. Many British policy-makers in the Cabinet, Foreign Office and Colonial Office held similar views to the prime minister and it is unclear who convinced whom. Nor is it certain that Macmillan or Macleod had any real colonial strategy. Rather than adopting a common policy indiscriminately, Macmillan's government seems to have responded pragmatically to events, taking account of political conditions that varied greatly from colony to colony. However, the speed of change after 1959 and the consistency of its direction indicate that something more than just a haphazard series of pragmatic responses to local conditions was at work. What caused Macmillan's government to change policy?

Summary diagram: Harold Macmillan and Empire

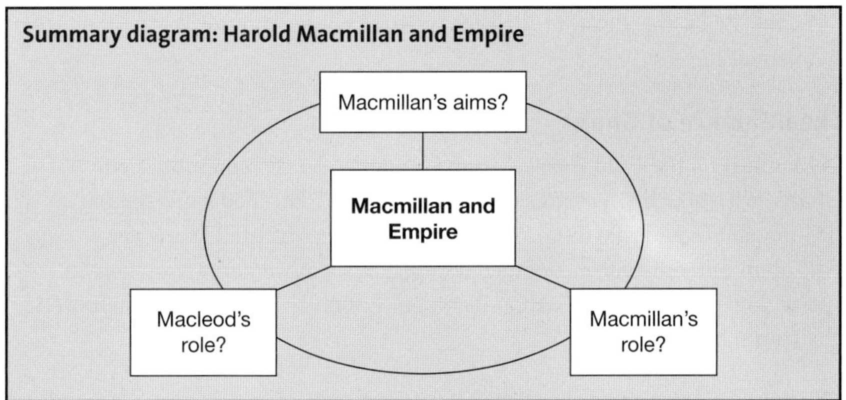

2 Decolonisation pressures

▶ *Why did Britain accept the need for decolonisation in the years 1959–63?*

By 1960, Macmillan, Macleod and most of the Cabinet accepted that a rapid withdrawal from Empire was likely to be less painful than a long campaign to retain control of colonial possessions. There were several reasons for this.

African nationalism

The upsurge of nationalist sentiment in Africa was a crucial factor in explaining the British government's change of policy.

The impact of the Second World War

The Second World War had stirred African nationalism.

- The Atlantic Charter (see page 118) inspired the African educated elite.
- The war sparked something of an economic revolution in parts of Africa. New factories rose to fill import gaps (for example, beer and cigarettes) and to process raw materials. Towns filled with wage-labourers who were susceptible to radical ideas.
- Africans were angered by increased British control and felt they were being exploited.
- A great shift of feeling on questions of race spread over the world after 1945. Until the Second World War, it had been regarded as perfectly reasonable to attribute national success to racial factors. The general Western assumption was that white people were racially superior to everyone else. But the example of Germany under Hitler showed that racial theories were unacceptable. By the 1950s, the idea that Africans were inherently inferior was no longer tolerable.

The influence of Ghana

In March 1957, the Gold Coast gained its independence, renaming itself Ghana, with Nkrumah as president (see page 138). This had a huge impact. If Ghanaians could rule themselves, why not other Africans? Moreover, Nkrumah immediately encouraged independence movements elsewhere in Africa. Throughout Africa, nationalist organisations won increasing support, challenging imperial rule.

The wind of change

Macmillan's conviction of the strength of African nationalism deepened as a result of a six-week tour of Africa in 1960. Speaking to the South African Parliament in Cape Town in 1960, Macmillan commented on the strength of 'African national consciousness'. The 'wind of change,' he said, 'was blowing through this continent. Whether we like it or not this growth of national consciousness is a political fact … our national policies must take account of it.'

French and Belgium colonies

It was not just British colonial rule which was threatened by growing nationalist activity. France and Belgium also faced challenges. The prolonged French struggle to keep Algeria resulted in the fall of the fourth French Republic. The new French president, Charles de Gaulle, finally offered Algeria full independence. He also granted independence to most of France's other African colonies. In 1960, Belgium followed France's example and decided to pull out of the Congo.

Britain could not ignore French and Belgian policies. As one colony was granted independence, others increased their demands and it became harder to sustain a case for delay elsewhere. In 1960, no fewer than sixteen new African states entered the United Nations, changing the balance of its membership. The newly independent states pressed for independence for other colonial territories. Britain, previously the pioneer of **devolution**, was left in the embarrassing position of appearing more illiberal than France. Moreover, it was difficult to justify denial of independence to British colonies whose size, economic and political development far outstripped that of France's former colonies. Pressure on Britain became more urgent as the Congo degenerated into anarchy in mid-1960. It seemed likely that trouble might spread into the British colonies bordering the Congo.

KEY TERMS

Devolution The handing over of powers.

Cold War The rivalry between the USA and its allies and the USSR and its allies after the Second World War.

Third World The developing countries of Africa, Asia and Latin America, which were not aligned with either the USA or the USSR.

How strong was African nationalism?

Some scholars regard the process of decolonisation as a series of successful liberation struggles. However, the view that nationalism made the collapse of British colonial rule inevitable is too simple. The strength of the nationalist movements has often been exaggerated by historians and politicians:

- Not all nationalist leaders won the hearts and minds of their people.
- Within virtually all of Britain's African colonies there was the fear that if independence came, power would be seized by one tribe, region or religious group. Britain, therefore, was in a position to play off one group against another as it had done effectively in the past.
- Britain could hope for support from conservative vested interest groups within the colonies if there was a threat of social upheaval.
- In the last resort, Britain had the military power to hold the nationalist movements in check. Portugal, a far weaker power, held on to its colonies much longer than Britain, and the white minority regime in Southern Rhodesia succeeded in maintaining power after 1964 (see page 168).

Lack of British will

What was lacking in Britain was not so much the strength to crush nationalist movements as the government's will to maintain colonial rule. There were several reasons for this:

- By 1960, Macmillan appreciated that any action, other than a rapid devolution of power, might produce insurrection. He realised that the brutal suppression of colonial peoples would damage Britain's standing and credibility in the eyes of the world as well as being condemned by many Britons.
- Aware that charges of imperialism and racism were weapons in the **Cold War**, Macmillan had no wish to alienate **Third World** opinion.
- Macmillan feared the spread of communism and the possibility of Africa becoming a battleground between East and West. In 1960, Russian intervention in Africa seemed imminent as Soviet military personnel were sent to exploit the situation in the Congo.

- Macmillan recognised that Britons, increasingly indifferent to Empire (see page 190), were unlikely to support new military burdens, particularly if this meant the reintroduction of National Service.

Most importantly, Macmillan, like many policy-makers, could see no good strategic or economic reasons for spending vast sums of money and risking the loss of thousands of lives trying to rule people who had no wish to be ruled. Bitter experience in Palestine, Egypt and Cyprus may have helped to weaken the British government's resolve to hang on to its Empire.

Thus, by 1960, Macmillan and most of his Cabinet accepted that a rapid withdrawal from Empire was likely to be less painful for all concerned than a long campaign to try to retain control of possessions that would eventually be lost anyway. Macmillan's desire was to construct new democratic states which would remain in the Commonwealth and be well disposed to Britain.

While some sections of the Conservative Party opposed rapid decolonisation, Macmillan encountered far less resistance than might have been expected. Most Conservatives accepted Britain's changing interests. Right-wing Conservatives, like Lord Salisbury, who opposed Macmillan's actions found there was little they could do. They were easily isolated because, in the last resort, the prime minister could rely on Labour support for his decolonisation policies. Nor could they rouse the British electorate. By the early 1960s, few Britons thought the Empire was worth fighting for. Encouraged by a media which was predominantly liberal, many frowned on coercive methods of maintaining colonial authority and were less prepared to accept arguments for maintaining minority rule which depended on assertions of white supremacy. More importantly, by the 1960s, the public was far more concerned with bread and butter issues – employment, education, health, housing – than with maintaining Empire. Most on the left regarded the Empire's dissolution as a good thing. Most on the right viewed its demise as – regrettably – inevitable.

KEY TERM

Pass laws Acts restricting the movement of black people in South Africa.

South Africa

White South Africans resisted the 'wind of change'. In March 1960, 67 Africans, campaigning to abolish South Africa's oppressive **pass laws**, were killed in clashes with police at Sharpeville. World-wide condemnation followed. In 1960, South African white people voted to make their country a republic. Given the change of status, the country had to apply to remain in the Commonwealth. While Macmillan supported its continued membership, African and Asian states threatened to leave if it remained. South Africa prevented a crisis by withdrawing its application.

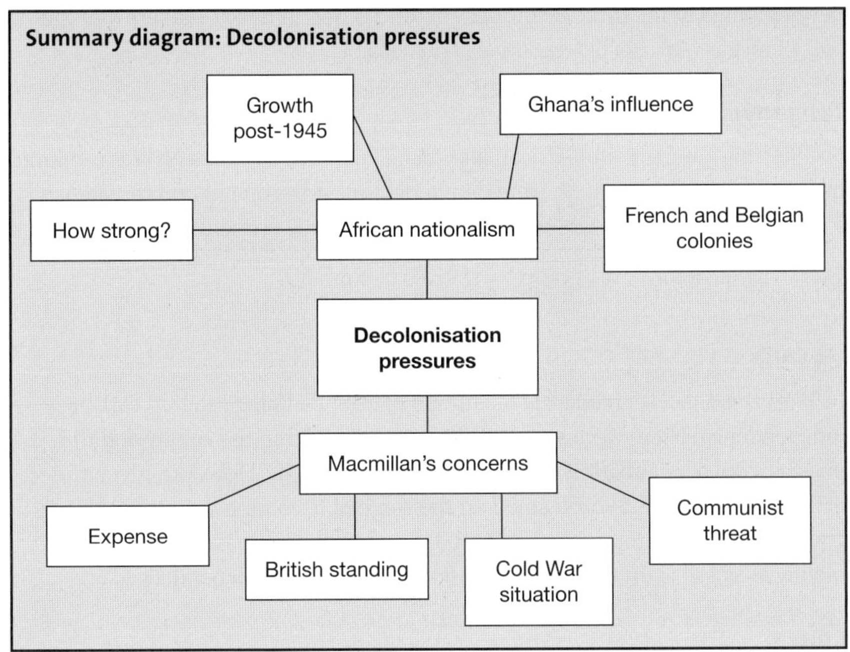

3 Decolonisation, 1957–63

▶ *Why did decolonisation occur so quickly in the period 1957–63?*

The process of decolonisation took place remarkably quickly.

Decolonisation in west Africa

The transfer of power was comparatively easy in west Africa:

- Ghana was granted independence in 1957 (see page 158).
- Nigeria, despite being deeply divided ethnically and religiously, became independent in 1960.
- Sierra Leone and the Cameroons followed in 1961.

Macmillan thought that Nigeria and the other west African territories were quite unready for self-government. But he believed that it should be granted because Britain had nothing to lose and possible influence to gain, while the alternative might be rebellion and repression.

Decolonisation in east Africa

In east Africa, Britain had once had hopes of establishing a federation which would include Tanganyika, Uganda and Kenya and which would be largely controlled by the white minority in Kenya. However, by the late 1950s, developments in the three territories convinced British policy-makers that the idea of an east African federation was not feasible.

Tanganyika

By 1959, the Tanganyikan African National Union, led by Julius Nyerere, enjoyed massive African support. Nyerere demanded self-government and threatened strikes and boycotts. Aware that Tanganyika had little economic or strategic importance, Britain promised it independence by December 1961. In 1963, Tanganyika joined with Zanzibar to become Tanzania.

Uganda

In 1959, there had seemed little likelihood of Uganda being granted early independence. There were serious tribal divisions within the colony and the possibility of a bloodbath if Britain withdrew too rapidly. However, given the tribal differences, Uganda seemed on the verge of becoming ungovernable, or governable only by repression. Britain decided that it was best to pull out as rapidly as possible. In October 1962, Uganda was given independence.

Kenya

Kenya was the most valuable of Britain's east African possessions. The 50,000 white population controlled most of the best land and dominated the Kenyan legislative council, blocking black political advancement. While there were some liberal developments in Kenya in the late 1950s, there seemed little prospect of majority rule or independence for Kenya. Old attitudes died hard:

- Little had been done to reconcile the Mau Mau detainees (see pages 143–4).
- Jomo Kenyatta, the suspected Mau Mau leader, who had been arrested in 1953 (and found guilty after a rigged trial) was still in prison.
- In March 1959, eleven prisoners were beaten to death at Hola Camp. Outrage in Britain grew as it emerged that no one would be prosecuted for any offence.

British officials were aware that developments in Tanganyika and Uganda would not be ignored in Kenya. Moreover, Kenya's white people were far from united. Some, especially those who were in the British government service, were prepared to break the mould of Kenyan politics and form a multiracial party. British policy-makers capitalised on this. At a London conference in January 1960, attended by white and black Kenyan politicians, the ban on African political movements was lifted and a constitution was devised which gave elected Africans a majority in the Kenyan legislature. Once the principle of self-government under majority rule was established, the process towards full democracy and full independence proved impossible to stop. Kenyatta, released from prison, became leader of the Kenyan African National Union. In December 1963, Kenya became independent under Kenyatta's premiership.

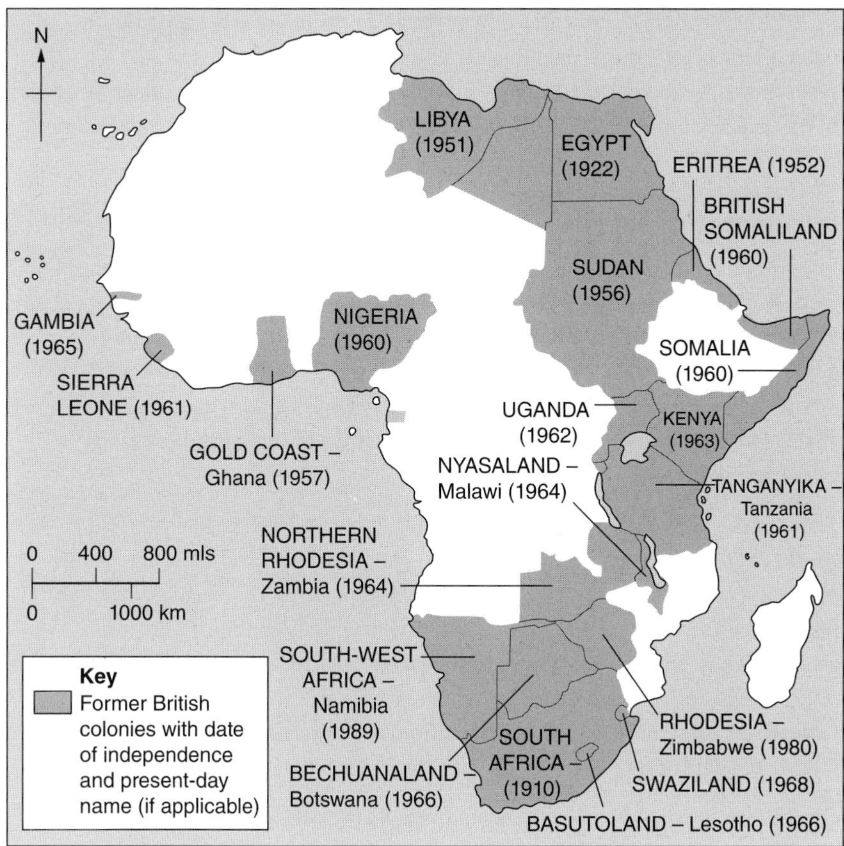

Figure 8.1 British decolonisation in Africa.

Decolonisation in central Africa

In central Africa the end of colonial rule was more difficult. Britain controlled:

- Northern Rhodesia (with 70,000 white people and 2 million Africans)
- Nyasaland (with 7000 white people and 2.5 million Africans)
- Southern Rhodesia (with 221,000 white people and 3.5 million Africans).

Britain's control of these territories was complicated by their membership of the Central African Federation (created in 1953), which was dominated by Southern Rhodesian white people, whose numbers had been swelled by an influx of British immigrants after 1945. Virtually no steps had been taken by the Federation to give black Africans any form of political representation. Although they gained a modest share in the Federation's rising prosperity (largely arising from the mining of copper and the sale of tobacco), black people still earned less than a tenth of white incomes.

In 1957, Macmillan's government was firmly committed to the idea of the Federation, even though most black people were bitterly opposed to it. British policy-makers hoped that white domination would gradually be offset by greater black representation. Nevertheless, the prospect of black majority rule seemed remote.

Problems in Nyasaland

In 1959, politics in central Africa became increasingly troubled. White people were worried by increasing disorder and growing support for Dr Hastings Banda (in Nyasaland) and Kenneth Kaunda (in Northern Rhodesia). Nyasaland's government, supposedly to prevent an armed coup, declared a state of emergency in March 1959. Banda and 100 other activists of the Nyasaland African Congress were imprisoned. In the police/military operations which followed, 51 Africans were killed.

These measures proved to be counter-productive. An independent inquiry, headed by Lord Devlin, condemned the Nyasaland government's action and accused it of running a 'police state'. No previous British colonial government had been so savagely criticised by an official inquiry. Although Macmillan's government rejected Devlin's report, it was reluctant to support more repressive policies. Macmillan, appreciating the extent of black hostility towards the Federation, feared that Northern Rhodesia and Nyasaland could become a bloody British Algeria.

Torn between the desire to conciliate black leaders and the fear that white people, who controlled all the military forces in the region, might simply declare independence, Macmillan and Macleod were uncertain about how to proceed. Each harboured doubts about a rapid transfer of power. But as rioting and violence in Nyasaland continued, the danger of a breakdown of authority loomed large. Accordingly, in July 1960, Nyasaland was given a constitution which ensured a black majority in its legislative council.

The Monckton Commission

A Royal Commission set up to advise on the Federation's future reported in October 1960. The Commission, headed by Walter Monckton, concluded that African distrust of the Federation had reached 'almost pathological' proportions and sweeping changes in its structure were necessary. It recommended that more power should be devolved to the territories and parity of representation for white and black people should be introduced immediately into the Federation's assembly.

Northern Rhodesia

Macmillan's government, which supported the Monckton Commission's findings, tried to persuade the Rhodesian white people to reach agreement with black leaders. In line with this policy, Macleod announced the creation of a conference to discuss Northern Rhodesia's constitution. Sir Roy Welensky, prime minister of the Federation, with the support of most Rhodesian white people, was determined to fight what was correctly perceived to be a move towards black majority rule in Northern Rhodesia. Complex and bitter negotiations on Northern Rhodesia's future followed. Hopes of finding a formula for a genuine multiracial state foundered on the intransigence of both white and black politicians. In Northern Rhodesia, Kaunda organised a campaign of civil disobedience, extending to sabotage and murder. It would soon, he warned, make the Mau Mau insurgency look like 'a child's picnic'. Fearing racial conflict, Macmillan was not sure whether to back the white settlers or to support black majority rule. To appease right-wing Conservative pressure, he moved Macleod from the Colonial Office, replacing him with R.A. Butler. However, this made little difference. In March 1962, Macmillan's government, convinced that the move to increased black representation was irresistible, accepted majority rule in Northern Rhodesia.

The end of the Central African Federation

The British government hoped that the granting of majority rule in Northern Rhodesia and Nyasaland would end the objections to the Federation. Instead, black leaders were now in a stronger position to campaign for independence from the Federation. Nyasaland was the first to do so. In October 1962, elections in Northern Rhodesia, under the new constitution, resulted in a victory for African parties, the two largest of which united to demand secession. It was clear that the Federation's days were numbered.

In the December 1962 elections, pro-Federation supporters in Southern Rhodesia were defeated by a new white party, the Rhodesian Front. The new government was determined to achieve independence under white rule and regarded the Federation as an obstacle to this. R.A. Butler presided over negotiations which began at the Victoria Falls in June 1963. The Victoria Falls Conference agreed that the Federation should be dissolved on 31 December 1963 and that Nyasaland (Malawi) and Northern Rhodesia (Zambia) should be given full independence in 1964.

The problem of Southern Rhodesia

The collapse of the Federation ended Britain's dream of multiracial rule. It also brought with it a further problem – that of Southern Rhodesia, where the white people refused to concede black majority rule. Macmillan's government was divided on whether to give Southern Rhodesia independence. While some Conservatives supported white rule, which they thought would be more efficient than black rule, others opposed giving independence to a white minority government. Southern Rhodesia thus remained a problem.

Decolonisation elsewhere

As well as abandoning Africa, Britain also decolonised in other areas.

The West Indies

In the West Indies, Britain's main concern was to try to ensure that new units of government were economically and politically viable. In 1958, it persuaded ten West Indian islands to form the West Indian Federation. However, local jealousies and the problems of distance conspired to make the Federation unworkable. In 1962, Jamaica and Trinidad (coupled with the nearby island of Tobago) decided to leave. Together they contained 83 per cent of the land, 77 per cent of the population and 75 per cent of the Federation's wealth. Accordingly, the Federation collapsed. The larger islands became independent; the smaller islands became Associated States with Britain retaining responsibility for their diplomacy and defence.

Cyprus and Malta

As opposition to British rule in Cyprus mounted again in 1958, some 30,000 British servicemen were sent to the island. They arrested almost 2000 EOKA suspects (see page 145). 'Black October' 1958 saw 45 people killed. Macmillan, deciding that the island was not worth fighting for, opened new talks with Archbishop Makarios. After prolonged negotiations an agreement was hammered out:

- Cyprus was to become independent within the Commonwealth in 1960.
- Its Greek and Turkish communities were each to have almost complete autonomy.
- Britain retained sovereignty over two bases.

It seemed a masterly solution, but trouble between Greek and Turkish Cypriots continued, reaching civil war proportions by 1963.

Malta, once a vital naval base, lost its importance as Britain's naval presence in the Mediterranean decreased. Plans to make Malta (with a population of 300,000) a part of the UK collapsed because Britain was unwilling to give the island sufficient financial assistance to bring up the standard of Maltese welfare to that of Britain. Instead, many Maltese demanded independence, which was granted in 1964.

Conclusion

In 1965, Gambia became independent. Bechuanaland (Botswana) and Basutoland (Lesotho) followed suit in 1966. Thus, by 1966 Britain had granted independence to all its African colonies, except Southern Rhodesia. It had done so much more quickly than planned. This meant that most colonies were less well prepared for self-rule than Britain had hoped. But it also meant that Britain disposed of its Empire without having the bitter experience of France in Algeria.

Most white people in Africa believed that Macmillan caved in far too easily to African nationalist pressure. Most historians, however, suggest that Britain divested itself of Empire with some dignity and skill. There was remarkably little bloodshed and no major political crisis in Britain. Britons watched the process of disintegration with detachment. In Africa, Britain retained the appearance of power up to the point of departure. This was not the case in reality. Given that it was not prepared to fight, Britain had few cards to play against determined opponents. It displayed some skill in masking this weakness and in devising the institutional machinery that allowed a peaceful withdrawal. For African leaders, constitutional legitimacy and the symbolic inheritance of colonial authority were valuable prizes. Thus, the transfers of power were invariably amiable, stately affairs. 'It was a pleasing pantomime in which all could delight', writes historian John Darwin (2012).

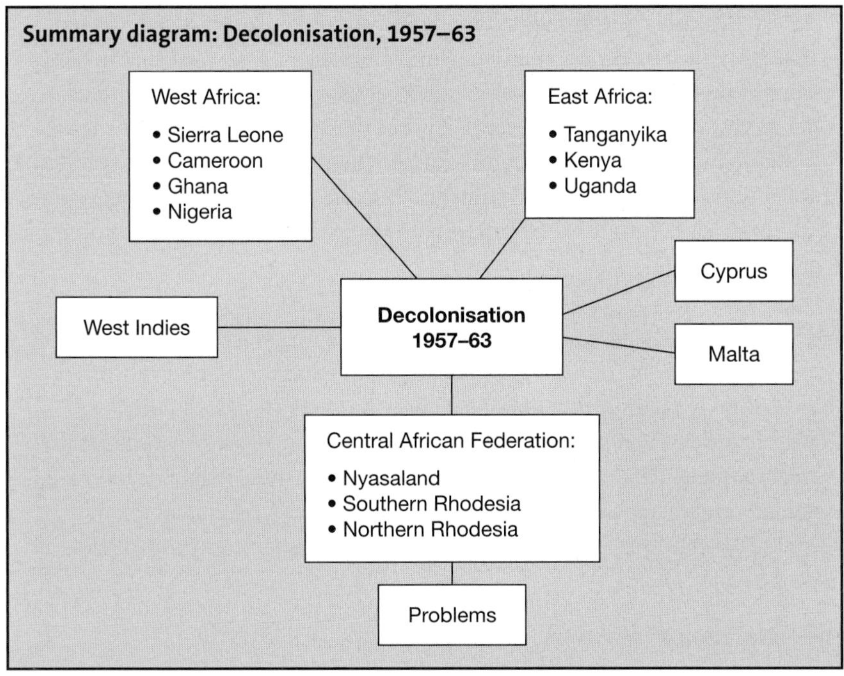

The post-colonial situation, 1964–7

▶ *To what extent did Britain cling on to Empire after 1964?*

The Empire, 1964–7

Although Britain had lost most of its colonies by 1964, some areas – and problems – remained.

Southern Rhodesia

In 1965, white Southern Rhodesians, refusing to concede black majority rule, declared independence from Britain. No other country recognised the new government. Britain's new Labour government, led by Harold Wilson, imposed an ineffectual trade boycott but made it clear that his government would not use force to invade Rhodesia – a move that would have been unpopular in Britain. The critics of Wilson's action argued that Britain could certainly overthrow the Southern Rhodesia government of Ian Smith if it so chose. Thus, it appeared as if Wilson must be deliberately choosing not to do so. It seemed that the only reason for this was that the British government sympathised with Smith on racial grounds. But the argument was not convincing. If Britain was as racially prejudiced and as strong as its critics claimed, then it would not have withdrawn from its African colonies at all. Southern Rhodesia remained a problem for the next fifteen years. South Africa supported Southern Rhodesia, undermining the economic blockade.

East of Suez

Ironically, the retreat from Africa, the West Indies and the Mediterranean coincided with a new effort to maintain British influence 'east of Suez'. Conservative and Labour leaders (as well as American leaders) feared that if Britain abandoned its role in the Middle and Far East there would be increased instability and the possibility of communist takeover. Consequently, some 100,000 British service personnel were based east of Suez in the mid-1960s – at huge expense.

The Federation of Malaysia

In 1957, the Federation of Malaya became independent but Britain assumed responsibility for its defence. By 1961, fearful of growing communist influence in South-East Asia, Britain supported the idea of a Federation of Malaysia which would include Malaya, Singapore and the three remaining British colonies of North Borneo, Brunei and Sarawak. Britain agreed to continue the defence commitments made in 1957. In 1963, the Federation was officially set up. It soon had problems:

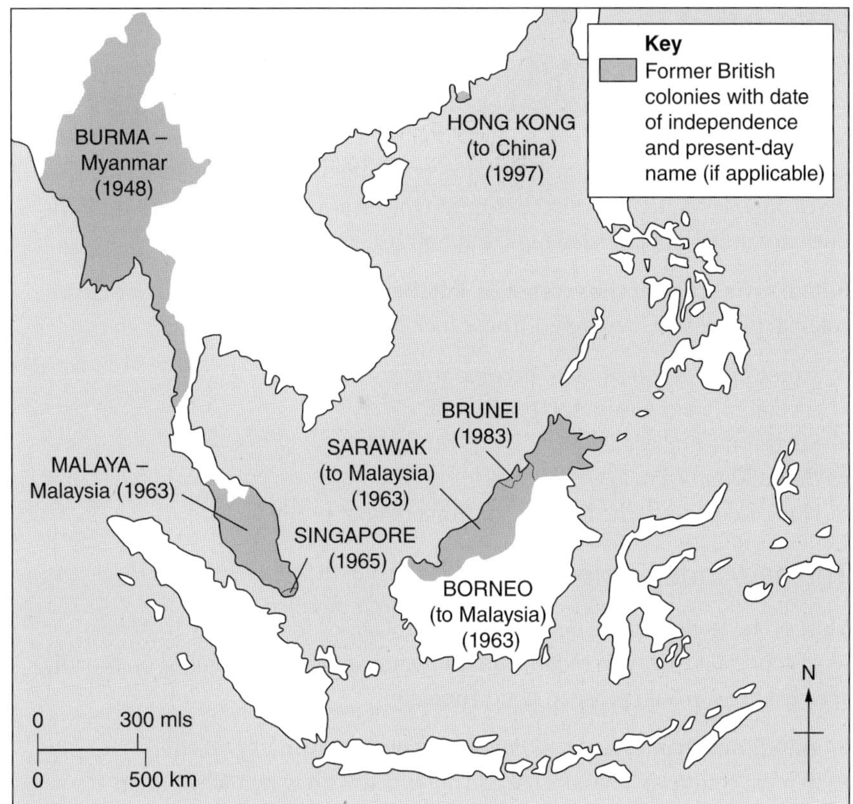

Figure 8.2 British decolonisation in South-East Asia.

- Indonesia, hopeful of annexing North Borneo and Sarawak, opposed the Federation and for the next three years tried to bring about its disintegration. Britain provided Malaysia with vital military assistance.
- In 1965, Singapore separated from Malaysia, largely because the Chinese majority in Singapore did not like Malay political control of the country.

Aden

In the late 1950s, Aden, a useful 'springboard' for defending British interests in the Middle East and the Indian Ocean, became a major British base. However, the colony was threatened by Arab nationalism both from without (especially from neighbouring Yemen) and from within Aden itself. To try to provide some support for Aden, Britain created a new South Arabian Federation in 1963 – a collection of small, undemocratic sheikhdoms. This did not solve matters and terrorism in Aden increased. Britain finally abandoned the base in late 1967 after a long, futile struggle.

British retreat

In November 1967, the value of sterling came under intense pressure, forcing Britain to devalue the pound by fifteen per cent. Harold Wilson appointed a new chancellor of the exchequer, Roy Jenkins, an ardent supporter of Europe and no less ardent opponent of Britain's post-imperial commitments. Against fierce opposition, Jenkins forced through the decision to end Britain's military presence in both the Persian Gulf and South-East Asia by 1971.

Britain's world power thus vanished. But the Empire was not quite over. Some colonial possessions remained. These included:

- scores of areas too small to become sovereign nations
- several military bases, notably Gibraltar
- Southern Rhodesia
- the Falkland Islands
- Hong Kong, until the lease with China ran out in 1997.

The new independent states

Most of the leaders of the newly independent states (particularly in Africa) were confident that with independence their economies, organised on broadly socialist lines, would prosper. Unfortunately:

- grandiose schemes for economic development invariably failed
- in most countries a handful of corrupt officials grew rich while their populations did not benefit.

Some former colonies soon became single-party states or military dictatorships. Many African countries were plagued by ethnic, regional and religious divisions. Nigeria suffered a major civil war between 1967 and 1970, resulting in an enormous loss of life.

However, some former colonies:

- successfully adopted Britain's style of government, especially those in the Caribbean
- were economically successful, for example, Malaysia and Singapore.

The Commonwealth

Between 1960 and 1966, 23 new countries became members of the Commonwealth. British governments promoted the Commonwealth, envisioning a multiracial fraternity which would help all its members. But most of the hopes underpinning the Commonwealth were not realised. As early as 1964, *The Times* called the Commonwealth 'a gigantic farce'.

In many respects, government attempts to 'sell' the Commonwealth were a means of trying to sustain British prestige by concealing the decay of British power. Tory politician Enoch Powell described the Commonwealth 'as a sticking plaster for the wound left by the amputation of Empire'.

By the 1960s, the Commonwealth was moving away from any special commitment or deference to Britain. Indeed, new members hoped to use the organisation to help influence British policy, particularly with regard to Southern Rhodesia.

A united policy on almost any issue was impossible to achieve. If the small group of deeply pro-British Dominion prime ministers in the early twentieth century were unwilling to have a united imperial foreign policy, it was unlikely that the diverse and greatly enlarged membership of the second half of the century could do so.

Even the old bonds of friendship with Australia, New Zealand and Canada were strained. All three countries now looked to the USA for defence. In Canada the old emphatic assertion of Canada's Britishness disappeared. A symbol of this was the replacement of the Red Ensign by the Maple Leaf flag. Australia and New Zealand were shocked by Britain's application to join the EEC in 1961. Both countries increasingly recognised that Asia, not Britain, held the key to their futures.

Nevertheless, the Commonwealth continued to hold together, providing technical, educational and professional assistance to its members. On occasions, it proved a useful instrument of international cooperation.

The European Economic Community

Anxious to preserve its special trade relationship with the Commonwealth, Britain did not join the European Economic Community (EEC) in 1957. However, in the early 1960s, Macmillan determined to join the EEC. Britain's share of the world's manufacturing exports was declining and it had a growing trade deficit. There was also a shift in the focus of Britain's trading activity away from the Commonwealth and towards Western Europe. The Commonwealth, in spite of its size, could not compare with the EEC's purchasing power. While Britain's initial applications to join the EEC were rejected in 1963 and 1967, Britain ultimately joined in 1973 – an indication that it had abandoned its hopes of a viable Commonwealth. The sterling area collapsed by 1972.

Migration to Britain

After 1945, Britain was short of workers. A 1948 Nationality Act allowed the 800 million subjects of the Empire to live and work in the UK without a visa. The first immigrants came from the Caribbean. Nearly 500, for example, came on the *Empire Windrush* from Jamaica in 1948. In 1953, some 3000 Commonwealth immigrants came. Immigration thereafter steadily increased. In 1961, 136,000 immigrants arrived, mainly from India and Pakistan. A multiracial Britain was thus one of the main results of Empire. It was, says historian Bernard Porter (2004), 'one for which the Empire, despite all its high multi-racial pretensions, had very poorly prepared her people'.

In 1961, the Commonwealth Immigration Act was introduced to impose limits on entry to Britain. The government argued that unrestricted immigration was encouraging racial division in Britain. By the 1960s, opinion clashed about Commonwealth immigration. Liberals believed that Britain was enriched by transfusions of new blood. But many Britons opposed the influx, sharing Enoch Powell's 1968 vision of the 'Tiber foaming with much blood'.

Conclusion

The British Empire had been the product of circumstances that occurred in the nineteenth and early twentieth centuries – the supremacy of the Royal Navy, the Industrial Revolution resulting in Britain becoming the workshop and banking house of the world, and the relative weakness of rival states. The Empire, the largest the world has ever seen, disappeared with astonishing speed. Between 1945 and 1965, the number of people under British colonial rule shrank from 700 million to 5 million. Within a generation, some 26 countries became independent. A number of factors helped to precipitate this collapse:

- loss of Britain's prestige following the Second World War
- post-war British military weakness
- American and Soviet opposition to imperialism
- emergent nationalism in the colonies
- global opposition to Western imperialism and its retreat on nearly all fronts
- Britain's recurrent economic crises
- Britons preference for welfare at home rather than expenditure abroad.

Relatively few Britons regarded the end of Empire as a national humiliation. Government ministers and officials did their utmost to brand the critics of 'scuttle' as anachronistic and reactionary. Most Britons accepted the Empire's demise as inevitable and were right to do so. The Empire always had within it the germ of its own destruction. Its commitment to trusteeship meant that it was ultimately doomed. The end of Empire was probably good for Britain. The country lacked the strength to carry out its overseas responsibilities and needed to adapt to its reduced global position.

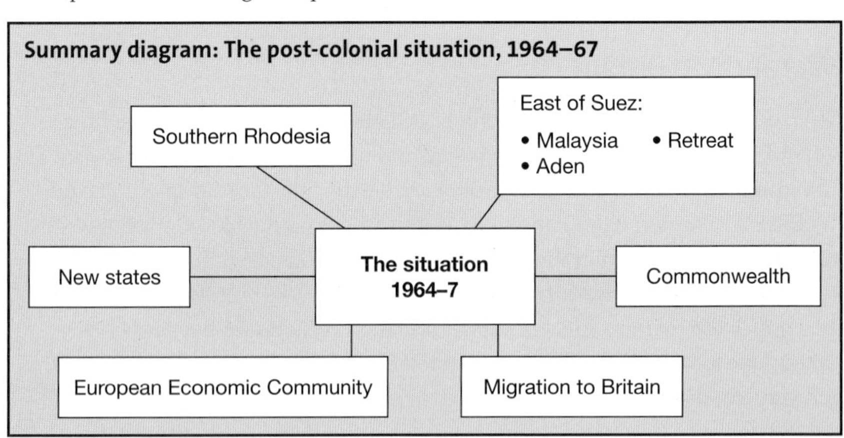

Key debate

▶ *To what extent was the British Empire a force for good?*

Historians continue to debate whether the Empire was a force for good or evil.

EXTRACT 1

From Robert Johnson, *Histories and Controversies, British Imperialism*, Palgrave Macmillan, 2003, p. 76.

In the long term, the legacy of colonisation has not been entirely negative. Mixed societies based on the ethics of Christianity, the rule of law and free enterprise have flourished. The legacy of British education, science and technology are evident. The former colonies of settlement model their political systems on British democratic institutions, with free elections, universal suffrage, secret ballots and freedom of assembly and expression. The British conception of property and its protection has been transferred even to the descendants of indigenous populations who claim 'ownership' of the land. The close connection between the former colonies and Britain continues … In this sense, the advocates of colonisation achieved their aim of spreading the British people and their values overseas.

EXTRACT 2

From Piers Brandon, *The Decline and Fall of the British Empire 1781–1997*, Vintage Books, 2008, p. 655.

On the debit side were arrogance, violence, exploitation, jingoism, racism and authoritarianism. At its heart was a betrayal of the civilised values which the British claimed to espouse. They had professed libertas [liberty] but practised imperium [authority], subjugating alien lands in the name of freedom. In the words of a disapproving journalist, 'much of the world, including Hong Kong, will remember us as perfidious Albion, an inheritance of Empire that will outlive all of us'. No doubt hypocrisy was integral to the British Empire, which deployed fine words to hide its ultimate reliance on coercion.

The positive

- The Empire had been an agent of cultural change. It had resulted in the expansion of trade, swifter methods of transport, new communications techniques, new kinds of schooling, new notions of leisure and taste, and a different religion. While some indigenous peoples had opposed the changes, there were also many people in every colonial society to whom the new cultural forms were deeply attractive. The treatment of women, for example, improved considerably in many parts of the Empire. In some countries, it is possible to credit British rule with free speech, good governance, democratic institutions, the rule of law and the ideal of fair play.

- The Empire brought peace, security and stability to people who had lacked them.
- It delivered the products of science and technology to vast tracts of the world, and showed their inhabitants how they could master their environment through sanitation, agriculture and building development.
- Historian Niall Ferguson (2002) claims that 'no organisation in history has done more to promote the free movement of goods, capital and labour than the British Empire in the nineteenth and early twentieth centuries'.
- The Empire was essentially a liberal empire. Its functionaries claimed that a commitment to freedom was fundamental to their civilising mission. In this respect, as Lloyd George told the Imperial Conference in 1921, the British Empire was unique: 'Liberty is its binding principle'. To people under the imperial yoke such affirmations must have seemed brazen instances of British hypocrisy. But in the twentieth century, the British put their principles into practice. They fulfilled their duties as trustees, giving their dependent colonies the independence long enjoyed by the white Dominions. The Empire thus realised its long-cherished ideal of becoming what *The Times* called in 1942 'a self-liquidating concern'. Its relatively bloodless end can be perceived as a triumph.
- While the Empire is now regarded with a mixture of embarrassment, indifference or even post-imperial guilt, in the period covered by this book it was a source of considerable pride to most Britons. It was perceived as conferring great power status on Britain, providing Britain with reliable sources of food and raw materials and a captive market for British exports, and providing the Royal Navy with bases from which it was able to dominate the world's sea lanes.
- The Dominions had a strong sense of shared Britishness. This inspired the extraordinary levels of sacrifice which helped Britain to win both the First and Second World Wars.

The negative

- The Empire was based on racial attitudes which were bitterly resented by non-white peoples.
- Indigenous races were excluded from power.
- Resistance to British rule provoked vicious reprisals such as Britain inflicted after the Indian mutiny and during the Mau Mau emergency and the Malayan insurgency.
- Britain's legacy was not generally good. In Africa, most governments swiftly abandoned democratic practices and eroded civil liberties.
- The colonies were economically exploited by Britain.

Chapter summary

Between 1957 and 1967, the British Empire was quickly dismantled. Most of the dismantlement came during the premiership of Macmillan (1957–63). Macmillan, initially committed to maintaining the Empire, faced considerable pressure from nationalism and decided that it was not worth expending money and lives to maintain British rule in large parts of Africa. He was aware that most Britons were indifferent to Empire. Thus, by 1964 most of Britain's colonies in Africa had gone. British efforts to pursue a costly 'east of Suez' role effectively came to an end in 1967. The Empire had gone: the Commonwealth remained, but had little impact on the world stage. Historians continue to debate whether the Empire was a good or bad thing for Britain and the world.

Refresher questions

Use these questions to remind yourself of the key material covered in this chapter.

1 What were Macmillan's imperial aims in 1957?
2 Why had Macmillan decided to jettison Britain's African colonies by 1960?
3 How strong was African nationalism?
4 What was the British public's view of Empire by the early 1960s?
5 Why was it easier for Britain to grant independence in west Africa than east Africa?
6 Why did the Central African Federation pose a major problem for Britain?
7 Why did British governments wish to join the EEC?
8 Was the British Empire a good or bad thing?

Question practice

ESSAY QUESTIONS

1 'The strength of African nationalism in the period 1918–63 made the collapse of British colonial rule inevitable.' Assess the validity of this statement.
2 'Britain had little control over the process of African decolonisation in the period 1918–63.' Assess the validity of this view.
3 'Britain handled its African colonies with considerable skill in the period 1920–63.' Assess the validity of this view.
4 'Britain continued to play an important imperial role in the period 1930–67.' Assess the validity of this statement.

INTERPRETATION QUESTION (A LEVEL)

1 Using your understanding of the historical context, assess how convincing the arguments in these three extracts are in relation to assessing the reasons for the decline of British imperial power in the period 1957–67.

EXTRACT A

From W.M. Roger Louis, 'The dissolution of the British Empire', in *The Oxford History of the British Empire: The Twentieth Century*, edited by Judith M. Brown and W.M. Roger Louis, Oxford University Press, 1999, pp. 354–5.

The immediate causes of the end of the British Empire are to be found not only in the nationalist movements in Empire itself but also in the lessons learned from the Algerian revolution and in the danger of Soviet intervention in the Congo. It seemed altogether more prudent to settle with African liberation movements in eastern and central Africa before war broke out between blacks and whites or before the Africans turned to the Russians for sponsorship … If the Americans looked forward to transforming the Empire in the long run into independent states within the Western alliance, in the short run they propped it up against the challenge posed by the Soviet Union and Communist China. Paradoxically, one consequence was that the cold war sometimes presented nationalists with the opportunity of playing the superpowers against each other or against the British. Actual or prospective superpower intervention could increase nationalist prospects … The international climate thus expedited the advance to independence, but the circumstances varied from region to region, from colony to colony. With the United States and the Soviet Union competing against each other in the colonial world, the local strength of nationalism or insurgency often determined the actual timing of decolonisation.

EXTRACT B

From Alan Farmer, *Britain: Foreign and Imperial Affairs 1939–64*, Hodder & Stoughton, 1994, p. 135.

In the early 1960s colonial rule almost everywhere came to an end far more quickly and far less satisfactorily than the British government intended. The idea that some colonies were unprepared, too poor or too small to become independent was tacitly abandoned. Most whites in Africa believed that Macmillan had caved in far too easily to African nationalist pressure. Most historians, however, are of the opinion that Britain divested herself of Empire with some dignity and skill. There was remarkably little bloodshed abroad and no major political crisis in Britain. The British public, reassured from all sides that Britain would remain a world power, watched the process of disintegration with indifference. It was generally assumed that formal Empire would be replaced by informal influence, sealed by economic ties and defence treaties.

EXTRACT C

From Bernard Porter, *The Lion's Share: A Short History of British Imperialism 1850–2004*, Pearson, 2004, p. 320.

Britain still clung to hopes of salvaging something from the wreckage, some vestige of colonial control: economic control: economic control in the form of oil installations in Aden or copper royalties in Zambia; or political control by backing 'moderate' parties against extremists: parties which could too easily be branded as British 'stooges' and could not hope to retain power when their patrons had gone. Sometimes this backing may have gone to the lengths of rigging pre-independence elections. There was some hard bargaining but usually Britain lost because (as in India in 1947) she had nothing really substantial to bargain with … She could not threaten to withhold independence. In most cases (again as in India) independence raced forward inexorably: a date set, then brought closer; then independence granted sooner still. It was not the most dignified way to go. Yet it was done. Britain in the 1960s was hustled and harried out of most of her old colonies … and without too much bloodshed.

CHAPTER 9

Conclusion

Between 1857 and 1967, the British Empire rose and fell. While that Empire is now regarded with a mixture of guilt, embarrassment and indifference, for much of the period covered by this book, it was a source of considerable pride to most Britons. However, it was not perceived quite so positively by those indigenous peoples who were under British rule. This concluding chapter will consider the changing nature of Britain's imperial experience from 1857 to 1967 by examining the following issues:

★ The Empire's growth and contraction
★ Influences on imperial policy
★ The role of economic factors
★ The impact of the Empire on British attitudes and culture
★ The response of indigenous people to British rule
★ The role of key individuals and groups
★ The nature of the Empire

1 The Empire's growth and contraction

▶ *Why did the British Empire grow and then contract?*

Economic and naval supremacy were crucial factors in enabling Britain to acquire an enormous Empire. However, Britain's acquisition of Empire was not the result of a co-ordinated policy of conquest. Nor was the eventual surrender of Empire the result of any master plan.

Imperial growth, 1857–1914

It is possible to see the British political establishment for several decades after 1850 as reluctantly imperialist. Arguably, many nineteenth-century British governments preferred 'informal' imperialism to expensive 'formal' annexation. But, given the vast area brought under British control after (and indeed before) 1857, the notion of 'accidental' or even 'reluctant' imperialism is not particularly persuasive. New territories came under British rule in the mid- and late-nineteenth century largely because of local circumstances. In many cases they were acquired for strategic reasons or to safeguard trading interests.

Throughout the nineteenth and early twentieth centuries, India was the most important part of the Empire. The largest single element of British army spending was devoted to the Indian army. While the Royal Navy's first task was to defend Britain, its second was to protect the trade route to India. Lord Curzon claimed that 'as long as we rule India, we are the greatest power in the world. If we lose it, we shall drop straightaway to a third-rate power.' After the Indian Mutiny, the whole civil and military system of British India was reorganised. The British government adopted full responsibility for most of the subcontinent.

The territory controlled by the Raj continued to expand in the late nineteenth century. So did the British Empire elsewhere. In the 'scramble for Africa' between 1880 and 1900, 90 per cent of the continent was appropriated by European powers. Britain, concerned that it might find itself barred from markets and sources of raw materials, acquired nearly 5 million square miles, almost as much as France, Germany, Belgium and Italy combined.

British governments used chartered companies in the 1880s and 1890s to seize and administer new territories. These companies, ensured that British taxpayers did not have to bear the cost of colonial expansion. But there were disadvantages in giving commercial companies licences to rule territories. They discouraged free competition and their exploitative functions were not always compatible with their subjects' welfare. Moreover, their actions could force the British government to take unpalatable action. Eventually, the areas under the companies' control were taken over by the government.

By 1914, the British Empire amounted to a fifth of the world's land surface and population. Most British governments, even Gladstone's Liberal governments, were reluctant to abandon territory. There was an awareness that the British electorate would not countenance the loss of Empire. By the 1870s, the Conservative Party was generally regarded as the party of imperialism. While this did not guarantee the Tories electoral success, perceived weakness on the imperial front could make the Liberals unpopular, for example, the events leading to the death of Gordon at Khartoum in 1885.

Queen Victoria's Diamond Jubilee procession in 1897 seemed proof that Britain had never been greater. But this impression was misleading. Beneath the external display, there was a growing sense of vulnerability. While Britain remained the world's greatest manufacturing and trading power, its lead was being cut back year by year as the result of industrial and commercial developments in other countries. Britain also seemed to have insufficient armed forces to defend its scattered possessions. The Royal Navy was a particular source of concern. Other countries were increasing their numbers of ships, forcing Britain to embark on expensive naval building programmes. While the British Empire looked strong on maps, in reality, there were problems. A bigger Empire resulted in Britain having more frontiers to defend. In the 1890s, for example, northern India was threatened by Russia, Egypt by France, and British territory in southern Africa by the Boer Republics.

Imperial fervour in Britain possibly reached its height in the Boer War (1899–1902). Thereafter, imperial sentiment cooled. The Liberal Party, which won the 1906 and 1910 elections, had no great vision of Empire. Nevertheless, Liberal governments made no effort to abandon it.

Imperial power or decline, 1914–39?

Britain's victory in the First World War seemed to prove the value of Empire. The Empire's contribution to Allied victory was considerable. The Dominions provided some 1.3 million men while over 1.4 million Indian troops were also mobilised. The Empire's economic resources greatly assisted the Allied war effort. The outcome of the war resulted in Britain acquiring new territories from Germany and Turkey. By the early 1920s, the British Empire was at its zenith. Britain also had huge influence in its informal empire, especially in the Middle East. No other power enjoyed the same degree of global influence.

However, the First World War did not really strengthen Britain's imperial position. The country was economically weakened by the war and it had been forced to sell many of its overseas investments. Declining economic power made it difficult for Britain to sustain its global military commitments.

There continued to be little system in the Empire's constitutional structure. While the Dominions were essentially self-governing, most of the 80 or so other imperial territories were still under various forms of British rule. Although Britain and the Dominions had cooperated effectively in the First World War, this did not continue after 1918. Hopes that Britain and its Dominions might act with a united voice in world affairs proved impossible to realise. The Balfour Declaration (1926) and the Statue of Westminster (1931) ensured that an Empire based on central authority was transformed into the Commonwealth of Nations. Dominions now had the right to change their constitutions and even withdraw from the Commonwealth.

Britain faced unrest in Egypt and in Palestine. It had even greater problems with India. Throughout the interwar years, the Congress Party, dominated by Gandhi, demanded independence. Britain used force to maintain control but also made considerable concessions to Indian nationalists.

It is possible to claim that Britain's imperial power was played out by 1939. Arguably, British governments and people lacked the resolution and conviction to hold down the growing resistance to imperial rule. The end of the Raj seemed nigh. Politicians were probably deluding themselves in believing that by ingenious constitutional arrangements they could prolong the Empire indefinitely.

However, it may be that the Empire was not in irreversible decline or even in retreat by 1939. Certainly few people in 1939 predicted a rapid end of Empire. Britain, despite its economic difficulties, was quite capable of sustaining its imperial commitments. Indeed, the economic situation, in particular Britain's dependence on imported food and need for export markets, seemed an excellent reason for the Empire's maintenance. The Dominions continued to be essentially satellite states. Although the formal bonds of Empire had disappeared, many people in the Dominions still felt attached to Britain by ties of sentiment and self-interest. In most of Britain's dependent colonies, there was little pressure for home rule. For all its imperfections, the Empire appeared to be a necessary part of any stable world order. By 1939, Britain had still not resigned itself to Indian independence. Given the German and Japanese threat, it seemed essential that India remain under British control. Arguably, therefore, the evolution of Britain's imperial system would have been very different but for the Second World War.

Decline and fall, 1939–67

Britain's victory in the Second World War seemed proof of the Empire's strength and solidarity. When Britain declared war on Germany in 1939, Australia, New Zealand, Canada and South Africa did the same. During the war, the Empire provided Britain with 5 million servicemen and essential food and raw materials. But the war weakened Britain and its hold on Empire. Although Britain emerged victorious, it was apparent that it did so largely because of the might of its two main allies: the USA and the USSR. Britain could not compare in military and economic strength with either superpower – both of which were anti-imperialist in outlook. By 1945, Britain was in dire economic straits. The destruction of houses, factories and shipping had cost the country a quarter of its wealth. Most foreign assets had been sold to pay for imports. If Britain was too poor to buy what the Dominions and colonies produced, too poor to invest in their economic development and unable to provide the manufactured goods they needed, one of the most significant factors holding the Empire together was lost.

The Labour Party, led by Attlee, came to power in 1945. While some Labour MPs wanted to jettison the Empire, this was not the opinion of Attlee's Cabinet. Most Labour ministers recognised that without colonies, Britain would no longer be a great power. Moreover, its economic prosperity would be threatened. But Attlee was committed to granting independence in India. Independence for India and Pakistan, in 1947 (followed by independence for Burma and Ceylon), marked the beginning of the end of the Empire. The precedent of India, the first non-white colony to become independent, was certain to influence the course of events elsewhere. If Britain lacked the will to rule in India, the jewel in the crown, then it was almost inevitable that its entire Empire would soon be lost.

But the granting of independence to India and Pakistan was not seen by Attlee's government as the start of a general process of decolonisation. Churchill, who returned to power in 1951 and who was far more committed to Empire than Attlee, pursued similar policies to his Labour opponent. British policy-makers continued to hope that the Commonwealth would become a third force, balancing the power of the USA and the USSR. But the prospect of building a strong Commonwealth stood little chance. The countries of the new

Commonwealth had little in common in religious, ethnic, political and economic terms with those of the old Dominions, which now tended to look to the USA for security.

In 1955, Sir Anthony Eden became prime minister. Like Churchill, he was determined to maintain British influence in the world, particularly in the Middle East. Eden's policies culminated in the Suez Crisis (1956) – a disaster from Eden's perspective. In 1957, Eden resigned. He had tried to act like the leader of a great power and failed. Suez is often seen as a watershed, separating the years in which Britain's survival as a world power seemed possible, from the years after: years which saw the rapid end of the Empire and the scaling down of Britain's global commitments. But the results of Suez should not be exaggerated. Eden's departure apart, Suez had relatively little impact on British politics. The Conservatives, under Macmillan, easily won the 1959 election. Britain's colonial withdrawal after 1960 was not a direct consequence of Suez. Arguably, Suez merely exposed underlying trends in the decline of British power.

Between 1957 and 1963, Macmillan's government granted independence to virtually all Britain's colonies in Africa. Britain probably had the military power to hold the African nationalist movements in check. What it lacked was the will to do so. By 1960, Macmillan appreciated that any action, other than a rapid devolution of power, might produce insurrection. He realised that brutal suppression of colonial peoples would damage Britain's standing in the world and be condemned by many Britons. Aware that charges of imperialism and racism were weapons in the Cold War, Macmillan had no wish to alienate Third World opinion. So he decided on rapid withdrawal from Africa – a process that was likely to be less painful than efforts to retain control of possessions that would eventually be lost anyway. His hope was to construct new democratic states, which were well disposed towards Britain. Given the speed of British withdrawal, most colonies were less well prepared for self-rule than Britain had planned.

For several more years, Britain tried to maintain its influence in the Middle and Far East. Some 100,000 British service personnel were based 'east of Suez' in the mid-1960s. But economic difficulties in 1967 resulted in Britain making drastic cuts to its forces in Asia and announcing its determination to quit its 'east of Suez' role within a few years. Thus, by 1967, the once mighty British Empire had shrunk to a few island bases scattered around the world. The Commonwealth survived but was a talking shop rather than a political or economic power.

The British Empire had risen largely because of Britain's military and economic might and the commitment of its people and governments to maintain and expand the territory under Britain's control. After 1945, Britain's military and economic might did not compare with that of the USSR and the USA. Moreover, the British people and its governments were no longer so committed to maintaining the Empire. In an age which was anti-imperialistic, the Empire quickly faded away.

Influences on imperial policy

▶ *What influenced imperial policy?*

While British imperial expansion was not the result of a co-ordinated policy of conquest, British governments were invariably determined to maintain Britain's perceived commercial and strategic interests. Throughout much of the period 1857–1967, most British governments and, so far as historians can tell, most Britons recognised the value of Empire. They believed it:

- conferred great power status on Britain
- provided Britain with reliable sources of food and raw materials and a captive market for British exports
- provided the Royal Navy with important bases from which it was able to dominate the world's sea lanes.

Prior to 1870 there was no great enthusiasm to expand the Empire. The loss of the American colonies (in 1783) suggested that colonies were bound to proclaim independence at some future stage. Given this expectation, there seemed little point in acquiring them. Nevertheless, even in the period 1844–70, at a time when there was supposed indifference to Empire, Britain acquired/annexed New Zealand, the Gold Coast, Hong Kong, Natal, Sierra Leone, Lower Burma, Basutoland and large areas of India.

If and when the Empire was challenged, whether by external threat (for example, from Russia, Germany or France) or by internal threat (for example, in India in 1857–8), Britain was ready to enforce its authority. Perceived threats to its imperial interests often led to Britain taking on more extensive responsibilities. Britain's presence in an area was thus often a springboard for further expansion. In the 1880s and 1890s, Britain's established interests seemed vulnerable. If Britain stood still, it might lose ground. Accordingly, politicians took stronger measures to secure imperial interests than previously. The territorial gains which accrued were considerable, especially in Africa.

British governments feared competition. If other countries seized territory, Britain's colonies might be threatened, as might British economic interests. Until the 1930s, Britain had the military and economic power to stand up to its imperial rivals. However, by the 1930s Britain was threatened by the growing strength and ambitions of Germany, Italy and Japan. Britain's economic and financial difficulties reduced its capacity to sustain large forces all over the world. British governments reduced imperial garrisons wherever possible. With the exception of the Indian army, colonial military units were of modest strength and could not be relied on to suppress a local insurrection if unsupported by British troops. Britain had to hope that major internal security problems did not break out simultaneously or coincide with an international crisis.

Britain's changing economic situation had a major impact on colonial policy. In the mid-nineteenth century, Britain's commercial ascendancy stretched far beyond the boundaries of its formal Empire: its industrial, banking and commercial power meant it had huge influence in China, the Middle East and Latin America. It seemed that the country no longer needed extensive colonies. However, by the 1880s Britain's commercial dominance was contracting. As Britain's 'informal' empire was challenged, its formal empire expanded. This was no accident. Imperial expansion in the 1880s, rather than a sign of British power, was as much a reflection of decline. Instead of enjoying a vague ascendancy over the world as a whole, Britain now had a more definite proprietorship over just part of it. It took over large tracts of the world to prevent them falling into the hands of its competitors who would use high tariffs to keep British goods out.

Britain continued to support free trade until the 1930s, but faced by the Great Depression, the British government introduced tariff protection and imperial preference in 1932. By the mid-twentieth century, more than half of Britain's trade was with the Empire/Commonwealth. Britain, in consequence, was determined to maintain its imperial system.

By the 1870s, British governments were aware that public opinion was often strongly imperialist. This influenced the way governments responded to imperial matters. Popular newspapers, such as the *Daily Mail* and the *Daily Express*, supported imperialism, their views affecting and also reflecting public and governmental opinion.

The men who made colonial policy, while determined to maintain British interests, hoped to do so at the cheapest possible cost. Lord Salisbury, Conservative leader from 1886 to 1892 and again from 1895 to 1902, was regarded as a strong supporter of imperialism. But even he believed that retrenchment should be a cardinal text of colonial policy.

Britain was always keen that colonies paid for themselves. Wherever possible, it relied on cheap methods of control. This meant that in many colonies Britain worked in collaboration with traditional leaders. Great efforts were made to avoid upsetting indigenous peoples, which might lead to rebellion and undue expense. By the early 1960s, Macmillan's government could see no good economic reasons for spending vast sums of money trying to rule people who had no wish to be ruled. The Empire was thus abandoned more quickly than had been intended.

The role of economic factors

- *What part did economic factors play in the development of the British Empire?*

Economic factors were of vital importance with regard to both the growth and contraction of the British Empire.

Economic concerns, 1857–1914

The acquisition of overseas territory had initially been based on the notion of mercantilism (see page 5). However, by the 1850s British politicians were committed to the notion of free trade. Unlike conventional imperialism, which profited the imperialists at the expense of their subjects, free trade, in theory, profited both Britain and its trading partners. In the 1850s and 1860s, free exchange of goods certainly supplied Britain's wants adequately and cheaply. Historians Ronald Robinson and John Gallagher (1953) claimed that British imperialism, an 'imperialism of free trade', was shaped as much by informal imperialism as by formal annexation. In most parts of the world, British concerns were the same: the safeguarding of commercial interests. If this could be done without expensive annexation, so much the better. Arguably, British informal influence in China, the Middle East and Latin America in the late nineteenth century was as significant as formal colonisation.

Britain dominated world trade and industrial production until the 1870s. However, by 1880 it was clear that other countries, notably Germany and the USA, were growing in industrial strength, challenging British pre-eminence. While Britain continued to support free trade, its industrial rivals imposed high duties, designed to protect their own economic interests. If Britain's competitors acquired colonies, Britain might be unable to trade with large parts of the world. To make matters worse, in the 1870s and 1880s, Britain suffered from economic depression. Falling profits and growing unemployment added to the fears of scarcity of markets. It seemed that the country must secure export outlets by expanding its Empire. Thus, British governments involved themselves in the 'scramble for Africa' and in developments in China. There was a realisation that Africa and China did not amount to much economically at the time. But there was concern over future developments. Britain had no wish to rule China. Its aim was to prevent other countries ruling it. It essentially achieved its aim and also ensured Britain's trading rights in large parts of China.

Given that most of its main economic rivals imposed high tariffs on British goods, some Britons supported the introduction of imperial protectionism. Tariff reform was particularly associated with Joseph Chamberlain. In 1903, he called for greater imperial economic unity. He proposed that:

- protective tariffs should be levied on manufactured goods, safeguarding British industry against unfair practices
- there would be no tariffs on colonial imports.

The issue of tariff reform split the Conservative/Unionist coalition wide open. The Liberal Party, committed to free trade, won the 1906 election and Chamberlain's hopes of establishing a kind of imperial common market, protected by high tariffs, bit the dust.

In theory, the British colonies continued to operate in a free trade environment. But in practice most were dominated by Britain as supplier and as a buyer. In most colonies, the encouragement to produce goods for the British market helped Britain more than it did the producers. Colonial production tended to be focused on a narrow range of commodities. This lack of diversity made colonial economies vulnerable to market shifts.

Economic concerns, 1914–67

Pre-1914, Britain had traded more with the outside world than with its formal possessions. Nevertheless, the Empire provided a good market for British goods. The Empire countries varied greatly in the economic benefits that they conferred on Britain. India dwarfed all the others, accounting for nearly 40 per cent of Britain's colonial exports. Australia, Canada, South Africa and New Zealand (in that order of importance) were Britain's next most important imperial trading partners, taking over 40 per cent of its colonial exports. The rest of the dependent colonies had relatively little economic significance.

Post-1919, the Empire was increasingly important to Britain's trading position as the country found it difficult to sell its goods to the rest of the world. The Great Depression of the early 1930s had a major impact on Britain's economic relations with its colonies. In 1932, Britain abandoned free trade and introduced the Import Duties Act, which imposed a ten per cent tariff on most imports. An Imperial Economic Conference at Ottawa (1932) accepted the principle of imperial preference. The conference resulted in a series of agreements over details of preferential trade between Britain and the Dominions. Although imperial protection did not fulfil the hopes of those who had been pressing for complete Empire free trade, it had some positive effects. Britain's trade with the Empire/Commonwealth increased considerably. Between 1935 and 1939, some 40 per cent of Britain's imports came from, and 49 per cent of Britain's exports went to, the Empire/Commonwealth. The trade agreements went some way to increasing imperial cohesion. Protectionist policies and preferential trade with the Dominions helped to sustain British industry through the harsh economic climate of the 1930s. Britain remained the world's greatest trading nation, albeit the country now had a balance of payments deficit.

Britain was left economically weakened by the Second World War. Trade with the Empire/Commonwealth was vital if the British economy was to revive. Revive it did. This was partly due to the sterling area. Most of the Dominions and dependencies used the British pound sterling as the basis of their currencies, banking their overseas earnings in London. Britain, moreover, remained the most important market for members of the sterling area. Various measures, agreed to in 1947, tied sterling area members far more closely than before to a common trade policy, obliging them to purchase more of their imports from Britain. The sterling area thus became a closed economic bloc in a way that the Empire had never been.

For most of the 1950s, half of British trade was with Empire and Commonwealth countries. Anxious to preserve its special relationship with the Commonwealth, Britain did not join the European Economic Community (EEC) in 1957. However, in the early 1960s, Macmillan decided it was in Britain's interest to join. Britain's share of the world's manufacturing exports was declining and the country had a growing trade deficit. There was also a shift in the focus of Britain's trading activity away from the Commonwealth and towards Western Europe. The Commonwealth, in spite of its size, could not compare with the EEC's purchasing power. While Britain's initial application to join the EEC was rejected in 1963, it ultimately joined in 1973 – an indication that it had abandoned its hope of creating a viable economically linked Commonwealth.

Did Britain benefit economically from its Empire?

Britain probably benefited economically from its Empire. However, while it did not spend much on the Empire's administration, it did spend a considerable amount on its defence. Britain's hope that the colonies would contribute to their own defence costs was barely realised – although India did help to foot the bill for the Indian army. Generally, British taxpayers paid most of the Empire's defence costs. Arguably, many of the things which supposedly made the Empire worthwhile – emigration, high returns on capital investment, increased trade – were insufficiently powerful to transform the vast defence expenditure into an overall balance of financial gain.

The impact of the Empire on British attitudes and culture

▶ *How did the Empire influence British attitudes and culture?*

For much of the nineteenth century, imperial affairs were not an especially important or divisive issue in British politics. This changed in the 1870s.

The situation, 1857–1914

In 1872, Conservative leader Disraeli injected the issue of Empire into domestic politics by criticising the Liberal government's imperial policies. As prime minister from 1874 and 1880, Disraeli put the consolidation of British power in India at the heart of his imperial crusade. His main aim was probably simply to associate the Conservative Party with patriotism in order to make a new appeal to the electorate. His strategy failed to prevent his defeat in the 1880 election. Nevertheless, imperialist sentiment in Britain was strong in the 1880s and 1890s and governments that appeared to ignore British interests did so at their peril.

Imperial fervour probably reached its height in the Boer War (1899–1902). But imperialist sentiment did not diminish much thereafter. By the early twentieth century, the most popular newspapers – the *Daily Mail* and the *Daily Express* – strongly supported British imperialism. Imperial enthusiasts created organisations to work for imperial unity. Britons were bombarded with imperial imagery in a variety of forms. The fact that so many Britons emigrated – some 1.5 million in the five years before 1914 – also strengthened imperial consciousness. First-generation emigrants retained close links with Britain and helped to keep alive the sense that Britain was the centre of a Greater Britain which reached out to all corners of the globe. Young Britons were instilled with imperial pride. School textbooks stressed the achievements of men and women who helped to establish the Empire. The success of the Scout and Guide movements stressed the obligations and rewards of imperial citizenship.

Probably the greatest imperial enthusiasts came from the public schools, as well as army and naval officers, colonial administrators and businessmen. The extent of working-class support has generated controversy. While some historians have doubted whether the working class was ever particularly supportive of the Empire, others think large numbers of workers were won over to – or manipulated into – supporting imperialism. Certainly, many working-class Britons served all over the world in the armed forces, with the result that they and their families had at least an interest in imperial matters.

In the late nineteenth and early twentieth centuries, most Britons seem to have felt a sense of pride in the Empire and derived satisfaction from the thought that they constituted a successful imperial race. While the term Anglo-Saxon race was often used, it was envisaged more as a distinct set of values and institutions rather than in biological terms. In fact, the most common justification of Empire rested less on race than upon the concept of 'mission'. There was a strong belief that Britain brought better conditions of life to less fortunate peoples.

Britain's initially poor performance in the Boer War helped to shatter some of the national complacency. Many feared that the Empire might be brought down by decadence. There was much talk of the need for national efficiency. Only by becoming efficient, it was claimed, could the Empire survive and prosper. The upbringing and education of all children, rich and poor alike, was seen as crucial if Britain was to remain a great imperial power.

But not all Britons supported imperial expansion. Opponents of Empire – radical Liberals, Irish Nationalists, Socialists – claimed that the Empire exposed Britain to wars, distracted attention from social problems at home and led to exploitation of indigenous peoples. After the Boer War, imperialism became less popular. The pro-imperialist Conservative/Unionist coalition was heavily defeated in the 1906 and 1910 elections.

The situation, 1914–67

Britain showed no enthusiasm to abandon its Empire between the wars. Imperialist supporters, like Lord Beaverbrook, owner of the *Daily Express*, did their best to sell the idea of Empire to Britons. Lord Reith, head of the BBC, saw radio as a force that might help to unite the Empire. In 1932, the BBC began an Empire Service which broadcast to all the countries of the Empire. Racial prejudice made it difficult for most Britons to take seriously the idea of non-Europeans governing themselves. Even Labour MPs believed that self-determination was not realistic in most colonies for a long time to come. The only colonial people to be granted self-rule between the wars were the 30,000 white settlers in Southern Rhodesia who ruled over 1 million Africans.

After 1945, many Britons, raised to believe in the virtues of parliamentary democracy, found it difficult to reconcile this with the paternalistic idea of Empire. On the left, there were increasing doubts about the justice of imperial rule and the rights of indigenous peoples. Nevertheless, prior to 1960 there was little public pressure to jettison Britain's remaining colonies. There was an awareness of the Empire/Commonwealth's economic importance. In 1951, it supplied nearly half of Britain's imports and took 54 per cent of British exports. Moreover, it still seemed vital if Britain was to remain a world power. Most Britons also believed that Britain still had some responsibility to its colonial peoples. Most of the electorate continued to vote for the Conservative Party – the party of Empire – throughout the 1950s.

After 1960, the attitude of most Britons to imperial rule changed. Although some Conservatives opposed the rapid transfer of power into the hands of black Africans, Macmillan encountered far less resistance than he expected. By the early 1960s, most Britons, encouraged by a predominantly liberal media, frowned on coercive methods of maintaining control and were less prepared to accept arguments for maintaining minority rule, which depended on assertions of white supremacy. The public was far more concerned with bread and butter issues – employment, education, health and housing – than with maintaining the Empire. Accordingly, Britons watched the process of imperial disintegration largely with indifference. Most on the left regarded the Empire's end as a good thing. Most on the right viewed its demise as – regrettably – inevitable. Most, left and right alike, seem to have believed that Britain had done a reasonably good imperial job, bequeathing to former colonies a legacy that included parliamentary government, health care, education, applied technology, and respect for the rights of the individual. It should be said that this legacy was far from firmly based in many of the new states.

By the 1960s, rather than Britons going out to settle the world, large numbers of people from the Caribbean, India and Pakistan determined to make new lives for themselves in Britain. A multiracial Britain was to be one of the main legacies of the Empire. It was one for which the Empire, despite all its high multiracial pretensions, had done little to prepare Britons.

5 The response of indigenous people to British rule

How did the indigenous peoples respond to British rule?

British imperial rule is often seen as despotism exercised by pompous and bigoted administrators. In reality, the number of British officials was usually so small and the financial resources of most colonies so slim that colonial rule had to rely on locally recruited subordinates to staff both its bureaucracies and its security forces. British officials had little option but to cooperate with native leaders, who remained the main source of authority in the countryside. British rule did have some virtues. Many administrators had a strong sense of duty to the people they governed. British administration did bring some economic investment, the establishment of law and order, the setting up of schools, and the end of practices such as cannibalism and human sacrifice. Urbanisation and the building of railways produced work opportunities for indigenous people, as did the growth of large-scale agriculture and mining.

British politicians, journalists, missionaries and explorers claimed that Britain intended to bring civilisation to indigenous peoples and was preparing colonial subjects for home rule. But central to this argument was the fact that freedom was some distance away. Outside the settlement colonies, there was little democracy. Most British administrators remained aloof from the people they ruled. While believing their duty was to help the indigenous peoples over whom they presided, most saw themselves as a superior race. They were not expected to be over-friendly with the natives for the harm this might do to their authority.

Inequality and discrimination

The Empire was thus a place of deep inequality between coloniser and colonised. Oppression, constraint and the uneven distribution of wealth and privilege were the norm. British rule eventually affected every aspect of indigenous peoples' lives – job opportunities, property ownership, marriage, laws, religious practice, education and entertainment – sometimes for better but often for worse. Indigenous workers' wages were far lower than those of white workers and they had few rights. Leaving a 'job' without lawful cause, careless work or insulting a master could lead to withdrawal of wages, flogging or imprisonment. Large numbers of Indians were used as an indentured workforce, not just in India but in the Caribbean, Africa and the Pacific. In many respects, the settlement colonies treated their indigenous peoples more unfairly than Britain treated the peoples in the Crown colonies. Aborigines in Australia found themselves outcasts, native tribes in Canada were forced to settle on reservations, New Zealand Maoris lost much of their land, while South Africa established a rigid apartheid system.

Lack of investment

Relatively little British investment went into the colonies. Accordingly, most indigenous people lived in poverty, their lives often blighted by the threat of hunger and disease. More than 6 million died in famines in India in the 1870s, while 3 million died in 1943. Cholera, plague and a host of other diseases had a devastating impact in parts of India and Africa. It had long been British policy that colonies should be financially self-supporting. Not much was done therefore to fulfil what Britain claimed was its 'positive trust' to its colonial subjects. In most African colonies, fewer than one in ten children went to (substandard) schools. A governor of Tanganyika described his colony as 'lying in mothballs' between the wars – an apt description of what happened in most dependencies.

Labour politicians had long talked of 'developing' the colonies but most had little idea what developments should occur or how this should be done. Anxious to develop colonial economies to provide Britain with urgently needed raw materials after 1945, scores of 'experts' descended on Africa, in particular, with schemes for agricultural improvement. Most of the schemes proved to be a disaster, helping neither Britain nor the colonial economies. Nevertheless, by 1950 the Labour government claimed that it had abolished the old type of capitalist imperialism. In reality, far from helping their economic development, Britain had exploited its colonies for all they were worth, restricting investment, and controlling their trade and the prices of their main commodities. This so-called 'second colonial occupation' led to increased resentment.

Colonial nationalism

By the late 1950s, many Africans were determined to throw off British rule. In 1960, Macmillan commented on the strength of 'African national consciousness' and talked of a 'wind of change' blowing through Africa. It was not just Britain's colonial rule that was threatened by growing nationalism. In the early 1960s, France and Belgium granted independence to most of their African colonies. As one country was granted independence, it became harder to sustain a case for delay elsewhere. Macmillan's government thus granted independence to huge swathes of Africa. It is possible to regard the process of decolonisation as a series of successful liberation struggles. However, the view that nationalism made the collapse of British colonial rule inevitable is too simplistic. Not all so-called nationalist leaders won the hearts and minds of their people. Within virtually all of Britain's African colonies there was the fear that if independence came, power would be seized by one tribe, region or religious group. Britain was thus in a position to play off one group against another as it had done effectively in the past. But crucially, there were few indigenous peoples who showed any wish to support British rule. Most celebrated Britain's departure.

6 The role of key individuals and groups

▶ *How important was the role of key individuals and groups?*

British imperial expansion was not fuelled simply by British governments. Adventurers (like John Speke) and philanthropists/missionaries (like David Livingstone) also played an important role. Missionaries, more than any other class of colonisers, lived and worked among local peoples. They were usually the only conduit for Western health care and education in remote areas. Missionaries were not the agents of the British state; indeed, they were often at odds with colonial officials. Nevertheless, they were part of the imperial conquest in that most tried to promote Western values. Along with humanitarians, doctors and teachers, missionaries called on colonial governments to end what they saw as barbaric practices. This led to the common and sincerely held view that 'backward' peoples benefited from colonial administrations that educated them and helped them to curb disease and poverty.

British governments did not exert much control over missionaries. Nor did they necessarily exert control over other 'men on the spot'. Men such as Rhodes in southern Africa, working with local power brokers, did their best to realise their own ambitious schemes. Once the schemes were launched, they usually sought the support of British governments to complete the process.

Clearly, leading politicians, from Gladstone through to Wilson, were important in determining the process of expansion and decolonisation. Nationalist leaders, like Gandhi, also played crucial roles in building support for independence. Such leaders left their marks on events. But they were often simply responding to situations rather than controlling them. Great men and women can make history. But their greatness is usually inextricably linked with the situations in which they find themselves and in which they operate.

Historians Peter Cain and Tony Hopkins, in the 1980s, claimed that City of London financiers had a major impact on imperial expansion. According to Cain and Hopkins, 'gentlemanly capitalists' were able to 'persuade' governments to act in their best interests. However, many scholars have challenged this interpretation. There is little evidence of financiers actually 'persuading' governments to act as they wished. Successive British governments took relatively little notice of business lobbies. Instead, they acted in what they perceived to be the 'national interest'. Britain's overarching commercial and strategic interests were their main concern.

7 The nature of the Empire

▶ *Was the British Empire a force for good or evil?*

For much of the period covered by this book, Britain ruled the greatest Empire the world has ever seen. Little more than ten per cent of the people in the Empire were British or of British origin. There were more Hindus and Muslims in the Empire than Christians. But the Empire was essentially British, defended by the Royal Navy, and held together by the symbolic institution of the monarchy, the English language, the British legal system and British administrators.

For most of the Empire's existence, British scholars, writers, politicians and journalists praised Britain's imperial mission. Today, those same groups are far less certain about that mission. Debate still rages about the nature of the Empire. Some politicians and scholars consider it a 'bad thing' which brought little benefit to Britain or the world. But others are equally adamant that it was a 'good thing' for both Britain and its colonies. The debate seems certain to continue. It is hard to generalise about an entity that affected so much of the world for so long. It could be, for example, that British rule was beneficial for some colonies – and for Britain itself – at some periods but not at others. Nor were the experiences of Empire the same in every colony. Colonies of settlement, like Australia and New Zealand, had a very different experience from Crown colonies, like India and Nigeria. India and Nigeria, themselves, had very different experiences from each other. It should also be remembered that today's morality is different from that of people in the past. Moreover, the British Empire, far from being a fixed entity, was constantly changing. Thus, almost any overarching statement about whether the Empire was a force for good or evil needs to be treated with care.

Indeed, it is worth considering the extent to which the British Empire was a 'force' at all. Certainly, from 1857 to 1939, the Empire appeared to be hugely powerful. By 1919, Britain could claim to rule a quarter of the world's land surface. It possessed the world's greatest navy, a deterrent to other great powers, and an army strong enough to deal with revolts by embittered colonial elements. Britain, with support from the Empire, emerged victorious from both the First and Second World Wars.

However, it can be argued that the British Empire was something of a paper tiger. From start to finish, it was a hotchpotch of territories which had little in common except links with Britain. There was little system in the Empire's constitutional structure. While Australia, New Zealand and Canada were essentially self-governing countries in 1857, the other imperial territories were at different stages of political development. The British government generally left day-to-day management of the Empire to officials in the Colonial Office. They, in turn, entrusted responsibility to administrators in the colonies themselves. Frederick Lugard, appointed high commissioner of northern Nigeria in 1900, found himself ruling a vast area with a civilian staff totalling 104 and a military force of 2000–3000 Africans, commanded by 200 British officers and non-commissioned officers. Because Britain relied on cheap methods of control, tribal leaders, royal families or influential indigenous cliques retained considerable powers. Arguably, the Empire was something of a bluff, held together less by force than by a mixture of cajolery and guile and by local collaboration.

AQA A level History

Essay guidance

At both AS and A level for AQA Component 1: Breadth Study: The British Empire, c1857–1967, you will need to answer an essay question in the exam. Each essay question is marked out of 25:

- for the AS exam, Section B: Answer **one** essay (from a choice of two)
- for the A level exam, Section B: Answer **two** essays (from a choice of three).

There are several question stems which all have the same basic requirement: to analyse and reach a conclusion, based on the evidence you provide.

The AS questions often give a quotation and then ask whether you agree or disagree with this view. Almost inevitably, your answer will be a mixture of both. It is the same task as for A level – just phrased differently in the question. Detailed essays are more likely to do well than vague or generalised essays.

The AQA mark scheme is essentially the same for AS and the full A level (see the AQA website, www.aqa.org.uk). Both emphasise the need to analyse and evaluate the key features related to the periods studied. The key feature of the highest level is sustained analysis: analysis that unites the whole of the essay.

Writing an essay: general skills

- *Focus and structure.* Be sure what the question is asking and plan what the paragraphs should be about.
- *Focused introduction to the essay.* Be sure that the introductory sentence relates directly to the focus of the question and that each paragraph highlights the structure of the answer.
- *Use detail.* Make sure that you show detailed knowledge, but only as part of an explanation being made in relation to the question. No knowledge should be standalone, it should be used in context.
- *Explanatory analysis and evaluation.* Consider what words and phrases to use in an answer to strengthen the explanation.
- *Argument and counter-argument.* Think of how arguments can be juxtaposed as part of a balancing act to give contrasting views.
- *Resolution.* Think how best to 'resolve' contradictory arguments.
- *Relative significance and evaluation.* Think how best to reach a judgement when trying to assess the relative importance of various factors, and their possible interrelationship.

Planning an essay

Practice question 1

To what extent was Britain responsible for the tension in southern Africa in the period 1881–99?

This question requires you to analyse why British policy helped bring about the Second Boer War in 1899. You must discuss the following:

- How British actions led to worsening relations between Britain and the Transvaal and Orange Free State (your primary focus).
- Other factors, not least Boer actions, that increased tension (your secondary focus).

A clear structure makes for a much more effective essay and is crucial for achieving the highest marks. You need three or four paragraphs to structure this question effectively. In each paragraph you will deal with one factor. One of these *must* be the factor in the question.

A very basic plan for this question might look like this:

- Paragraph 1: the effects of the discovery of gold in Transvaal on British policy.
- Paragraph 2: the effects of British (and Boer) actions in the early 1890s, such as the response to the *uitlander* situation and the Jameson raid.
- Paragraph 3: British (and Boer) actions in the years 1896–9 which led to the outbreak of war in 1899.

It is a good idea to cover the factor named in the question first, so that you don't run out of time and forget to do so. Then cover the others in what you think is their order of importance, or in the order that appears logical in terms of the sequence of paragraphs.

The introduction

Maintaining focus is vital. One way to do this from the beginning of your essay is to use the words in the question to help write your argument. The first sentence of the answer to question 1, for example, could look like this:

While British actions in the 1880s and 1890s undoubtedly increased tensions in southern Africa, the Boers must also share some responsibility for the outbreak of the Boer War in 1899.

This opening sentence provides a clear focus on the demands of the question, although it could, of course, be written in a more exciting style.

Focus throughout the essay

Structuring your essay well will help with keeping the focus of your essay on the question. To maintain a focus on the wording in question 1, you could begin your first main paragraph with 'weakness':

British fear of the threat of Transvaal was to lead to increased tensions in southern Africa in the 1880s.

- This sentence begins with a clear point that refers to the primary focus of the question (British responsibility for tensions in southern Africa) while linking it to a factor (Britain's fear of the Transvaal threat).
- You could then have a paragraph for each of your other factors.
- It will be important to make sure that each paragraph focuses on analysis and includes relevant details that are used as part of the argument.
- You may wish to number your factors. This helps to make your structure clear and helps you to maintain focus.

Deploying detail

As well as focus and structure, your essay will be judged on the extent to which it includes accurate detail. There are several different kinds of evidence you could use that might be described as detailed. These include correct dates, names of relevant people, statistics and events. For example, for question 1 you could use terms such as the Bloemfontein conference. You can also make your essays more detailed by using the correct technical vocabulary (for example, *uitlanders*).

Analysis and explanation

'Analysis' covers a variety of high-level skills including explanation and evaluation; in essence, it means breaking down something complex into smaller parts. A clear structure which breaks down a complex question into a series of paragraphs is the first step towards writing an analytical essay.

The purpose of explanation is to account for why something happened, or why something is true or false. An explanatory statement requires two parts: a *claim* and a *justification*.

In question 1, for example, you might want to argue that one important reason for the outbreak of the Second Boer War was the stubbornness of President Kruger and the Transvaal Boers. Once you have made your point, and supported it with relevant detail, you can then explain how this answers the question. For example, you could conclude your paragraph like this:

While Milner's actions in 1899 undoubtedly increased tensions between Britain and Transvaal**[1]**, it was President Kruger who finally decided to declare war on Britain in October 1899**[2]** and did so with the confident (if ill-founded) expectation of success**[3]**.

1 Claim.
2 Relationship.
3 Justification.

Evaluation

Evaluation means considering the importance of two or more different factors, weighing them against each other, and reaching a judgement. This is a good skill to use at the end of an essay because the conclusion should reach a judgement which answers the question. For example, your conclusion to question 1 might read as follows:

Clearly**[1]**, British policy in the two decades before 1899 helped increase tensions with the Boer governments of the Transvaal and the Orange Free State. However**[2]**, it remains far from certain that Salisbury's government actually wanted war with the Boers in the late summer of 1899. In the final analysis, therefore**[3]**, it was President Kruger's actions which made war inevitable. He, not Salisbury, was the man who issued the fatal ultimatum in October 1899. It was he who then proceeded to declare war on Britain.

1 Clearly.
2 However.
3 Therefore.

Words like 'however' and 'therefore' are helpful to contrast the importance of the different factors.

Complex essay writing: argument and counter-argument

Essays that develop a good argument are more likely to reach the highest levels. This is because argumentative essays are much more likely to develop sustained analysis. As you know, your essays are judged on the extent to which they analyse.

After setting up an argument in your introduction, you should develop it throughout the essay. One way of doing this is to adopt an argument–counter-argument structure. A counter-argument is one that disagrees with the main argument of the essay. This is a good way of evaluating the importance of the different factors that you discuss. Essays of this type will develop an argument in one paragraph and then set out an opposing argument in another paragraph. Sometimes this will include juxtaposing the differing views of historians on a topic.

Good essays will analyse the key issues. They will probably have a clear piece of analysis at the end of each paragraph. While this analysis might be good, it will generally relate only to the issue discussed in that paragraph.

Excellent essays will be analytical throughout. As well as the analysis of each factor discussed above, there will be an overall analysis. This will run throughout the essay and can be achieved through developing a clear, relevant and coherent argument.

A good way of achieving sustained analysis is to consider which factor is most important.

Here is an example of an introduction that sets out an argument for question 1:

The British governments of the 1880s and 1890s bear considerable responsibility for the increasing tension in southern Africa – tension which culminated in the outbreak of the Second Boer War in October 1899**[1]**. Convinced that the Boer republic of Transvaal was a potential threat to British interests in southern Africa, successive British governments – but particularly those of Lord Salisbury, who was prime minister from 1886 to 1892 and again from 1895 to 1902, sought ways to challenge the Transvaal**[2]**. So did some British businessmen, not least the diamond- and gold-mining magnate and Cape Prime Minister Cecil Rhodes. However, as this essay will show, the Boers, especially President Kruger of the Transvaal, must also shoulder some of the responsibility for the rise in tension and also for the actions which brought about war in October 1899**[3]**.

1 The introduction begins with a claim.
2 The introduction continues with another reason.
3 Concludes with outline of argument of the most important reason.

- This introduction focuses on the question and sets out the key factors that the essay will develop.

- It introduces an argument about which factor was most significant.
- However, it also sets out an argument that can then be developed throughout each paragraph, and is rounded off with an overall judgement in the conclusion.

Complex essay writing: resolution and relative significance

Having written an essay that explains argument and counter-argument, you should then resolve the tension between the argument and the counter-argument in your conclusion. It is important that the writing is precise and summarises the arguments made in the main body of the essay. You need to reach a supported overall judgement. One very appropriate way to do this is by evaluating the relative significance of different factors, in the light of valid criteria. Relative significance means how important one factor is compared to another.

The best essays will always make a judgement about which was most important based on valid criteria. These can be very simple, and will depend on the topic and the exact question. The following criteria are often useful:

- Duration: which factor was important for the longest amount of time?
- Scope: which factor affected the most people?
- Effectiveness: which factor achieved most?
- Impact: which factor led to the most fundamental change?

As an example, you could compare the factors in terms of their duration and their impact.

A conclusion that follows this advice should be capable of reaching a high level (if written, in full, with appropriate details) because it reaches an overall judgement that is supported through evaluating the relative significance of different factors in the light of valid criteria.

Having written an introduction and the main body of an essay for question 1, a concluding paragraph that aims to meet the exacting criteria for reaching a complex judgement could look like this:

Thus, the actions of the British governments of Lord Salisbury certainly helped to increase tension in southern Africa. So did the actions of Cecil Rhodes, who was something of a loose cannon, sometimes acting as an agent of the British government and sometimes acting semi-independently. Rhodes, Salisbury, Chamberlain and Milner must all be held in part responsible for the outbreak of the Second Boer War. But the Transvaal Boers must also share responsibility for the increased tension and for the war itself. Convinced that Britain wanted to end the Transvaal's independence and unwilling to concede rights to the *uitlanders*, President Kruger believed war to be inevitable. He therefore prepared for it. His resolve was stiffened by the fact that his leading generals assured him that the Boers would win and that the outcome would be a United States of Southern Africa under Transvaal leadership. Thus, it was the Boers who foolishly declared war on Britain in October 1899.

Interpretations guidance

Section A of the examination for AQA Component 1: Breadth Study: The British Empire, c1857–1967 contains extracts from the work of historians. This section tests your ability to analyse different historical interpretations. Therefore, you must focus on the interpretations outlined in the Extracts. The advice given here is for both the AS and the A level exams:

- For the AS exam, there are two extracts and you are asked which is the more convincing interpretation (25 marks).
- For the A level exam, there are three extracts and you are asked how convincing the arguments are in relation to a specified topic (30 marks).

An interpretation is a particular view on a topic of history held by a particular author or authors. Interpretations of an event can vary, for example, depending on how much weight a historian gives to a particular factor and largely ignores another one.

Interpretations can also be heavily conditioned by events and situations that influence the writer. For example, judging the merits or otherwise of British rule in India will tend to produce different responses – someone writing in the late nineteenth or early twentieth century might see the Raj as largely successful. Someone writing in the late twentieth century or early twentieth century might see the Raj as very flawed.

The interpretations that you will be given will be largely from recent or fairly recent historians, and they may, of course, have been influenced by events in the period in which they were writing.

Interpretations and evidence

The extracts will contain a mixture of interpretations and evidence. The mark scheme rewards answers that focus on the *interpretations* offered by the extracts much more highly than answers that focus on the *information or evidence* mentioned in the extracts. Therefore, it is important to identify the interpretations:

- *Interpretations* are a specific kind of argument. They tend to make claims such as 'The expansion of the British Empire in Africa in the late nineteenth century was essentially the result of economic factors.'
- *Information or evidence* tends to consist of specific details. For example: 'Britain defended its interests in Africa whenever they were threatened in the period 1880–1899.'
- *Arguments and counter-arguments*: sometimes in an extract you will find an interpretation which is then balanced in the same paragraph with a counter-argument. You will need to decide with which your knowledge is most in sympathy.

The importance of planning

Remember that in the examination you are allowed an hour for this question. It is the planning stage that is vital in order to write a good answer. You should allow at least one-quarter of that time to read the extracts and plan an answer. If you start writing too soon, it is likely that you will waste time trying to summarise the *content* of each extract. Do this in your planning stage – and then think how you will *use* the content to answer the question.

Analysing interpretations: AS (two extracts)

The same skills are needed for AS and A level for this question. The advice starts with AS simply because it only involves two extracts rather than three.

With reference to these extracts and your understanding of the historical context, which of these two extracts provides the more convincing interpretation of Disraeli's imperial policies in the period 1874–80? (25 marks)

Extracts A and B are used for the AS question. Extracts A, B and C are used for the A level question.

EXTRACT A

A view of Disraeli's imperial policy in the period 1874–80. (From Frank McDonough, *The British Empire 1815–1914*, Hodder Education, 1994, p. 74.)

However, there is good reason to believe that Disraeli's Indian obsession and the popular jingoism it encouraged were matters of political style rather than of political substance. When what he did (rather than what he said) is considered it is possible to understand why many historians have reached the conclusion that Disraeli's championing of imperialism was mainly show. There was no new administrative or economic policies for the Empire enacted by Disraeli as Prime Minister. Despite all his talk at Crystal Palace about the misguided decision to offer self-government to the colonies of settlement, he completely ignored the colonies of settlement when he was in power. In fact, it seems that he virtually ignored the Empire as a whole.

EXTRACT B

A view of Disraeli's imperialism in action. (From Graham Goodlad, *British Foreign and Imperial Policy 1865–1919*, Routledge, 2000, p. 4.)

The electoral victory of February 1874 offered Disraeli an opportunity to give practical expression to his professed concern for the defence of the empire. Several steps towards the consolidation of British power in the tropics were taken in the first years of the government. In West Africa, a new authority, the Gold Coast Protectorate, was created, British residents were installed in three of the Malay states, while in the southern Pacific, Fiji was annexed to the empire. In 1875 Disraeli engineered one of the most dramatic coups of his career when he purchased for Britain shares in the Suez Canal Company.

EXTRACT C

Disraeli's imperial policy (only relevant for A level). (From Piers Brendon, *The Decline and Fall of the British Empire 1781–1997*, Vintage Books, 2008, p. 163.)

As Prime Minister from 1874 to 1880, Disraeli prosecuted a similar policy (to Gladstone), being equally reluctant to accumulate costly encumbrances, especially in the tropics. He was furious when 'prancing proconsuls' dragged Britain into wars with Zulus and Afghans. However, Disraeli would add to the Empire if he could thereby augment British greatness. Moreover, he sometimes responded to local circumstances, such as native disorders, which threatened British merchants, missionaries or settlers. Thus in 1874 he extended British authority in Malaya and took control of Fiji.

Analysing Extract A

From the extract:

- Disraeli's support of imperialism was mainly show.
- He introduced no new imperial policies.
- He showed little interest in imperial matters.

Assessing the extent to which the arguments are convincing:

- Deploying knowledge to corroborate that Disraeli did seem to support imperialistic policies (for example, in his Crystal Palace speech).
- Deploying knowledge to highlight the fact that his apparent support for the British Empire may have been simply to win political support.
- Suggesting that the last sentence may be an overstatement of the case: Disraeli's government showed a greater interest in imperial matters than the extract suggests (for example, the purchase of the Suez Canal shares).
- The extract mentions Disraeli's Indian obsession but then ignores the fact that Disraeli did devote considerable attention to the defence of India.
- The extract omits any reference to British imperial expansion in the years 1874–80 – expansion mentioned in Extract B.

Analysing Extract B

From the extract:

- Disraeli was concerned with matters of imperial defence.
- He took actions to consolidate Britain's position in the tropics.
- He purchased the Khedive of Egypt's Suez Canal shares in 1875.

Assessing the extent to which the arguments are convincing:

- Deploying knowledge to agree with the view that Disraeli did take positive steps to enhance and defend the British Empire.
- Deploying knowledge to suggest that – in many respects (as Extract A suggests) – Disraeli does seem to have been something of a reluctant imperialist once in power.
- Examining the extent to which Disraeli's imperial policy was more active than that of his predecessor, Gladstone.
- Examining the situation in 1879–80. If Disraeli did so little on the imperial front, why did Gladstone come out of retirement and launch his passionate Midlothian Campaign in opposition to Disraeli?

Comparing the analysis of each extract should give the direction of an overall conclusion and judgement about which of the extracts is more convincing. In this case it may be that Extract B is more convincing because it does provide some evidence in support of its views rather than simply make sweeping assertions.

The mark scheme for AS

The mark scheme builds up from Level 1 to Level 5, in the same way as it does for essays:

- Do not waste time simply describing or paraphrasing the content of each source.
- Make sure that when you include your knowledge it is being used to advance the analysis of the extracts – not as knowledge in its own right.
- The top two levels of the mark scheme refer to 'supported conclusion' (Level 4) and 'well-substantiated conclusion' (Level 5).
- For Level 4, 'Supported conclusion' means finishing your answer with a judgement that is backed up with some accurate evidence drawn from the source(s) and your knowledge.
- For Level 5, 'well-substantiated conclusion' means finishing your answer with a judgement which is very well supported with evidence, and, where relevant, reaches a complex conclusion that reflects a wide variety of evidence.

Writing the answer for AS

There is no one correct way! However, the principles are clear. In particular, contextual knowledge should be used *only* to back up an argument. None of your knowledge should be standalone – all your knowledge should be used in context.

For each extract in turn:

- Explain the evidence in the extract, backed up with your own contextual knowledge, for Disraeli's imperial policies being more assertive than those of Gladstone or simply show with no substance.
- Explain the points in the extract where you have evidence that contradicts Disraeli's imperial policies being simply for show.

Then write a conclusion that reaches a judgement on which is more convincing as an interpretation. You might build in some element of comparison during the answer, or it might be developed in the last paragraph only.

Analysing interpretations: A level (three extracts)

For the AQA A level exam, Section A gives you three extracts (see page 200), followed by a single question.

Using your understanding of the historical context, assess how convincing the arguments in each of these three extracts are in relation to Disraeli's imperial policies. (30 marks)

An analysis of Extracts A and B has already been provided for the AS question (see page 201).

Analysing Extract C

From the extract:

- Disraeli's imperial policies were very similar to Gladstone's.
- He was not interested in winning new colonies in the tropics.
- He was pushed into taking action by circumstances over which he had little control.

Assessing the extent to which the arguments are convincing:

- Deploying knowledge to corroborate the notion that Disraeli's imperial policies were similar to those of Gladstone.
- Deploying knowledge to explain that there were marked differences between the policies of Disraeli and Gladstone.
- Suggesting that all politicians and governments react to events over which they have little control; the reactions of Disraeli and Gladstone to those events, however, may well have been different.
- The extract minimises the proactive nature of Disraeli's imperial policies.

Writing the answer for A level

First, make sure that you have the focus of the question clear – in this case, the focus is on the nature of Disraeli's imperial policies and how convincing the extracts are on that subject. Then you can investigate the three extracts to see how convincing they are.

You need to analyse each of the three extracts in turn. A suggestion is to have a large page divided into nine blocks.

Extract's main arguments	Knowledge to corroborate	Knowledge to contradict or modify
A		
B		
C		

- In the first column, list the main arguments that each uses.
- In the second column, list what you know that can corroborate the arguments.
- In the third column, list what might contradict or modify (you might find that you partly agree, but with reservations) the arguments.
- You may find, of course, that some of your knowledge is relevant more than once.

Planning your answer

Decide how you could best set out a detailed plan for your answer:

- Briefly refer to the focus of the question.
- For each extract in turn, set out the arguments, corroborating and contradictory evidence.
- Do this by treating each argument (or group of arguments) in turn.

- Make comparisons between the extracts if this is helpful. The mark scheme does not explicitly give credit for doing this, but a successful cross-reference may well show the extent of your understanding of each extract and add to the weight of your argument.
- An overall judgement is not required, but it may be helpful to make a brief summary, or just reinforce what has been said already by emphasising which extract was the most convincing.

The mark scheme for A level

For each of the three extracts, the mark scheme makes it clear that a good answer will:

- Identify the arguments presented in each extract.
- Assess the extent to which the arguments are convincing, using own knowledge.
- Take every opportunity to make a balanced answer wherever this is appropriate, by corroborating and contradicting the arguments in each extract.

The mark scheme progresses upwards like this:

- *Level 1*: general comments about the three extracts or accurate understanding of one extract.
- *Level 2*: some accurate comments on the interpretations in at least two of the three extracts, but with limited comments or with description.
- *Level 3*: some supported comments on the interpretations, putting them in their historical context. Some analysis of the content of the extracts, but little attempt to evaluate them.
- *Level 4*: good understanding of the interpretations provided in the extracts, with knowledge to give a good analysis and some evaluation.
- *Level 5*: very good understanding and strong historical awareness to analyse and evaluate.

Notice that there is no reference in the mark scheme to *comparing* the extracts or reaching a judgement about the most convincing.

Glossary of terms

Afrikaans Language spoken by Boers, meaning 'African-Dutch'.

Afrikaner A person born in South Africa of Dutch/ Boer descent.

Annexation Taking permanent possession of a country.

Apartheid Segregation and separate development of races.

Autocratically Non-democratic rule which is often conducted by one person.

Bantu An African people who speak a common group of languages. In the apartheid era, the white minority used 'Bantu' or 'native' to refer to Africans in South Africa, often in a derogatory way.

Boers People of Dutch origin who settled in southern Africa.

Breech-loading Firearms that loaded at the side rather than down the barrel (like a musket).

Cession The process of giving up power or ceding territory.

Chanak crisis An international crisis which almost resulted in a war between Britain and Turkey in 1922.

Cold War The rivalry between the USA and its allies and the USSR and its allies after the Second World War.

Colonial Service The people who worked for the British Colonial Office.

Commonwealth A group of states united by a common interest or joint history.

Confederation An association of states which unite permanently by treaty. Those states retain specific local powers.

Conscription Compulsory enrolment for service, either in the armed forces or in particular areas of work.

Customs union A group of states having free trade among themselves, and a common tariff policy towards non-member states.

Deficit A shortfall of revenue, as compared with expenditure.

Dervishes Members of an Islamic sect who opposed Egyptian/British rule in the Sudan in the late nineteenth century.

Devolution The handing over of powers.

Diarchy A form of government in which two bodies are vested with power.

Dominions Britain's self-governing colonies (for example, Australia and Canada).

Dumping Exporting commodities for sale at below the cost of production to ruin overseas competition.

East India Company A commercial company that established considerable political power in India in the eighteenth and early nineteenth centuries.

Emir A North African chieftain.

Entente A friendly agreement not involving a binding commitment.

Envoy A diplomat sent to transact business with a foreign government.

Evangelists People who do their best to spread (what they believe to be) good ideas.

Executive power The right to administer and manage.

Free trade International trade that takes place without tariffs being imposed.

Gold Coast Present-day Ghana.

Gross national product (GNP) The total value of all goods and services produced within a country plus the income from all investments abroad.

Guerrilla war Conflicts in which irregular forces harass an enemy rather than fight pitched battles.

Hinterland Inland territory.

Holocaust Hitler's attempt to eliminate all the Jews in Europe after 1941.

Indenture A written agreement, often between workers and employers, agreeing terms of employment – usually for a long period.

Indian National Congress Initially a society set up by educated Indians, it eventually became a major political force, campaigning first for home rule and then for independence for India.

Indigenous People who are native to the area they inhabit.

Industrial Revolution The economic and social changes arising out of the change from industries carried out in the home with simple machines to industries in factories with power-driven machinery. This led to a great change in the scale of production.

Irish Home Rule The idea that Ireland should have its own Parliament and be essentially independent from the rest of Britain.

Jewel in the crown The greatest asset.

Jingoism Extreme patriotism. (The word came from a popular song of the 1870s when Disraeli threatened war with Russia. According to the lyrics, 'We don't want to fight but by jingo if we do; we've got the ships, we've got the men; we've got the money too'.)

Khaki fever British soldiers wore khaki (brown)-coloured uniforms.

Laissez-faire The principle that governments should not interfere in social and economic matters.

League of Nations An organisation, similar to the present-day United Nations, established in 1919 to help preserve world peace.

Little Englanders Opponents of British imperialism.

Mandate The power conferred upon a state by the League of Nations to govern and protect a region.

Manifest destiny A God-given right. The term is more widely used with regard to the USA's expansion westwards in the course of the nineteenth century.

Martial law The imposition of military power by a government in time of emergency, resulting in the temporary suspension of ordinary administration and policing.

Mercantilism The belief, widely held in Europe in the seventeenth and eighteenth centuries, that economic self-sufficiency is the key to national wealth and prosperity. European states envisaged that colonies would provide them with valuable raw materials and also provide markets for their goods.

Middle East The mainly Turkish and Arabic-speaking area around the eastern end of the Mediterranean Sea and in the Arabian Peninsula.

Missionary A person sent on a mission to convert people, usually to a particular form of religion.

Mother country The home country of colonists.

Mughals A Muslim dynasty which claimed to rule much of India from 1526 until 1858.

Northern Rhodesia Modern Zambia.

Ottoman Empire The huge empire controlled by the Ottoman Turks in the Middle East.

Pass laws Acts restricting the movement of black people in South Africa.

Passive resistance Deliberate refusal to do what law or regulation demands and submission to the consequent penalties.

Paternalistic A system or tendency in which well-meaning supervision is apt to be seen as unwelcome interference.

Portuguese East Africa Modern Mozambique.

Protectionism The introduction of high import duties to protect a nation's industries from foreign competition.

Protectorates States or territories which have effectively been taken over and run by another (more powerful) state without being officially annexed.

Raison d'être The main purpose.

Raj Used to describe British rule in India, 1858–1947. It encompasses attitudes and styles of living as well as Britain's actual governing of India.

Rajahs Indian and other Asian princes or kings.

Rand millionaires British and German mining magnates who made fortunes from Transvaal gold. The rand was the Boer currency.

Reservations Areas of land set aside for use by particular groups.

Satellite states Countries which rely on and obey the dictates of a more powerful state.

Scorched-earth policy This involves burning farms, destroying crops, rounding up animals and poisoning the wells of the enemy.

SEATO The South-East Asian Treaty Organisation was set up in 1954.

Self-determination The power of people (of a particular group/nation) to choose their own form of government.

Southern Rhodesia Modern Zimbabwe.

Sovereignty Ultimate power.

Suzerainty Having supreme power over someone.

Third World The developing countries of Africa, Asia and Latin America, which were not aligned with either the USA or the USSR.

Uitlanders White foreigners living in the Transvaal and the Orange Free State.

USSR The Union of Soviet Socialist Republics, formed in 1922.

Zionists Jews who wished to establish a national home in Palestine.

Further reading

General texts of the period 1857–1967

P. Brendon, *The Decline and Fall of the British Empire 1781–1997* (Jonathan Cape, 2007)

A provocative and very readable account of the British Empire's decline

J.G. Darwin, *Unfinished Empire: The Global Expansion of Britain* (Penguin, 2013)

A comprehensive (and at times controversial) analysis of how the British Empire worked

N. Ferguson, *Empire: How Britain Made the Modern World* (Penguin, 2004)

An important and readable text

A. Jackson, *The British Empire: A Very Short Introduction* (Oxford University Press, 2013)

A concise but very useful book

L. James, *The Rise and Fall of the British Empire* (Abacus, 1995)

This remains a useful work

P. Levine, *The British Empire* (Routledge, 2013)

Well worth a read

T.O. Lloyd, *The British Empire 1558–1983* (Oxford University Press, 1984)

The good news is that you only need to read half the book!

M. Lynch, *The British Empire* (Teach Yourself/Hodder Education, 2005)

An excellent introduction to the topic which contains useful facts and figures

B. Porter, *The Lion's Share: A History of British Imperialism 1850–2011* (Routledge, 2014)

Incisive and lucid: an essential text

Texts covering the years 1857–1914

R. Hyam, *Britain's Imperial Century 1815–1914: A Study of Empire and Expansion* (Palgrave Macmillan, 2003)

A very good introduction to British imperial activity pre-1914

F. McDonough, *The British Empire 1815–1914* (Hodder Education, 1994)

A short and solid overview of events

A. Porter, editor, *The Oxford History of the British Empire: The Nineteenth Century* (Oxford University Press, 1999)

A superb collection of essays by experts in their field

Texts covering the years 1914–67

J.M. Brown and W.M. Roger Louis, editors, *The Oxford History of the British Empire: The Twentieth Century* (Oxford University Press, 1999)

This is a vital book, incorporating a series of essays by various experts

J.G. Darwin, *Britain and Decolonisation* (Macmillan, 1988)

A perceptive and persuasive text, well worth reading from cover to cover

J.G. Darwin, *The End of the British Empire: The Historical Debate* (Blackwell, 1991)

A short and interesting read, especially for those who have already established the 'shape' of the topic in their minds

R. Hyam, *Britain's Declining Empire: The Road to Decolonisation, 1918–1968* (Cambridge University Press, 2006)

A good introduction to decolonisation

K.O. Morgan, *The People's Peace. British History 1945–1989* (Oxford University Press, 1990)

This book examines British domestic, foreign and imperial policy in the period

D. Reynolds, *Britannia Overruled: British Policy and World Power in the Twentieth Century* (Longman, 1991)

This text examines the problems Britain faced in foreign and imperial matters in the twentieth century

A. Thompson, editor, *British Experiences of Empire in the Twentieth Century* (Oxford University Press, 2016)

Insightful views of the impact of empire on Britain

Texts specifically on India

Chandra Bipan *et al.*, *India's Struggle for Independence 1857–1947* (Penguin, 1989)

Written by five experts, this is a detailed examination of the struggle for Indian independence

L. James, *Raj: The Making and Unmaking of British India* (Abacus, 1998)

A good introduction to the Raj

K. Lalvani, *The Making of India: The Untold Story of British Enterprise* (Bloomsbury Continuum, 2016)

A very positive view of the Raj

S. Tharoor, *Inglorious Empire: What the British Did to India* (Penguin 2018)

A very critical assessment of British rule in India

J. Wilson, *India Conquered: Britain's Raj and the Chaos of Empire* (Simon & Schuster, 2017)

Another book critical of the Raj

Britain and Africa

L. James, *Empires in the Sun: The Struggle for the Mastery of Africa* (Weidenfeld & Nicolson, 2017)

A good introduction to the scramble for Africa

T. Pakenham, *The Scramble for Africa* (Abacus, 1992)

The first full-scale study of the European scramble for Africa in the late nineteenth century

T. Royle, *Winds of Change: The End of Empire in Africa* (John Murray, 1998)

A succinct account of the end of British rule in Africa

Britain and the Middle East

R.T. Harrison, *Britain and the Middle East 1619–1971* (Bloomsbury Academic, 2016)

A more accessible, but still comprehensive, survey

E. Podeh, editor, *Britain and the Middle East: From Imperial Power to Junior Partner* (Sussex Academic Press, 2007)

Probably the most detailed and authoritative book on Britain's role in the region

The Suez Crisis

K. Kyle, *Suez* (Weidenfeld & Nicolson, 1991)

An authoritative account of the Suez crisis

W.M. Roger Louis and R. Owen, editors, *Suez 1956: The Crisis and its Consequences* (Clarendon, 1989)

An interesting collection of essays on the Suez debacle

Biographies

R. Blake, *Disraeli* (Faber & Faber, 2010)

Still the best biography of Disraeli

T.L. Crosby, *Joseph Chamberlain: A Most Radical Imperialist* (Tauris, 2011)

Probably the best short introduction to Chamberlain's political career

L. Fischer, *The Life of Mahatma Gandhi* (HarperCollins, 1997)

A detailed account of Gandhi's eventful life

M. Gilbert, *Churchill: A Life* (Heinemann, 1991)

A single-volume book by Churchill's best biographer

A. Horne, *Macmillan, Vol. II 1957–1986* (Macmillan, 1989)

This will give you a superb feel of both the man and the period

R. Jenkins, *Gladstone* (Pan, 2002)

An interesting biography by a more recent Liberal politician

R. Rhodes James, *Anthony Eden* (Weidenfeld & Nicolson, 1986)

A sympathetic 'official' biography of Eden

B. Roberts, *Cecil Rhodes: Flawed Colossus* (Thistle Publishing, 2015)

A readable, well-written and fair-minded analysis of Rhodes

Index